Also by LIS WIEHL

—

WINNING EVERY TIME

The **51%** Minority

THE
51%
MINORITY

How Women Still Are
Not Equal and What You
Can Do About It

Lis Wiehl

BALLANTINE BOOKS | NEW YORK

Published in the United States by Ballantine Books,
an imprint of The Random House Publishing Group,
a division of Random House, Inc., New York.

BALLANTINE and colophon are registered
trademarks of Random House, Inc.

ISBN 978-0-345-46921-2

LIBRARY OF CONGRESS CATALOGING-IN-PUBLICATION DATA

Wiehl, Lis W.
The 51% minority : how women still are not equal and
what you can do about it / Lis Wiehl.

p. cm.
Includes bibliographical references and index.
ISBN 978-0-345-46921-2 (alk. paper)
1. Women's rights—United States.   2. Women—United States—
Social conditions—21st century.
I. Title.   II. Title: Fifty-one percent minority.
HQ1236.5.U6W54 2007
305.420973—dc22   2006049937

Printed in the United States of America on acid-free paper

www.ballantinebooks.com

2 4 6 8 9 7 5 3 1

FIRST EDITION

Book design by Barbara M. Bachman

To our grandmothers and mothers, who came before,

our daughters, who come after,

and to us, the 51% Minority,

who must make the case today

CONTENTS

ONE STEP FORWARD, TWO STEPS BACK

Recently, I was at a dinner party and a raucous conversation ensued concerning the current political climate. There was much discussion of civil liberties, the Supreme Court, and, of course, the war in Iraq, but then the gentleman seated to my right, a successful gay professional, said something that alarmed me. "I certainly wouldn't want to be a woman today," he told the table. "It's a no-win situation. You're damned if you do and damned if you don't with every single decision, and your body is a political playground. At least as a gay man, I know where I stand. As a woman, you're stuck in some weird societal purgatory."

"Yeah," another man agreed. "Isn't it strange that women are fifty-one percent of the population and still get the short end of the stick on almost every front?"

The conversation was a punch in the gut. Not because it was disrespectful, but because I realized it was true. As women, not only are we expected to make incredible sacrifices and compromises that men are never expected to make, but we are then criticized for doing so (often even by ourselves) each and every step along the way.

The following night the conversation was still bouncing around my mind when, between my job as a professor and my job as a television legal analyst, I was making an on-the-fly, less-than-perfect dinner for my two children, nine-year-old Danielle and thirteen-year-old

Jacob. I looked at my young daughter as she animatedly talked about her day, and I pondered her future. *As she grows, is she going to get the same opportunities and advantages that my son is?* "Hey, Dani," I asked her. "Do you think there are more males or females in this country?"

"More men!" Jacob answered quickly. "That's why we're in control!"

"Nope!" I announced. "Women are fifty-one percent of the population."

"Then why don't we rule the world?" Dani asked. "We should take back the rights! *Take back the rights! Take back the rights!*" Jacob enthusiastically joined her in the chant. "*Take back the rights!*"

"Wait a minute," I told them. "You can't take back what you've never had."

They both looked at me. "So what is it exactly you want, then?" Jacob asked.

Hmmm, I thought. *Good question.*

It seems we have come a long way, baby. Commercials now hark that "choosy moms (and dads!) choose Jif!" And a woman has been president of the United States (at least on TV, until she got canceled). But is it only superficial? Are we just being pacified, yet still being served the same stale rap? Did we make some progress only to have it usurped while we were minding the kids? Have we taken two steps forward and one step back? Or worse . . . one step forward and two steps back?

True, we're no longer stuck in the narrow role of the middle-class American housewife that Betty Friedan described in *The Feminine Mystique*—certainly we'll all admit the women on *Desperate Housewives* are far from that—nor do we as a group feel harassed by the implied inequality of men holding doors for us. But are we treated equally under the law? Quite simply, *no!*

Women in America have fought for and achieved certain rights, such as the right to own property, the right to vote, and even the right to hold public office, but there's still gross inequity. For example, since 1789 only 34 women have served in the U.S. Senate, compared to

1,850 men. In the workplace, the pink-collar ghetto is alive and well. Though today we earn more than half of all bachelor's degrees, once out in the workforce we are still only making 73 cents for every dollar a man makes, and of the Fortune 500 companies, there are only eight women in the top positions. Our bodies are a veritable battleground, and not just over abortion. Several employers are now getting away with making women's weight part of their job description, but can you imagine a man being told he'd lose his job if he went bald? The average weight for women in their forties is twenty-five pounds heavier than it was in 1960, yet the "healthy" image from magazines is a look roughly twenty-five pounds lighter than it was then. Perhaps more frustrating is that we are continuously bombarded with stories and tricks on "how not to look fat" and more than a quarter of us feel the need to lie about our weight. Socially, we're still considered less than completely feminine if we're anything but demure—it's still daring to ask a man on a date, and downright audacious even to think of asking a man for his hand in marriage.

A recent survey by the Department of Labor shows that the average workingwoman spends about twice as much time as the average workingman on household chores and care of the children. On real estate deeds in many states, an unmarried woman is still listed as a "spinster." Funny how there isn't a male equivalent. And if you're not irritated yet, why is it that in many states women are denied prescription coverage for birth control even though men are allowed it for Viagra?

Yes, even with the drastic changes that have occurred in our society during the last twenty-five years, women still get, as my dinner companion so succinctly put it, the short end of the stick.

This is nothing new. Throughout the centuries, women have consistently gotten the short end of the stick when it came to freedom, power, and property. In some times and places, this was sugarcoated with idealization—women were pure, dainty creatures who ought not soil their pretty little hands with business or matters of state. (Never mind that poor women have always toiled with their hands.)

It was in the eighteenth century, when a collection of colonies decided that they were being treated unjustly, that the American woman's fight for equal treatment began. We've been left out from the beginning. In 1776 Abigail Adams wrote her husband, John, who was attending the Continental Congress in Philadelphia, "In the new code of laws, remember the ladies and do not put such unlimited power into the hands of the husbands." John Adams replied, "I cannot but laugh. Depend upon it, we know better than to repeal our masculine systems." And the men convening there drafted the Declaration of Independence, which states that "all *men* are created equal."

Yes, shortly after the "all men are created equal" line, it became self-evident that we women were somehow not. We weren't allowed to vote for the first president, or the second. In fact, it wasn't until the thirtieth president that we finally got to cast our vote, and we only got that right because in the late 1800s the women's suffrage movement began to demand it.

In January 1917, when we still didn't have the right, a group of women sitting in the gallery during Woodrow Wilson's State of the Union address unfurled a large yellow banner asking, "Mr. President, what will you do for woman suffrage?" and women started demonstrating in front of the White House. By July of that year, an annoyed President Wilson was tired of all the demonstrating and started arresting the suffragists. Rather than giving up, they rallied. One of the movement's leaders, Alice Paul, went on a hunger strike in jail, and they tied her down and force-fed her three times a day for three weeks. When she was released from prison, she fought harder. Finally, President Wilson got the point and said he would support women's right to vote. The Nineteenth Amendment to the Constitution was ratified in 1920.

In 1921, Alice Paul drafted what she considered the logical next step, a simple amendment: "Men and women shall have equal rights throughout the United States and every place subject to its jurisdiction." In 1923, an empathetic male introduced it before Congress. Here we are almost a century later, and we *still* do not have equality of rights under the law.

The 1930s saw a chastened nation enter an age in which survival became a larger issue than social progress. Women in the workplace were frowned upon, as they would be taking a job that might go to a husband and father, but when they were *needed* during World War II, women were actively encouraged and lionized by the media for filling male roles. So many men were off to war that women were hired for the kinds of higher-paid, often heavy labor jobs that they'd never have been offered a decade earlier. Women could help win the war by working, and six million Rosie the Riveters went into the workforce in higher paying industrial jobs.

It didn't last. When the boys came marching home, the girls were expected to move out of the way: "Give me back my wrench, and get back into the house where you belong." Though 98 percent of women polled at the time said they would like to use the skills they had acquired and continue working, one out of every four lost her factory job. In another poll in 1945, 57 percent of women and 63 percent of men said that married women whose husbands earned enough shouldn't be *allowed* to work.

In the 1950s, a campaign every bit as manipulative as the one that gave birth to Rosie the Riveter tried to sell women on the idea that ultimate happiness and satisfaction could be achieved only by devoting one's energies fully to home and hearth. Magazines such as *McCall's* and early television shows pushed an image of family togetherness in which the male ruled supreme and the woman, in her starched apron (to be removed in favor of something a little sexier before the husband's return in the evening) was intended to find her fulfillment by concentrating on the children and the nest, to the exclusion of all else.

The suburban tract house was filled with a gleaming array of modern appliances. These "advances" and workload somehow just weren't as fulfilling as the ads and articles promised, and physicians began prescribing more and more barbiturates and tranquilizers as women began having "nervous breakdowns" in droves. Psychiatrists and pundits proclaimed that women who wanted more were maladjusted and frigid, and probably to blame for everything from juvenile delinquency to homosexuality.

In 1959 Betty Friedan's *The Feminine Mystique* proposed that the problem with women's lives might be their circumstances rather than themselves. And then, with the advent of the birth control pill, a woman was no longer at the mercy of her fertility.

In 1964 Title VII of the Federal Civil Rights Act was passed making it unlawful to discriminate against any individual because of race, color, religion, sex, or national origin in matters of employment. Ironically, gender was added to Title VII by conniving lawmakers in hopes of spoiling its chances for passage. Fortunately, the effort failed and Title VII passed.

Throughout the 1960s and 1970s, women continued to enter the workforce, and those who enrolled in institutions of higher education increasingly strove for something besides what used to be scathingly referred to as the "MRS degree." They liberated themselves from their girdles and bras, and in the let-it-all-hang-out atmosphere of the times, more and more women began to simply talk to one another about their issues. As they shared life experiences and concerns, a collective epiphany happened: *It's not just me.* And the personal became political.

In 1972, the Equal Rights Amendment actually passed Congress after forty-nine years of trying—and seemed set to have at least thirty-eight states ratify it into law. Then in 1973, with *Roe v. Wade,* the United States Supreme Court declared abortion to be a private matter between a woman and her doctor. Everything is heading in the right direction, right?

Nope—enter the backlash. The ERA, it was said, would legislate single-sex education out of existence, make government-funded abortions a necessity, subject women to the draft, and make single-sex public toilets illegal. Women such as Phyllis Schaffly added their voices to the chorus of fear and loathing, and suggested that a radical minority of women were demanding societal changes that "normal" women were not willing to support. Not only did the amendment fall three states short of passage, "women's libbers" and "feminists" were branded bad people.

For the next twenty-five years, "women's libbers" and "feminists" were demonized, and more and more women were subversively co-erced into closing their mouths and settling for what our male leaders have deemed best for us since 1776.

This book isn't a diatribe. It is a heartfelt effort to point out where we as women don't have equality under the law and to suggest ways to make it better. Admittedly, we are still living in a world that views the struggle for equality as unladylike, unfeminine, but my hope is that as I make this case and you read of the real-life struggles of the women in these pages, you'll agree that equality is not, as Rush Limbaugh says, about being a "feminazi"; it's about being human. Equally human.

I'm a woman who went to law school with the belief that I could make a difference—that I could affect the lives of other people positively by fighting for what's right. Besides being a lawyer, a professor, and a TV commentator, I'm a divorced and recently remarried mother of two kids who has just used her life savings to buy a house. I work three jobs while helping with homework, chauffeuring my son to baseball, throwing slumber parties for my daughter, and trying to remember to turn in the Girl Scout cookie money. In short, I, like you, am a twenty-first-century woman.

Yes, one of the 150 million of you. And I'm here to tell you we're the majority—our nation is now 51 percent girls and women, 49 percent boys and men, and given the strength of our numbers, I believe we *can* and *must* be honest about our needs and desires and *bold* in our quest for equality. We must not accept the idea that we are a "special interest group," that our pregnancies are "disabilities," and that our work efforts don't measure up dollar for dollar to men's. What's good for us is good for all. We can demand to be heard and we can demand that our wishes be acted upon.

So, here we sit in the breaking dawn of the twenty-first century, and we've actually taken a step (or two) backward. Sure, we've come a long way from the 1876 ruling by a Minnesota court that decreed women did not need access to a legal education because they were too busy taking care of their children to study. But here it is 2007 and the

Supreme Court is down to one woman, *Roe v. Wade* is in danger of being overturned, and we women are still being kept in our place by men in leadership positions deciding what's best for us, all the while maintaining the status quo.

So, what does "women's rights" mean to a woman in the twenty-first century? What women want today is certainly different from what it was 100 years ago, but it's also radically different from the wants of our mothers and our mothers' mothers. It's not about burning bras, or about bashing men. We're women with a different set of needs than those who came before. But what are those needs? What's missing from our lives? Where is the playing field not level? And what are our *actual* legal rights?

In a September 2005 *New York Times* article headlined "Many Women at Elite Colleges Set Career Path to Motherhood," reporter Lisa Belkin stirred the pot by suggesting that many women at the nation's most elite colleges aspired to play the "traditional female role" after college, putting aside careers in order to make raising children their main commitment. One young woman (a Yale pre-law student with a 4.0 average) said her mother had always told her that she'd have to choose between career and motherhood because "you can't be great at both at the same time."

Belkin's survey of Yale undergraduates found that a whopping 60 percent said they'd cut back or stop working once they had children. The piece was followed by a tidal wave of letters that reflected divergent views from both men and women. The passionate responses made me want to find out more. I developed a survey to find out what it means to be a woman today and what we want as we look toward the future. Dani, my nine-year-old, wanted to participate too. Here is her list of the rights she wants, spelling errors and all:

We're just as good as men!
Be the best you can be.
No holding back . . .
Fite the power.
Woman as Pope!

In addition to Dani, more than three hundred women across the country answered the survey—all ages, all demographics—and the results helped craft this book. As you'll see in the cases and issues in this book, today's women are concerned about ageism, about society's obsession with their looks over their abilities, about domestic violence, about equal pay, about being treated with respect, about *Roe v. Wade*, and about the future.

In talking to women from across the nation—young, old, fat, thin, rich, poor, famous, and famous only to their husbands and kids—I've discovered that today gender inequality is still rampant, in both transparent and covert ways. What women want are improvements in areas of social equality, domestic obligations, and employment opportunities.

You'll hear the stories of real-life women who are struggling for equal treatment and deserved respect. We'll examine their situations, their predicaments, and find out how their situation indicates a systemic problem. Are you entitled to your job back after your pregnancy? What legal options do women have if their company won't give them their jobs back? Can you be told you must dress in a more "ladylike" manner at work? Or worse, what do you do when your boss tells you to lose weight or else lose your job?

Our laws are meant to assist us in the pursuit of happiness, but are they helping us do that? Have we become complacent, not because we're not concerned, but because we've become so busy keeping the balls in the air and food on the table that we don't have time to make it better? Have we settled into our routines and become a group of women who feel responsible to the demands of others—our husbands, our children, our parents, our bosses—and forgotten about ourselves?

Why have our voices gone quiet? Have we taken one step forward and two steps back by becoming the we-can-do-it-all gender, the ultimate "wonder women"—accepting our lot and spinning faster and faster, changing our hats with every spin? Why have we lost the fire of our foremothers? My fear is that younger women today are taking their rights for granted and do not understand that the laws that em-

power us, such as *Roe v. Wade,* which granted us control over our bodies, were not always here and are in danger of being taken away.
Someone spoke up and fought for those rights, and many of them are
quietly falling away like petals from a flower.

It's daunting how much easier it is to erase rights we have than
gain new ones. If we don't protect what we have, our daughters will be
left worse off than we are. How can we help our daughters protect
and strengthen our rights, setting them on a path to reaching their
full potential? How can we help our sons develop into men who are
caring and aware? How can we help ourselves today?

These questions encourage us to find out who we are as women,
what we want, and how we can do our part to follow that dream. They
can only be answered by contemplating how far we have (and have
not) come and by examining which rights we still need to fight for
and who should be on the front lines of those battles. And the answers make the case for us to become the most fulfilled, empowered
women we can be, transforming ourselves from a group that follows
to a group that leads and *unites.* In this divided nation, I can think of
no more important task.

The **51%** Minority

CHAPTER 1

EQUAL = EQUAL

"I have the right to be president <u>and</u> mommy"

There's much speculation that we'll have a woman running for president of the United States as early as 2008. According to a Siena College Research Institute survey, 81 percent of voters across the country are ready to vote for a woman for president, 62 percent say the country is ready for a woman president, and 52 percent of voters feel that a president's gender wouldn't matter when it came to foreign affairs.

In the 86 years we've been able to vote, only one woman has been on a major party ticket: Geraldine Ferraro as running mate to Walter Mondale in 1984. "Even God herself couldn't have changed that outcome with the Reagan ticket," Ferraro says, reflecting on that election. "But I'll tell you, if a woman were president today, we wouldn't be at war in Iraq. And though the administration didn't *cause* Hurricane Katrina, a woman would have responded differently—the response would have been immediate, with much more empathy, and the guys who screwed up would have been fired immediately."

In her book *Closing the Leadership Gap*, White House Project founder Marie Wilson quotes the Rev. Patricia Kitchen: "For over 200 years, the United States has been steered by male leadership who tend to lead from a self-centered, self-preservation perspective. Women around the world are inclined to lead, their families and nations, from an other-centered perspective."

"For the most part women are much more collaborative and inclusive," Washington governor Christine Gregoire said. "Women won't just announce a decision—it's going to be done this way or that way. We have the attitude of 'Let's try to talk through the issues,' which avoids confrontation and controversy. That's my style and I've observed it in a lot of women."

"Outsiders often bring clarity of vision, as well as a sense of discovery and innovation," Anna Quindlen wrote in her "Last Word" column for *Newsweek*'s special report on how women lead. "Women are not the only ones capable of this. But the difficulties they've encountered while seeking representation and respect may provide the steel and strength needed to embrace change. You're less wedded to the shape of the table if you haven't been permitted to sit at it."

At the table of leaders and decision makers, we remain outsiders. For every ten men in executive roles in this country there is only one woman, a number that has changed little in twenty years. As for those who sit in judgment of the cases that establish legal precedent in this country, there are 629 male federal judges, 199 female. And in the history of our country 98.25 percent of our senators have been men.

What has this male dominated leadership decided? That they'll let us know what we can and can't do. Instead of making it easier on women, the Bush administration has made decisions that have made being a woman even harder. During this administration, child care programs have been underfunded and undermined, making such drastic cuts that only one out of seven children eligible for federal child care assistance receives help. By the Bush administration's own estimates, this change will result in 300,000 children losing child care assistance by 2009. This isn't helping children, this isn't helping women, and this isn't helping our society.

This administration's tax cuts have also affected women and children. In addition to the drastic cuts in child care programs, programs such as housing subsidies, Pell grants to help pay for college, and aid to state and local governments have been slashed in order to pay for these cuts. The average tax cut for millionaires was about $113,000 in 2003, five times the income that a typical single mother with children lives on for an entire year.

Think that's bad? According to the National Women's Law Center, it gets worse:

• The administration ended the equal pay initiative and has removed all materials on narrowing the wage gap from the Department of Labor's website. The Department of Justice has also dropped cases challenging sex discrimination in employment.
• The Department of Education has "archived" all Title IX guidance on preventing sexual harassment in schools, making it unavailable to administrators and parents trying to protect children from sexual harassment.
• The administration has placed individuals hostile to women's interests on advisory bodies, such as those responsible for domestic violence and reproductive health.
• The administration proposed cutting funding to emergency shelters, crisis hotlines, and other domestic violence services to 26 percent below previously authorized levels.
• The administration's plan to "restructure" Medicaid, changing it from an entitlement program to a block grant, will result in more women without health insurance.
• For the first time in history, states can now deny contraception and family planning services to poor women.
• The administration has backed laws criminalizing abortion, while cutting out family planning programs vital to women's health.
• Medical research is being undermined and scientific information distorted to serve an anti-abortion and anti-family-planning agenda. For example, the National Cancer Institute posted information on its website that falsely suggested there's a link between abortion and breast cancer.

"The administration's policies are reversing progress for women and girls across the board," Nancy Duff Campbell, co-president of the National Women's Law Center, said. "The few positive steps the administration has taken to help women are overshadowed by the overwhelming number of proposals that hurt them."

Perhaps most troubling is the fact that President Bush has appointed to the Supreme Court and federal courts judicial nominees who oppose critical rights for women and girls. Since federal judges are appointed for life, they have the opportunity to affect generations. Justice Antonin Scalia, for example, who has consistently voted against the protections of *Roe v. Wade*, was appointed by President Reagan in 1986, when Scalia was fifty. It should not go unnoticed that President George W. Bush has consistently appointed younger conservative judges.

His new appointments to the Supreme Court (two males—age fifty and fifty-five—to replace one male and one female) have consistently opposed women's rights, and their judicial philosophies seem against our progress toward equality. During his years as a legal adviser to President Reagan, new chief justice John G. Roberts Jr. opposed legal and legislative attempts to strengthen women's rights, questioning "whether encouraging homemakers to become lawyers contributes to the common good" and disparaging "the purported gender gap." In internal memos to Reagan that surfaced during his confirmation hearings, Roberts encouraged ignoring the Equal Rights Amendment that was pending in Congress and said that directing employers to give equal pay to women as men in jobs of "comparable worth" was "staggeringly pernicious" and "anti-capitalist."

As a Justice Department attorney, Justice Samuel Alito (President Bush's replacement for Sandra Day O'Connor) wrote a memo laying out a proposal for the eventual overturning of *Roe v. Wade*. On the bench, Judge Alito voted in favor of upholding a provision in the 1982 Pennsylvania Abortion Control Act that required married women considering an abortion to notify their husbands. Judge Alito's opinions in sexual discrimination and sexual harassment cases demonstrated his desire to make it easier for judges to dismiss cases before they ever get to a jury, and he wrote the Third Circuit decision that Congress did not have the power to require state governments to comply with the Family and Medical Leave Act. Fortunately, three years later the Supreme Court disagreed. But now he's one of them.

TAKING THE LEAD

Around the world, women are proving that we do make a difference when we're in positions of power. Court TV's Catherine Crier recalled a women's seminar she moderated during which several members of Congress, writers, and businesswomen were asked what they'd do if they were president of the United States. "Asked to summarize at meeting's end, I said that all the participants described their issues and policies in terms of 'stewardship.' None of them talked about manipulating power for power's sake or acquiring money or influence. I do believe this is a female perspective—one the world needs desperately. Women truly think in terms of future generations and the vast majority would put more effort into addressing education, health care, and poverty. Imagine women working to preserve the environment and therefore pushing energy independence and freedom from fossil fuels. Imagine how they would negotiate issues of war and peace before sending their sons and daughters into battle."

Though no woman has ever been nominated, we do have the right to be president of the United States—well, sort of. Article 2, section 1, clause 5 of the Constitution states: "No Person except a natural born Citizen, or a Citizen of the United States, at the time of the Adoption of this Constitution, shall be eligible to the Office of President; neither shall any Person be eligible to that Office who shall not have attained to the Age of thirty-five Years, and been fourteen Years a Resident within the United States." (Clause 1 says: "He shall hold his Office during the Term of four years." Presumably the eight males and one female of the Supreme Court will recognize the use of *he* in the generic sense.)

The White House Project, an organization dedicated to fostering the entry of women into leadership positions, including the presidency, and *CosmoGirl!* magazine have established an internship to groom seven ambitious young women for the chance to run in the presidential election of 2024. But that's five elections away. What about *now* in this country? Isn't it time? Hillary? Condoleezza? Kay Bailey Hutchison? Susan Collins? Or maybe a political outsider such as Oprah? Oprah, in an essay entitled "How I Got There" that she wrote for *Newsweek,* described the secret to her success: "I'm always aiming for the truth. I relate to the core of everyone's pain and promise. I understand that the common denominator in the human experience from the thousands of people that I've talked to is that everybody just wants to be heard."

And perhaps that's what our first woman president will do differently than the men before her: *she will listen.* A woman as commander in chief would certainly go a long way to help regain some of our losses in Supreme Court representation and in other areas of government. Looking at women leaders around the world, their tenures suggest a lot about how a female president might approach the job:

In Chile, President Michelle Bachelet Jeria created a balanced cabinet of ten men and ten women, fulfilling her campaign promise. The fifty-five-year-old divorced mother of three ran on the platform of creating balance. Bachelet's first three months in office were spent working on thirty-six measures she had promised to implement during her first one hundred days as president. They ranged from simple presidential decrees, such as reducing the age for free health care from sixty-five to sixty, to guaranteeing day care services for all preschool children in the neediest forty percent of the population.

The president of Finland, Tarja Halonen, sixty-three, has approval ratings that hover around 88 percent. She has been a strong supporter of human rights, international solidarity, and pacifism, and she's already being mentioned as a possible United Nations secretary general.

When Ellen Johnson-Sirleaf, sixty-eight, assumed the presidency of Liberia, the divorced mother of four boys and grandmother of six immediately cracked down on corruption. She fired all officials appointed by the former government and announced that civil servants would all be thoroughly investigated. To address the rape epidemic in that country, one of her first actions was to pass a law that made rape illegal.

Mary McAleese, the fifty-five-year-old president of Ireland, ran on the theme of "building bridges" and has been welcomed in Northern Ireland by both Catholics and Protestants. The president of Latvia, Vaira Vike-Freiberga, is hugely popular. The seventy-year-old was pivotal in improving relations with foreign countries, joining NATO and the European Union. Her approval ratings have ranged between 70 and 85 percent.

The president of the Philippines, Gloria Macapagal-Arroyo, a practicing economist, made the economy the focus of her presidency. She's implemented out-of-the-ordinary solutions to economic policy, such as her "holiday economics" program, under which the government adjusts holidays to form longer weekends. Her theory was that the long weekends would allow people to spend more time with their families and boost the economy by promoting domestic travel and tourism. Economic growth in the Philippines under her leadership has been record-breaking. Inflation there is the lowest since 1986 and the annual growth in the gross domestic product, 4.6 percent, is almost a percentage point higher than under any other president.

Prime Minister Helen Clark of New Zealand brought in significant changes to the welfare system and child tax credits in her "Working for Families" package. Her government has also changed industrial relations law and raised the minimum wage six times in as many years.

Chancellor Angela Merkel of Germany has the highest approval ratings recorded for a chancellor since 1949. Many economic commentators have referred to the "Merkel factor," which has caused a rapid rise in consumer confidence and market spending.

Women such as Portia Simpson-Miller, prime minister of Jamaica, and Khaleda Zia, prime minister of Bangladesh, are making a difference for the poor and the oppressed in their countries. Simpson-Miller has been an advocate for those in Jamaica who have historically been voiceless and faceless in the corridors of power, namely, women and the poor. Zia instituted compulsory free primary education in

Bangladesh and, though she is the mother of two boys, she has given girls the chance, for the first time, to receive a free education up until the tenth grade, including a stipend for food.

Yes, it would be great to have a woman president—not just to say we have a woman on the job but because she'll recognize that *what women need, we all need.* But let's get real. Not every woman wants to be president, nor does every man. Actually, many women don't want a job outside their home at all, considering the monumental task of raising kids to be quite enough. Society and other women should applaud whichever role we star in—as long as we've chosen that role and not been forced into it by societal expectations, lack of support, or biases.

Why, then, does it seem that men in this country are somehow better predisposed for leadership positions, such as CEO and president of the United States? Perhaps it's because we have been made to believe it. In a 2004 *Harvard Business Review* article entitled "Do Women Lack Ambition?" psychiatrist Anna Fels made the point that women—far more than men—consider and reconsider a decision to pursue a goal and often abandon it, not because they aren't ambitious but because societal norms tell women that they shouldn't be.

Fels examined studies that explored attitudes toward women versus those toward men from preschool on; the discoveries are deeply troubling. One project studied fourth, sixth, and eighth grade classrooms and found that "teachers praise boys more than girls, give boys more academic help, and are more likely to accept boys' comments during classroom discussions." In another study of how women and men are viewed in the workplace, researchers asked two groups of people to evaluate items such as articles, paintings, and résumés, all clearly marked with either male or female names, but reversed for each group. In other words, what one group believed was originated by a man, the other group believed was originated by a woman. "Regardless of the items, when they were ascribed to a man, they were rated higher than when they were ascribed to a woman."

Lawrence Summers, while president of Harvard, found it appropriately provocative to suggest at a prominent academic conference that fewer women succeed in math and the sciences because married women with children aren't willing to accept the sacrifices demanded by the eighty-hour workweek and that women somehow may be biologically unsuited to succeed in these areas. The firestorm of controversy that erupted after these comments made it clear that many people felt the remarks were purely sexist. And yet his comments raise troubling questions: Was Summers discouraging women from entering the sciences by suggesting to them, both deliberately and subliminally, that they won't succeed as scientists? Is he suggesting that only men should be scientists? Just how should the women pursuing Ph.D.'s in science and engineering at his school feel? And what about the women who are applying or have applied for teaching positions there?

When I was considering careers, my dad told me the tale of his first day in law school. The dean stood before the incoming class and said of their difficult journey ahead, "Look to your left, look to your right, gentlemen; one of you won't be here at graduation." Yes, his class was all men. Today women earn more than half of all bachelor's degrees, 57 percent of all master's degrees, and 44 percent of all law degrees. Women are receiving half of chemistry and 60 percent of biology bachelor of science degrees. In the 1970s women earned only 9 percent of all medical degrees; by 2004, 50 percent of all entering medical students were women. And, according to studies, the gender gap in these fields is definitively cultural, not genetic.

Summers eventually issued a two-page apology that was posted on the Harvard website, in which he said, "I was wrong to have spoken in a way that has resulted in an unintended signal of discouragement to talented girls and women." Perhaps it was the "untalented" ones to which his speech referred. Apologize as he tried, he had said it, couldn't take it back, and lost his job for publicly subscribing to the belief that women didn't *want* to work as hard as men. That, well, their brains aren't, um, made for this kind of stuff. I mean, they've got to be home!

Betty Friedan concluded *The Feminine Mystique* with some questions: "Who knows what women can be when they are finally free to become themselves? Who knows what women's intelligence will contribute when it can be nourished without denying love? Who knows of the possibilities of love when men and women share not only children, home, and garden, not only the fulfillment of their biological roles, but the responsibilities and passions of the work that creates the human future and the full human knowledge of who they are?"

Forty years later, how have we moved toward answering her questions? Are we finally free to become ourselves? Sort of. Are we able to prove our intelligence in the workplace without denying time and love to our children and families? Rarely. Are our husbands and partners sharing fully in the responsibilities of raising and nurturing our children? No.

One thing is for certain: after examining the laws in this country, we are no longer faced with the "problem that has no name." We're able to name it, and its name is inequality.

WHAT CAN WE DO?

Our laws have changed a lot over the course of the last hundred years. We've gotten the right to vote, to use contraception, to have control over our body, and to bring suit if we're discriminated against in the workplace. But society still isn't behind us—and perhaps we ourselves haven't fully embraced the goal.

"We live in a time when our individual rights are more threatened than at any time in decades," said Ellen Dial, president of the Washington Bar Association. "It is very sobering. I've told my daughter that it is a failure of my generation that we haven't solidified the advances made by the very brave women who led the fight for women's rights in this country. I don't know if it was a sense of complacency or the degree to which our lives got a lot more complicated, but I think women have been working hard to do well, and we've failed to make sure that basic freedoms of privacy and equality were forever installed in our legal system so they couldn't be taken away again. We haven't done what we could have done."

But we're not helpless. We can't sit around waiting on a benevolent male ruler to decide our fate. We may still earn less than men, but women make up 73 percent of all shoppers in the United States and spend 80 cents of every dollar. As we all know, money talks. With that spending muscle, we wield an extraordinary amount of power.

What's more, we're a majority of the population and, according to the United States Census Bureau, the majority of the voting population. In 2000, women voters surpassed men voters in the U.S. presidential elections for the first time. Fifty-four percent of voters are female, and 61 percent of the eligible female population voted, compared to 58 percent of males—a difference of about eight million votes.

In a survey commissioned by Votes for Women 2004, a project of the Communications Consortium Media Center, 61 percent of women voters felt that "women's equality under the law" was the top issue that candidates did not talk about enough. Second, at 60 percent, was "equal pay for women," followed by "prevention of violence against women," at 58 percent, and "appointing women to leadership positions in the administration," at 54 percent. A majority of voters, 55 percent, agreed that if U.S. women had equal rights under the law, it would strengthen their economic well-being. Women are most often the ones who have to leave work to relieve the babysitter or can't afford a babysitter because we can't get a job that pays enough for us to make a living and pay for child care. Even worse, the fact that the men working next to us are making 25 percent more for the same work because they have "a family to provide for" is a travesty and must be stopped.

Washington governor Christine Gregoire focuses a great deal of attention on the issues facing women and children. "Before women got into office," she said, "men didn't have to focus on those issues. Now, if you don't have a focus on those issues, you won't get very far. Women have found the power of the electoral box."

Today there is power in our numbers. We have to understand that we can determine the outcome of any election, and in so doing, we should demand nothing less than equality. We should all, whether male or female, have an equal opportunity to pursue the American dream with equal rights so that through honesty, hard work, and determination we can have an equal chance of living the best life.

Men and women are different—there's no denying that. But it's time the white males in power think outside themselves and realize that we need more than we've gotten. And if they aren't going to realize it, we'll realize it for them.

What we decide to do with that equal footing—whether it's in the home or outside the home—isn't as important as having it in the first place, so that we can succeed in doing whatever we put our minds to. We all want an equal chance of winning when the cards are dealt. And we must work toward a different future for ourselves and our daughters, such that they are given that equal chance—that equal right—to pursue their dreams.

"We have to stop taking no for an answer," television anchor Rita Cosby declared. "We need to realize that we can often turn the no into a yes. With tenacity, vision, appreciation for others, and a little push of the envelope, I believe we can achieve our wildest dreams and well beyond! We should be afraid *not* to try." And we certainly shouldn't have laws working against us.

CHAPTER 2

EQUAL PAY

"I have the right to equal pay for equal work"

Women earn 73 cents for every dollar men make. That's right, we have to work *three and a half months longer* than men in order to make the same amount they do in a year. Each year, the National Committee on Pay Equity (NCPE) denotes a day in late April as "Equal Pay Day." A state holiday in California, it's the day women's earnings finally catch up to what men made the previous year. What does that mean in terms of numbers? Well, women are losing out on average more than $300,000 over the course of a lifetime—that's the difference between owning a home and renting, sending your children to college or not, retiring comfortably or scraping along on Social Security. For women of color the difference is even greater. In one year, the average black woman earns approximately $12,000 less than the average white man. Over a thirty-five-year career, this adds up to $420,000. And for the average Hispanic woman, the news is even worse. They earn $17,837 less than the average white man annually. Over a thirty-year career, that's more than a half million dollars!

Surely there must be some other factor, such as education or job task, that leads to the discrepancy. But there isn't. NCPE studies show a wage gap in numerous professions even when comparing women and men who have the same job, education, qualifications, and time in the workforce. For example, a survey of public relations professionals showed that women with less than five years of experience make $29,726, while their male counterparts earn $48,162. A study of women in the telecommunications industry showed that among video programmers, women with advanced degrees earn 64.6 percent of the salary of their male colleagues, and women with college degrees earn 80 percent. Women attorneys earn nearly $375 per week less than male attorneys, women doctors earn nearly $680 per week less than male doctors, women professors earn $245 per week less than male professors, and women schoolteachers earn $86 per week less than male teachers.

"This wage disparity is a lifelong problem for women," says Washington senator Patty Murray, "because it follows them into retirement. Women are twice as likely to live in poverty over age sixty-five. Women are more dependent upon Social Security for a greater percentage of their retirement income. And because of lower lifetime wages, many women are unable to contribute to private pensions or retirement savings."

In 1995, the U.S. government's Glass Ceiling Commission published its findings that there were barriers continuing "to deny untold numbers of qualified people [read: women] the opportunity to compete for and hold executive level positions in the private sector." At that time, women held 45.7 percent of America's jobs, but 95 percent of senior managers were men. More shocking was that when women did make it to a managerial position, their earnings on average were a mere 68 percent of what their male counterparts made.

I ask you, does this sound like equal pay?

THE RIGHTS WE HAVE

After hearing these statistics, you may be surprised to learn that there is a forty-three-year-old federal law banning wage discrimination based on sex. Signed into law on June 10, 1963, by President John F. Kennedy to a lot of fanfare, the act made it illegal to pay women lower rates than men simply because of their sex.

The need for the law had become apparent. Women, who had served patriotically in war industry jobs while men were off fighting World War II, not only had made less in the same positions but also had been pushed out of their jobs when the men came back from war. Requests by the National Labor Board that companies voluntarily make "adjustments which equalize wage or salary rates paid to females with the rates paid to males for comparable quality and quantity of work on the same or similar operations" went unheeded. Between 1950 and 1960 women were making, on average, more than 40 percent less than their male counterparts in the same job, and there was no attempt to hide the fact. It was as obvious as the classified ads run in every newspaper across the country: "Help Wanted—Male." Jobs were categorized according to gender, and most employers looking to fill the higher-paying jobs were seeking men. When it came to the jobs that were for the "low man on the totem pole," the women's totem pole was even lower: *identical* jobs were listed under "male" and "female" with different pay rates!

So President Kennedy signed an act whose intentions were good— equal pay for equal work—but whose results for the average woman weren't very effective. Between then and now, the closing of the wage gap has been at a rate of less than half a penny a year. Why? Because in law the exception can swallow the rule, and loopholes often provide an effective out for the corporations that underwrite much of our political system. Here's the law (I know it's long, but you need to read it in order to see how our laws provide legal loopholes that protect corporations more than women):

MINIMUM WAGE

SEC. 206

—

(d) (1) No employer having employees subject to any provisions of this section shall discriminate, within any establishment in which such employees are employed, between employees on the basis of sex by paying wages to employees in such establishment

at a rate less than the rate at which he pays wages to employees
of the opposite sex in such establishment for equal work on jobs
the performance of which requires equal skill, effort, and responsibility, and which are performed under similar working conditions, except where such payment is made pursuant to (i) a
seniority system; (ii) a merit system; (iii) a system which measures earnings by quantity or quality of production; or (iv) a differential based on any other factor other than sex: *Provided*, That
an employer who is paying a wage rate differential in violation of
this subsection shall not, in order to comply with the provisions
of this subsection, reduce the wage rate of any employee.

And here are the *exceptions* to the law, aka the small print:

EXEMPTIONS

SEC. 213

—

(a) The provisions of sections 206 (except subsection (d) in the
case of paragraph (1) of this subsection) and section 207 shall
not apply with respect to—

(1) any employee employed in a bona fide executive, administrative, or professional capacity (including any employee employed
in the capacity of academic administrative personnel or teacher in
elementary or secondary schools), or in the capacity of outside
salesman (as such terms are defined and delimited from time to
time by regulations of the secretary, subject to the provisions of
subchapter II of chapter 5 of title 5 [the Administrative Procedure
Act], except that an employee of a retail or service establishment
shall not be excluded from the definition of employee employed in
a bona fide executive or administrative capacity because of the
number of hours in his workweek which he devotes to activities
not directly or closely related to the performance of executive or

administrative activities, if less than 40 per centum of his hours worked in the workweek are devoted to such activities); or

(2) [This section was repealed but related to employees of a retail or service establishment.]

(3) any employee employed by an establishment which is an amusement or recreational establishment, organized camp, or religious or non-profit educational conference center, if (A) it does not operate for more than seven months in any calendar year, or (B) during the preceding calendar year, its average receipts for any six months of such year were not more than 33⅓ per centum of its average receipts for the other six months of such year, except that the exemption from sections 206 and 207 of this title provided by this paragraph does not apply with respect to any employee of a private entity engaged in providing services or facilities (other than, in the case of the exemption from section 206, a private entity engaged in providing services and facilities directly related to skiing) in a national park or a national forest, or on land in the National Wildlife Refuge System, under a contract with the Secretary of the Interior or the Secretary of Agriculture; or

(4) [This section was repealed but provided exemptions to employers in retail establishments.]

(5) any employee employed in the catching, taking, propagating, harvesting, cultivating, or farming of any kind of fish, shellfish, crustacea, sponges, seaweeds, or other aquatic forms of animal and vegetable life, or in the first processing, canning or packing such marine products at sea as an incident to, or in conjunction with, such fishing operations, including the going to and returning from work and loading and unloading when performed by any such employee; or

(6) any employee employed in agriculture (A) if such employee is employed by an employer who did not, during any calendar quarter during the preceding calendar year, use more than five hundred man-days or agricultural labor, (B) if such employee is the parent, spouse, child, or other member of his employer's immediate family, (C) if such employee (i) is employed as a hand harvest laborer and is paid on a piece rate basis in an operation which has been, and is customarily and generally recognized as having been, paid on a piece rate basis in the region of employment, (ii) commutes daily from his permanent residence to the farm on which he is so employed, and (iii) has been employed in agriculture less than thirteen weeks during the preceding calendar year, (D) if such employee (other than an employee described in clause (C) of this subsection) (i) is sixteen years of age or under and is employed as a hand harvest laborer, is paid on a piece rate basis in an operation which has been, and is customarily and generally recognized as having been, paid on a piece rate basis in the region of employment, (ii) is employed on the same farm as his parent or person standing in the place of his parent, and (iii) is paid at the same piece rate as employees over age sixteen are paid on the same farm, or (E) if such employee is principally engaged in the range production of livestock; or

(7) any employee to the extent that such employee is exempted by regulations, order, or certificate of the Secretary issued under section 214 of this title; or

(8) any employee employed in connection with the publication of any weekly, semiweekly, or daily newspaper with a circulation of less than four thousand the major part of which circulation is within the county where published or counties contiguous thereto; or

(9) [This section was repealed, but provided overtime provision exemptions to employers in motion picture theaters.]

(10) any switchboard operator employed by an independently owned public telephone company which has not more than seven hundred and fifty stations; or

(11) [This section was repealed, but provided overtime provision exemptions for telegraph agency employers.]

(12) any employee employed as a seaman on a vessel other than an American vessel; or

(13) [This section was repealed, but provided overtime provision exemptions to small logging crews.]

(14) [This section was repealed, but exempted tobacco growers.]

(15) any employee employed on a casual basis in domestic service employment to provide babysitting services or any employee employed in domestic service employment to provide companionship services for individuals who (because of age or infirmity) are unable to care for themselves (as such terms are defined and delimited by regulations of the Secretary).

. . .

(g) The exemption from section 206 of this title provided by paragraph (6) of subsection (a) of this section shall not apply with respect to any employee employed by an establishment (1) which controls, is controlled by, or is under common control with, another establishment the activities of which are not related for a common business purpose to, but materially support the activities of the establishment employing such employee; and (2) whose annual gross volume of sales made or business done, when combined with the annual gross volume of sales made or business done by each establishment which controls, is controlled by, or is under common control with, the establishment

employing such employee, exceeds $10,000,000 (exclusive of ex-
cise taxes at the retail level which are separately stated).

Translated into regular-speak for you and me, what's left is that
"equal pay for equal work" does not really mean that women have to
be paid equally. The loopholes protect the employer more than the employee. Don't misunderstand—since its inception in 1963, thousands
of women, from factory workers to grocery store clerks to college professors, have used the Equal Pay Act to fight wage discrimination. But
the act doesn't apply to employees who are employed in an executive,
administrative, or professional capacity (including any academic administrators personnel or teachers in elementary or secondary
schools), or in the capacity of outside salesman. That covers a lot of
positions, right?

And then, to get more specific, it also doesn't apply to anyone employed by an amusement or recreational establishment, organized
camp, religious or nonprofit educational conference center that does
not operate for more than seven months in any calendar year, or during the preceding calendar year, if its average receipts for any six
months of such year were not more than one third of its average receipts for the other six months of such year. (Got it?) The Equal Pay
Act also does not apply if you are working in the fishing or agriculture
sectors, or if you are employed by any weekly, semiweekly, or daily
newspaper with a circulation of less than four thousand. There is also
an exemption from the law for any domestic service employee who
provides babysitting services or companionship services for older or
disabled individuals (traditionally women's work).

Geraldine Ferraro, sponsor of the Women's Economic Equity Act
of 1984, which ended pension discrimination against women, provided job options for displaced homemakers, and enabled homemakers to open IRAs, put it bluntly: "Roadblocks still exist. Women aren't
getting equal money because with these loopholes most corporations
will take the chance and would sooner pay for the rare judgments
against them than deal with 'lesser beings' that do 'less quality work.' "

"Substantially Equal"

What's worse is—though a number of court cases have established that jobs need be only *substantially equal,* not identical, in order to be compared for purposes of the act—when it comes to proving that jobs are "substantially equal" and the law has been violated, it is often an impossible feat and many cases fail in court for this reason.

In one recent case in Maryland that went on to be heard by the Supreme Court, two women who supervised a county 911 emergency center (as director and deputy director) made less than the male directors and deputy directors in all other county departments. After a county-commissioned study determined that employees deserved an increase in pay, Sandra Wheatley, fifty-two, and Jane Grogan, sixty, received a smaller increase than the males in other county departments. The two women had worked their way up in the department as the only females in management and were recognized for their abilities, but not in salary.

"It was an endless fight," Wheatley explains. "They kept patting me on the back telling me I was doing a fine job, but giving me no more money. I knew the men with the same responsibilities as me were making more, so I said I needed a raise. Two days later my boss told me, 'You'll be taken care of,' but when the dust settled, the six-thousand-dollar raise I got wasn't even half of what the male supervisors were making. I was not being taken care of because I was a woman, and that didn't sit well with me."

"They hired a man to come into my department under my supervision," Jane Grogan said, "and he got six thousand dollars more than I did! And I was supervising him. I questioned the discrepancy and the human resources director (a male) told me, 'Don't supervise him, just do his paperwork.' "

After years of struggling through the inequality of the system and pursuing the proper channels, filling out the proper paperwork, they were ultimately given the brush-off. "We got tired of playing their games. I asked for a meeting and Jane and I sat on one side of a table facing three men who were our superiors. We never got our questions answered and they were basically saying we had no reason to complain. When the meeting was over I thought, *I've been a good girl long enough. I'm going to find a lawyer.*"

Wheatley and her deputy, Jane Grogan, decided to consult attorney F. J. Collins in Baltimore. "I'm picky on discrimination cases I take," the attorney said, "because the courts make it so difficult to pursue them. I have to be careful. But I looked at this case and saw as plain as the nose on your face that this was an equal-pay claim. All the male directors were making more than the female directors. It was such a blatant example of disparity—all the men were making more than all the women."

In court the two women and their attorney presented undisputed evidence that they were paid less than male employees in the same grade classification within Wicomico County's pay system and, furthermore, that all of the male directors and deputy directors were paid more than the female directors and deputy directors. They argued that the essence of the job of all directors is the same. They supervise subordinates, conduct staff meetings, prepare budgets, answer to the same County Council, and otherwise manage their departments. None of the other directors or deputy directors has greater seniority or performance ratings than Sandra Wheatley and Jane Grogan, yet Wheatley earned approximately $25,000 less than the male directors and deputy directors and substantially less than the males in her grade.

And what did the courts say?

The lower court ruled against the women, insisting their jobs were "unique" and there were no male employees in the "same" position. On appeal before the Fourth Circuit Court of Appeals Wheatley and Grogan presented evidence that all managers—regardless of the department—performed the same supervisory skills, such as preparing budgets, monitoring employees, and conducting meetings. The Court of Appeals declined the argument, saying that all department director positions require different skills and require different levels of responsibility. The judges noted as an example that both the director and deputy director of public works were "required to hold graduate degrees in civil engineering. By contrast, Ms. Wheatley and Ms. Grogan perform their jobs well without possessing any advanced degrees at all. While it is certainly true that plaintiffs provide valuable services to the County, it would be disingenuous to argue that their jobs require skills substantially equal to the jobs which require engineers to direct the Department of Public Works."

Never mind that there are *eleven* different department heads, each overseeing different departments, but across the board the male directors and deputy directors were making much more than female directors and deputy directors. What's worse, after an internal study evaluated and classified employee pay scales, the women were assigned salaries *below* the midpoint of their class and all male directors and deputy directors were given salaries *above* their class midpoints.

"The court required there to be essentially a complete match," Collins, the attorney who argued the case, explained. "The job had to be an exact comparator. The fact that the female was making less than the male she was supervising was not enough. The court demanded that we had to find someone in the exact same job, which is, in reality, hard to find with the exception being an assembly line job."

It should not go unnoted that at each stage, beginning with their first internal office pleas, these women's situation was heard only by male ears. (At this point in the growing realization of our inequality, we should also note that women who end up in the court system have their cases heard and judged by predominately male ears. In fact, 76 percent of the federal judges in the United States are male.) "The reason why discrimination cases are lost so frequently," Collins says, "is because the courts undermine the jury system. This case was a slam dunk in front of a jury. The judge knew that and would not let a jury decide."

And what the male courts decided was this: "We are unpersuaded that 'equal work' under the Equal Pay Act can be established when two employees have similar titles but responsibilities that bear no more than the most general resemblance. We likewise affirm the district court's dismissal of plaintiffs' Title VII claims."

"The law looks pretty and says you can't do all this nasty stuff," Collins adds, "but people do it because they can. The courts will not enforce discrimination laws and will not let juries decide cases. Women are summarily dismissed."

According to the court, accepting the Equal Pay Act argument in this case would be asking "us to convert the EPA equality standard into a similarity test. We decline to hold that having a similar title plus similar generalized responsibilities is equivalent to having equal skills and equal responsibilities. Were we to adopt that position, we would deprive compensation structures of all flexibility and deny employers the chance to create pay differentiations that reflect differing tasks and talents."

But are those tasks and talents differing because they are performed by a "breadwinner" male as opposed to a "mother" female? Does it come down to the argument that we live in a society that inherently values women in the kitchen with a kid on a hip and another in the womb more than women leading others in the boardroom? To be more specific, do we as a society think that what men do is worth more money than what women do? About two-thirds of all working women are contributing half or more to their household income, yet there seems to be a pervasive belief that the man in a two-income family deserves to make more than the woman. Does the Equal Pay Act protect us from such thinking? The jury—uh, judge—is still out on that.

"Breadwinners"

Wal-Mart has been named defendant in the largest class action lawsuit in history, in which 1.6 million present and former female employees of Wal-Mart and Sam's Club are suing the giant for a systematic system of lower wages, denied promotions, and a sexist corporate culture. Similarly, a class action suit has been filed against

Costco Wholesale Corporation charging that Costco fosters a "glass ceiling" that excludes women from obtaining promotion to managerial positions. It should not go unnoticed that these are two of our nation's largest employers.

With an estimated 3,500 stores and 1.3 million employees, women are about two-thirds of Wal-Mart's workforce, one-third of its management, and only one-seventh of its store managers. In more than two hundred depositions already taken for the case, many of the women tell a frighteningly similar story—that men took priority over women for promotions, advancement, and higher salaries at the world's largest employer because men are the traditional family breadwinners. Wal-Mart denies the allegations, but the writing might be on the "Wal." Lawyers for the class estimate that the company could be liable for an award of more than $1 billion if the workers win the case. Other analysts are suggesting this number may go even higher.

U.S. District Judge Martin Jenkins of San Francisco ruled that the case met class action status in that it fulfilled the need to show a single issue, common to all plaintiffs, that outweighs individual differences. According to his eighty-four-page opinion, the issue here is sex bias and a "strong corporate culture that includes gender stereotyping." Jenkins noted that the evidence did not outright prove intentional, choreographed bias, but that the suit was justified in that the evidence supports "an inference that Wal-Mart engages in discriminatory practices" and that the "higher one looks in the organization, the lower the percentage of women." He noted that some of the plaintiffs' evidence is indisputable: women were paid less than men in every region and in most job categories, and the salary gap widened between men and women over time even when employees were hired for the same jobs.

"Men are here to make a career, and women aren't" seems to be the overarching mantra the women of the class action suit are attributing to Wal-Mart, and that, according to their experiences and conversations with their superiors, Wal-Mart is a company that believes women can make less and men should make more and have more professional responsibility because they are the "traditional breadwinners." The lead plaintiff, Betty Dukes, a fifty-four-year-old greeter in a California store, has worked for Wal-Mart for ten years (and as of this writing continues to work there), and despite her constant efforts to achieve a management position, has never been offered one. She also alleges that her complaints were met with a demotion and a pay cut.

According to court papers, women working full time for Wal-Mart earned about $1,100 less than men if they were hourly employees and about $14,500 less if they were salaried employees. Even when women did achieve equal ranking, they didn't receive equal pay. Male district managers made 35 percent more than their female counterparts; regional male vice presidents made 50 percent more than the females. And, unfortunately for qualified females at Wal-Mart, there was no application process for promotions, no system by which they could climb the hierarchy to higher positions. The only way up was to be anointed by a manager, most likely a male crowning another male. And according to the depositions taken thus far, when females complained, they were either ignored or terminated.

Wal-Mart maintains that there is no evidence of discrimination and has asked the Ninth Circuit Court of Appeals to decertify the case, suggesting that its own constitutional rights would be violated if the court deprived the company of the opportunity to defend itself against each woman's individual claim. Coincidentally, Wal-Mart has put in place a new pay system and given its (mostly) male managers "diversity goals."

"Comparable Worth"

Historical patterns of sex segregation remain strong across much of our workforce. Overall, just 15 percent of women work in jobs typically held by men, such as engineer, stockbroker, and judge, while fewer than 8 percent of men hold female-dominated jobs such as nurse, teacher, or salesclerk. Such a sex-segregated economy leaves women with some startling disadvantages: they earn less than men with the same education at all levels. Incredibly, male high school *dropouts* pulled down an average of $36,000 a year between 1983 and 1998, after inflation adjustments, while women with a bachelor's degree made $35,000. Women with a graduate degree averaged $42,000; men, nearly $77,000.

Why are women often concentrated in low-earning fields, and, in turn, why are those fields traditionally dominated by women so often paid less? Part of the problem is what is known as "comparable worth." Jobs that are traditionally male are valued more highly than jobs that are traditionally female despite the reality of the jobs themselves.

Women employees at Kohl's Supermarkets often worked in the bakery and deli departments; men often worked in the produce department for substantially higher pay. Female employees of Kohl's sued, claiming sex discrimination. The lawsuit failed, as it was determined that the jobs were not substantially equal, in that they required different skills. Is slicing ham intrinsically less difficult or valuable than stacking grapefruit?

Women are often believed to have a natural altruism, leading them to nurturing professions such as nursing and teaching. The belief that nursing was an extension of a woman's natural domestic role established it as a "women's" occupation, of lower societal value than "men's" occupations such as medicine—or even heavy equipment operation. This lack of value is reflected in lower salaries. Right now women make up approximately 90 percent of nurses in the United States, and even with a serious shortage of registered nurses in this country, nursing still pays significantly less than traditional "men's" work. Recent studies have shown that women in academic medicine earn a dramatic 41 percent less than men, showing that even though women have made great strides in the medical profession, they advance much more slowly than their similarly experienced male colleagues.

We, as a society, absolutely have to work on pay comparability. Studies have found that if an occupation is mostly worked by women, it pays less. Perhaps some of that disparity comes from differences in education or experience, but most of it comes down to one word—

discrimination. According to statistics analyzed by the Mothers Movement Online, the four leading occupations for women—cashiers, cooks, housekeepers, and waitresses—are among the occupations with the lowest median earnings.

In an article on the group's website, mothersmovement.org, entitled "Doing the Math on Earnings Inequality," Judith Stadtman Tucker points out that in 1999 the median earnings of child care workers, teacher's assistants, and kindergarten teachers were lower than those of service station and parking lot attendants. "Maybe it's just me," she writes, "but it seems like something is seriously out of whack with a society that pays workers more for taking care of cars than it does for teaching and taking care of people."

And the situation doesn't improve at our institutions of higher education. In academia women are vastly overrepresented in the lower ranks of adjunct and assistant professors and vastly underrepresented among full-fledged, tenured professors. Dr. Barbara Lavin-McEleney began working for Marist College in 1976, teaching criminal justice. She was later granted tenure and promoted to associate professor. She complained several times that she was not being paid equally—first to her department chair, then to the vice president of academic affairs, and finally to the college president—but the college did not act on her complaints. In 2001 she brought a suit against the college in which she showed that she was paid less than other, comparably experienced associate professors.

She had been hired in 1976, and her salary increases over the course of her twenty-five-year career had been percentage increases. Recent hires were paid more current salaries. Even though the school argued that her salary was competitive and fair based on the market value of her discipline, the jury determined that she was paid about $5,800 a year less than her male counterparts.

I've had experience with this myself. As a professor at the University of Washington law school, I became director of the trial advocacy program, one of the largest programs in the school, and after a short time on the job learned that I was being paid $5,000 less than the director of another, smaller program, who happened to be male.

The unfairness of this unequal pay incensed me, and, as a role model for other women at the school, I could not in good conscience get paid $5,000 less than a man for the same work. In fact, I was willing to resign over it. I assembled my facts regarding salary rates, the comparative experience of my fellow director and me (mine was greater), and the amount of work involved for each of us (my program enrolled more students) and went to the university provost, laying out the numbers and declaring that as a lawyer I had learned—and now was teaching to my students—the importance of obtaining justice. I couldn't honorably instruct my students—especially aspiring women lawyers—if I didn't seek it for myself. The provost agreed to grant me the $5,000 raise that would give me parity with my colleague. But what if he hadn't? Would I have had a chance in a court of law?

Furthermore, why should women have to go to court to climb the corporate ladder? First, we're making less money, and then, adding insult to injury, we have to spend money in order to wage a prolonged fight against companies with deep pockets, which in the end may prove futile, leaving us frustrated, broke, and with our reputation at work tarnished. Rather than having to sue our employers to achieve better positions and pay, wouldn't it be a whole lot easier to be paid fairly and given equal chance to succeed? Why is it that if we work as hard as men, we aren't rewarded equally for it?

RIGHTS WE SHOULD DEMAND

Despite some big settlements and a few groundbreaking cases, change has been too slow in coming. The Equal Pay Act was signed more than forty years ago, so why is it that we're still making only three-quarters of what men are making for the same work? First, we are still viewed in the marketplace primarily as "mothers who work." Second, there's an American aversion to discussing what we earn. Many people are hesitant to talk about their wages, even with trusted co-workers. Third, we aren't very good at negotiating; we have trouble demanding what we need. Fourth, we are hesitant to raise the subject of discrimination for fear of retribution. And fifth, what we do as women isn't valued as highly as what men do, even when it's the same tasks.

Equal ≠ Equal

In a 2005 *Newsweek* article entitled "The Myth of the Perfect Mother," writer Judith Warner wrote that in America "motherhood" is an "awful burden" instead of a joy and that we ought to "blame society." She suggests that rather than demanding help from Washington, we privatize our problems and internalize them. Having children should be a joy, not a burden to our lives. What child would want to grow up living beneath the shadow of preventing his mother from earning equal pay at the very least, and ideally achieving her workplace goals?

In 1969, six years after the Equal Pay Act was written into law, Judge Harold Carswell ruled in the Fifth Circuit Court of Appeals that employers could refuse to hire women who have children, in obvious defiance of Title VII of the 1964 Civil Rights Act, which prohibits discrimination on the basis of sex as well as race. The case involved Ida Phillips, who was denied employment by the Martin Marietta Corporation as an aircraft assembler simply because she had preschool-age children, though men with preschool-age children were hired.

In his dissent to the ruling, Chief Judge Brown of the Fifth Circuit said:

> The case is simple. A woman with pre-school aged children may not be employed, a man with pre-school children may. The distinguishing factor seems to be motherhood versus fatherhood. The question then arises: Is this sex related. To the simple query, the answer is just as simple: Nobody—and this includes judges, Solomonic or life-tenured—has yet seen a male mother. A mother, to over-simplify the simplest biology, must then be a woman.

In 1970, when Judge Carswell had been nominated as a Supreme Court justice, Betty Friedan testified against his appointment:

I am not a lawyer, but the wording of Title VII of the Civil Rights Act so clearly conveys its intention to provide equal job opportunity to all oppressed groups, including women—who today in America earn on the average less than half the earnings of men—that only outright sex discrimination or sexism, as we new feminists call it, can explain Judge Carswell's ruling.

Human rights are indivisible, and I, and those for whom I speak, would oppose equally the appointment to the Supreme Court of a racist judge who had been totally blind to the humanity of black men and women since 1948, as the appointment of a sexist judge totally blind to the humanity of women in 1969.

To countenance outright sexism not only in words, but by judicial flouting of the law in an appointee to the Supreme Court in 1970, when American women—not in the hundreds or thousands but in the millions—are finally beginning to assert their human rights, is unconscionable.

I trust that you gentlemen of the committee do not share Judge Carswell's inability to see women as human beings, too. I will however, put these questions to you.

How would you feel if in the event you were not reelected, you applied for a job at some company or law firm or university, and were told you weren't eligible because you had a child?

How would you feel if your sons were told explicitly or implicitly that they could not get or keep certain jobs if they had children?

Betty Friedan had given the problem a name—sexism. Judge Carswell's Supreme Court nomination was soon history, but is the thought? Does the pay differential come from the fact that we're somehow docked for our mothering *potential*, even if we don't have kids? Melissa, a thirty-year-old associate in a law firm, told me, "When I brought up my career goals in a meeting with my senior associate, he said for me not to be concerned so much about my future at the firm because I'd 'have children soon enough and stop working.' When I insisted that wasn't true, he said, 'I assure you that it is, but you just don't know it yet.' "

Interestingly, even if gender patterns (i.e., women taking off for pregnancy or working part time or flex time to spend more time with their families) are factored into the earnings gap, the difference between men's and women's earnings is still staggering. According to an analysis of the 2000 Census earnings data, men make more money than women in the same occupations at all points in the pay scale. And don't think education makes a difference in the inequality. In fact, the most dramatic inequality occurred at the high end of the earning spectrum for women with bachelor's or advanced degrees— women age thirty-five to fifty-four made just 55 percent of comparable men's earnings. I'm no statistician, but it seems to boil down to one thing—we earn less across the board simply because we're women. Subconsciously or consciously, employers view men as the primary wage earners, breadwinners, those who bring home the bacon, and women as working so that we can buy ourselves some lovely things—for what used to be called "pin money."

Women should be paid the same as men for the same work. Women should be allowed to do the same work if we so desire, regardless of whether we're married, or mothers, or single. Seventy percent of Americans say that men are treated better when it comes to salaries, and it's time to turn the boat around. Perhaps some employers are genuinely ignorant of the fact that their pay scales favor men, particularly white men, as a result of historical predispositions. We should demand that businesses take action toward examining their pay practices to ensure that all employees are treated equally. How do we do that? Hit 'em where it hurts—financial pressure. Women make up seventy-three percent of all shoppers in the United States and spend eighty cents of every dollar. So, it really is quite simple. We, my fellow 51 percenters, can stop giving money to companies that aren't fulfilling their equal pay obligations. If we did, women would be guaranteed equal footing on the climb up the corporate ladder.

Don't Shhh Me

Moving on to the second conundrum—the hesitancy to discuss what we make, even among our closest friends. The Equal Pay Act and Title VII of the Civil Rights Act are unfortunately hard to enforce and the legal cases difficult to prove and win. These laws are complaint-driven, and the information needed to prove the validity of a complaint is held with employers. Iowa senator Tom Harkin and District of Columbia congressional delegate Eleanor Holmes Norton have introduced the Fair Pay Act in Congress to remedy this situation, so that we can protect individual privacy but attain empowering knowledge. The act would require public disclosure of employer job categories and their pay scales without disclosing specific information on individual employees. In addition, it would also mandate that employers provide equal pay for jobs that are *comparable* in skill, effort, responsibility, and working conditions, and allow employees who allege pay discrimination based on sex, race, or national origin to either file a complaint with the Equal Employment Opportunity Commission (EEOC) or go to court. (Incidentally, an EEOC charge is a prerequisite in all work-related discrimination cases except those relating to equal pay.)

Currently, women who suspect pay discrimination are forced to file a lawsuit and enter into a drawn-out legal discovery process in order to determine whether they make less than the man working beside them. This translates to high court costs. A readily available written pay policy would keep employers in check and show employees that the system is based on objective criteria. It seems an easy fix for a dastardly problem. The expensive burden placed on women of filing a lawsuit and on businesses of defending them could be diminished if women could see up front that they were being treated fairly.

There should also be a mechanism to force employers into mandatory and binding arbitration in discrimination cases, which would cut out the entire judicial system and its onerous litigation costs and lengthy wait times of up to five years for a trial date. Putting discrimination cases in the hands of a binding arbitrator whose decision is final for both the employer and the employee will give women the opportunity for a swifter resolution and easier access to having allegations heard.

The Paycheck Fairness Act (introduced by New York senator Hillary Rodham Clinton and Connecticut congresswoman Rosa DeLauro) would also strengthen the Equal Pay Act by allowing complainants to seek compensatory *and* punitive damages against discriminating employers. The act would also increase resources available to the EEOC so that they could provide employers additional technical assistance and training on compliance with pay equity laws. We must pass legislation that lets employers know they can't get away with this discrimination. Employers who violate the Equal Pay Act should be "outed." Women will not tolerate exceptions that eat the rule. Let's strengthen the law by cutting out the exceptions.

Ask or Ye Won't Receive

A recent study has shown that large companies yield better returns to their stockholders if they have more women in senior management. It seems that women often have a knack for hiring good people and creating a healthy business climate. So why, then, are there so few women at the top? Barbara Corcoran, one of our country's most successful female entrepreneurs, says, "I've learned that women often underestimate their own earning potential and fail to realize how important they are to companies. Women prefer to work cooperatively, which makes them great leaders but poor negotiators. We'll give and give until we have no more to give."

Giving is great for team building, but it can leave women in the lurch when it comes time for promotions and rewards to be handed out. If you've brought skilled people into a project and then downplay your role in the project, a more competitive, aggressive person (often a man) will get the glory. This tendency makes women very well suited to accomplish management-level tasks while preventing them from actually getting there.

"Tell It Like It Is"

The fourth reason that change has been slow in coming is also addressed in the Paycheck Fairness Act. Many women say that if they were to discover an inequity in pay they would be hesitant to ask their employer about it. "Look," Vicki, a forty-four-year-old banker explained, "I'm already tenuous about the vulnerability of my position in this company of testosterone. If I were to say anything about my salary being disproportionate to my male co-workers, I would be labeled a 'whining woman.' I've seen it happen and those women went unhappily on their un-merry way." And Patricia, a twenty-six-year-old graduate student, was told by a former employer that "if I complained, I'd be sorry."

The Paycheck Fairness Act would shield us from retribution by adding a non-retaliation requirement to protect employees who press (or have pressed) a claim of discrimination on the basis of sex and would require the secretary of labor to conduct studies and improve outreach to employees in reference to pay differentials in the workplace. No one, particularly someone who is being wronged, should be punished for speaking up. This provision in the act is crucial to our advancement in the workplace and the human need to feel safe enough to speak the truth.

Unfortunately, President Bush has not only cut women in the workforce off at the pass in our quest for equal pay but also diminished several of our gains. The Supreme Court has one fewer woman, and Chief Justice John Roberts, when he was assistant White House counsel to the Reagan administration in 1984, scoffed at the notion that men and women should earn equal pay in jobs of comparable importance, going so far as to suggest that such a "radical redistributive concept" may as well have the slogan "From each according to his ability, to each according to her gender."

Despite the growing number of discrimination complaints, the administration also chopped the EEOC's budget by $9 million and demanded it reduce its caseload. Corporations (aka "big money") will now feel even less pressure to comply with our already hard-to-enforce antidiscriminatory guidelines. At the same time the administration cut the EEOC budget, it was giving money to groups such as the ultra-conservative Independent Women's Forum, which received $10 million to train Iraqi women for their elections. This group opposes the UN Convention on the Elimination of All Forms of Discrimination Against Women because the convention supports reproductive rights and advances causes such as equal pay for equal work, maternity leave with pay, and child care facilities for working mothers.

And if you don't like what is going on in the Bush administration, don't think about calling the White House Women's Office. It's closed. That's right; our seat at the president's table has been pulled away. What's worse is that, as noted by the National Council for Research on Women, vital data about women have been "deleted, buried, distorted, or has otherwise gone missing from government websites and publications," including twenty-five reports from the U.S. Department of Labor's Women's Bureau. Apparently, President Bush and his corporate sponsors believe that if we can't see the data, the discrimination doesn't exist.

We must tell them otherwise.

Share Responsibility

Remember the 73-cent statistic at the opening of this chapter? New research indicates that when you look at how much the typical woman *actually* earns over much of her career, the true difference is more like 56 cents! That's the conclusion of a new study by Stephen J. Rose, an economist at Macro International Inc., a consulting firm, and Heidi I. Hartmann, president of the Institute for Women's Policy Research in Washington.

Why the big discrepancy? The 73-cent statistic is based on women who work full-time for a full year. Only one-quarter of women, though, achieve this level of participation consistently throughout their working lives. So Rose and Hartmann looked at the pay of men and women over fifteen years, including those who worked part-time or dipped in and out of the workforce in order to care for children or elderly parents.

Family responsibilities still fall more heavily on women, and in the United States neither society nor employers have found good ways to mesh those with job demands. Making it worse still, the latest Bush budgets continue to slash funding for child care. The administration has frozen funding for after-school programs, cutting more than half a million kids, and an estimated 300,000 children will be cut from government-supported child care programs by the year 2009. Who does this hurt? Women. Particularly poor women.

Without child care, many women must take time off or work part time in order to be with their children. That choice itself is constrained by the widespread lack of day care and flexible job options. If she doesn't do it, who will? Despite all the brouhaha over Lisa Belkin's article about women "opting out" of careers, few women can afford to drop out altogether from the workforce in order to have kids. But, as we'll see when we discuss pregnancy discrimination, it's women who risk derailing their careers and permanently slashing their pay by starting a family. Just one year out of the workforce cuts a woman's total earnings over fifteen years by 32 percent, while a hiatus of two years slices it by 46 percent and a break of three years slashes it by 56 percent, according to Hartmann and Rose. Men lose almost as much, their average pay dropping by 25 percent if they take off a year, but fewer than 8 percent of men felt the need to do so.

Women take a big hit for going part time. On average, they work less: 1,498 hours a year versus 2,219 worked by the typical man. But before anyone decides that this means the pay gap is justified, consider the invisible second job still falling squarely on the shoulders of many of today's women—keeping the household going.

EQUAL PAY IS EQUAL POWER

The issue of equal pay for women is not just a women's issue. That $300,000 lifetime difference is significant to the well-being of an entire family. Until stronger legislation exists and there is widespread recognition of just how devalued traditionally "female" occupations continue to be, a host of systemic problems—from female-headed households mired in financial struggle to a lack of qualified workers in all-important caregiving jobs—will continue to prevent our society from being all that it could and should be.

When fifty thousand workingwomen were asked in the AFL-CIO "Ask a Working Woman" survey to rank the issues that are important to them, fair pay tops the list. A series of focus groups commissioned by the Center for Policy Alternatives and Lifetime Television found that 93 percent of African American women, 91 percent of Latinas, 90 percent of Asian American women, and 87 percent of white women said equal pay and benefits for women should be one of the top policy priorities in the United States.

We must balance this inequity. The scales of monetary justice must be equally weighted. Employers have to be forced to be gender-blind—and our laws need to allow for punitive damages and stricter financial penalties against employers who discriminate against women. The only way any of this will change is if we *make* it change. What's fair is fair. We're not asking for *extra* advantage, we're asking for *equal* advantage.

We shouldn't have to work twice as hard to receive half as much, and we shouldn't be kept out of the boardroom because of preconceived notions that we should be in the kitchen. We must use our voices, our votes, and our buying power to persuade our politicians and our bosses (both mostly male) that we deserve equal pay for equal work, for ourselves and for our families.

Equal pay is equal power. Without equal pay we will never have equal power.

CHAPTER 3

SEXUAL HARASSMENT

"I have the right to say 'Thanks, but no thanks' without repercussions"

When I was representing the House Democrats during the impeachment of President Clinton, I was the subject of several articles and tabloid TV shows that wanted to know "who the blonde is." The *Washington Post* gave out "awards" such as "Best Trained Attack Dogs" (to Barney Frank and Bill McCollum), and to me they gave the "Most Want to Be Stranded on a Desert Island With" award. Was I insulted? Not really. Did I feel harassed? No.

But there have been other scenarios where I've felt differently. During my tenure as a federal prosecutor, an opposing lawyer in a criminal case was purposely trying to belittle me by commenting on my appearance and femininity. In that circumstance—trying to put a drug lord in jail—I had no recourse to "come back" at him without demeaning myself in doing so in front of the jury. I had to approach the judge behind the scenes and ask that he put a stop to the defense attorney's belittling comments. In another example, an overtly sexual situation occurred this past summer while on vacation. One night before dinner a male in one of the couples with us sidled up to me at the bar and pressed himself up against me. He was excited to be there, if you know what I mean, and I couldn't get away from him fast enough. I felt dirty, and as though *I* had done something wrong. It wasn't until the next day that I could bring myself to talk about it, and my friends said I should have said something right at that moment and that I was "acting like a typical victim of sexual harassment" by blaming myself and saying I "must have been imagining it." I was shocked at the thought that I was blaming *myself.* Should I have made a scene right then and there and embarrassed him? Can I be sexually harassed when I'm out to dinner with friends? What about street hassling and wolf whistles and ogling?

"In many contexts the right response is 'Get a life!' " Deborah Rhode, a Stanford law professor and one of America's leading experts on gender discrimination and legal ethics, explains. "The vast majority of women don't welcome this form of attention. For centuries women were harassed but they had neither a label nor a remedy for the experience. We're now seeing a lot of responses by institutions to implement policies and procedures and training programs that are dealing with the issue at the preventative level. And that's a sign of enormous progress. But progress remains to be made. Our society is still trying to sort out where the boundaries are."

There's a time and place, and sometimes when it's the wrong time, we might decide it's better to slough it off. Court TV commentator Rikki Klieman recalled, "Once I walked into a courtroom where a judge literally asked me 'to do a pirouette.' Instead of reporting him to some judicial conduct commission, I did the twirl, laughed it off, and then never had anything but good results in front of him for decades. Humor and a smile may have gotten us a long way in the 1970s, but bet your bottom dollar, they still work today."

None of us wants to lose the humor at work or in our lives. We certainly don't want to become a sterile society where we're all walking on eggshells for fear of doing something that can get us sued or thrown in jail. Here, all it takes is a little common sense. I remember an exercise I did in an undergraduate psychology class on "personal space" in which the class was randomly put in pairs and we experimented on what was a comfortable distance from each other. We communicated with our partners and said "stop" when the space between us was one step too narrow. Our partner would take one step back, and that was the distance we needed in order to maintain comfort in a conversation.

The same type of approach can prevent sexual harassment. Most of us don't want our behinds grabbed by random men. (Though one female lawyer—who took part in an on-air debate with me after actor Christian Slater was slapped with misdemeanor charges for allegedly squeezing the butt of a fifty-two-year-old woman at two in the morning on Manhattan's Upper East Side—suggested she'd have run after him, not to arrest him, but to ask him to do it again.) These things are obvious, right? But humor can make the lines fuzzy. What one person finds funny, another might find embarrassing or, worse, humiliating. What one finds a compliment, another might find insulting.

We don't, however, want to be the girl who cried wolf. If a woman charges sexual harassment when it's not true or when it could have been dealt with directly, future complaints are less believable for her and other women. Accusations shouldn't be used as a sword to punish someone publicly for an inappropriate remark or action that could have been dealt with personally.

MSNBC's Rita Cosby, who is known for her Emmy award–winning tough interviews with world leaders ranging from Yasir Arafat to Henry Kissinger, tells the following story about dealing with a boss's inappropriate behavior: "I was very young at the time," she remembers, "and didn't know how to handle a boss sending me flowers and notes. I was intimidated. I am typically not afraid to speak out, but I felt overwhelmed, helpless. I never told people at work who the flowers were from; I was too embarrassed and went through such an internal struggle. I worried about the stigma if I confronted him, and finally confided in my friends.

"I got the courage to confront him, and I said, 'If you like me as a person, you'll stop what you are doing. You are hurting a valuable employee, and you're hurting someone you value as a person.' He was my boss, and I wanted to keep my job! After our talk, he changed. So, in being direct, I won. But I realized how tough it is for women to come forward if they aren't respected. Unless you've walked in those shoes, you can't judge. And I totally understand how people don't report more severe sexual harassment. How scared they are, how overwhelmed. At first, I felt paralyzed, and I worry for other women who are dealing with much worse, and don't have a boss who cares."

THE RIGHTS WE HAVE

Sexual harassment entered the national vocabulary in 1991 when Anita Hill came to Capitol Hill to testify against Clarence Thomas's confirmation for Supreme Court. She alleged that Thomas had made sexual advances to her when she was his assistant, saying things about penises, referring to his sexual prowess, and asking her the bizarre question that was played over and over on the news: "Who has pubic hair on my Coke?"

During her testimony before the all-male congressional committee hearing on October 11, 1991, the Yale-educated lawyer described a hostile work environment while working for Thomas at the Department of Education. An environment in which she, as Thomas's assistant, was allegedly constantly asked out and barraged with sexual talk from her boss. From her testimony:

> My working relationship became even more strained when Judge Thomas began to use work situations to discuss sex. On these occasions, he would call me into his office for reports on education issues and projects, or he might suggest that, because of the time pressures of his schedule, we go to lunch to a government cafeteria. After a brief discussion of work, he would turn the conversation to a discussion of sexual matters.
>
> His conversations were very vivid. He spoke about acts that he had seen in pornographic films involving such matters as women having sex with animals and films showing group sex or rape scenes. He talked about pornographic materials depicting individuals with large penises or large breasts involved in various

sex acts. On several occasions, Thomas told me graphically of his own sexual prowess.

Because I was extremely uncomfortable talking about sex with him at all and particularly in such a graphic way, I told him that I did not want to talk about these subjects. I would also try to change the subject to education matters or to nonsexual personal matters such as his background or his beliefs. My efforts to change the subject were rarely successful.

When Judge Thomas was made chair of the EEOC, I needed to face the question of whether to go with him. I was asked to do so, and I did. The work itself was interesting, and at that time it appeared that the sexual overtures which had so troubled me had ended. I also faced the realistic fact that I had no alternative job. While I might have gone back to private practice, perhaps in my old firm or at another, I was dedicated to civil rights work, and my first choice was to be in that field. Moreover, the Department of Education itself was a dubious venture. President Reagan was seeking to abolish the entire department.

For my first months at the EEOC, where I continued to be an assistant to Judge Thomas, there were no sexual conversations or overtures. However, during the fall and winter of 1982, these began again. The comments were random and ranged from pressing me about why I didn't go out with him to remarks about my personal appearance. I remember his saying that someday I would have to tell him the real reason that I wouldn't go out with him.

He began to show displeasure in his tone and voice and his demeanor and his continued pressure for an explanation. He commented on what I was wearing in terms of whether it made me more or less sexually attractive. The incidents occurred in his inner office at the EEOC.

One of the oddest episodes I remember was an occasion in which Thomas was drinking a Coke in his office. He got up from the table at which we were working, went over to his desk to get the Coke, looked at the can and asked, "Who has pubic hair on my Coke?" On other occasions, he referred to the size of his own penis as being larger than normal, and he also spoke on some occasions of the pleasures he had given to women with oral sex.

As we all know, despite Hill's testimony, Clarence Thomas is now one of the nine Supreme Court justices. Whether you believe Hill to be a courageous woman speaking up about a Supreme Court nominee's boorish behavior or, as those who sought to discredit her charged, a vindictive soul seeking fifteen minutes of fame, her congressional testimony opened the way for a national discourse on sexual harassment—and led many companies to establish sensitivity training programs in the hope of eliminating sexual harassment from the workplace.

Two months after Anita Hill testified before the country, U.S. District Court Judge James Rosenbaum made legal history by permitting the case of *Jenson v. Eveleth Mines* to proceed as the first-ever class action suit for sexual harassment. The case brought new meaning to "hostile working environment" and, as told by journalist Clara Bingham and lawyer Laura Leedy Gansler in their book *Class Action,* is a reminder of the psychological toll and emotional torture women sometimes endure in the pursuit of justice.

The story (recently made into the movie *North Country,* starring Charlize Theron) begins in 1975 when Lois Jenson, a single mother on welfare, was hired by Eveleth Mines as part of the company's compliance with affirmative action guidelines. As one of the first four women to enter the man's world of iron mining, she and others were subjected to relentless harassment. They were groped, propositioned, called obscene names, deliberately exposed to hard-core pornography, and physically attacked. Eager to be making a decent wage to support her family, Jenson endured. The four women were barraged by daily torment, including a man repeatedly ejaculating on the clothes stored in one woman's locker, two foremen driving two women into the middle of the woods and ordering them to "service them," and perpetual crotch grabbing. The miners would later call these events "jokes."

In 1984, Lois had had enough; she mailed a complaint to the Minnesota Human Rights department. The following week, her tires were slashed. And the fourteen-year legal fight for justice began.

In 1987, the state determined there was probable cause and moved for conciliation, but the mine co-owner and manager, Ogelbay Norton Company, refused the state's request to pay Lois $6,000 in punitive damages and $5,000 for mental anguish. The following year, attorney Paul Sprenger filed the case in U.S. District Court in Minneapolis and asked that the suit be certified as a class action. It wasn't until 1991 that Judge James Rosenbaum granted the request, thus establishing the precedent that sexual harassment claims can be the basis of a class action suit. (Until then, the courts had only examined specific instances involving an individual woman who was harassed by an individual man.) Rosenbaum's ruling determined that women could band together, sharing the financial and psychological burdens of filing a sexual harassment case, and helping to avoid the "nuts and sluts" defense—the argument that an individual woman is either a "nut," overreacting to an ordinary, harmless situation, or a "slut," a hussy who is on the prowl for sex.

In early 1992, Lois was diagnosed with post-traumatic stress disorder and stopped working at the mine. In December of that year, the trial began before U.S. district judge Richard Kyle in St. Paul, and five months later he ruled that Eveleth Mines was liable for not preventing sexual harassment and ordered the company to develop programs to educate all employees on sexual harassment. (During trial depositions, the miners had answered such questions as "Is rape sexual harassment?" with "It depends on if she asks for it.")

Retired federal magistrate Patrick McNulty of Duluth was named special master to oversee a trial to determine how much money the women should receive in damage awards. McNulty permitted the company's lawyers to request medical records of all the women dating from birth, and for six months the women were subjected to degrading grilling about their lives. In March 1996 (twelve years after Lois had bravely made her first formal complaint), McNulty issued a public 416-page report, revealing sordid details of the women's private lives, calling them "histrionic," and awarding them an average of $10,000 each. And so the victims were victimized again, even though they were granted a few dollars for their harassment.

In 1997, the Eighth Circuit Court of Appeals reversed McNulty's opinion, saying: "If our goal is to persuade the American people to utilize our courts as little as possible, we have furthered that objective in this case." A new jury trial for damages was ordered, and in December, on the eve of a new trial, a warped sort of justice was carried out: after spending $15 million in a losing effort to defend the right to maintain a hostile work environment, Eveleth Mines settled with the women for a total of $3.5 million. Lois Jenson had mixed feelings: "We never got a chance to set the record straight. We just wanted to be believed."

As we're discovering in our journey to equality, it is often ordinary women who dare to speak up and advance the rights of us all, at great cost to themselves. The case proved women could prevail *as a group* against sex-based employment discrimination. Paired with the Anita Hill testimony, employers across the country adopted substantial anti-sexual-harassment policies and these women's steadfastness and courage to see it through resulted in a dramatic cultural shift.

We now have laws recognizing that every human being is entitled to set boundaries between his or her intimate life and the rest of the world. (I say "his or her" because there have been cases of men being harassed at work by female superiors, but, as with most of the power imbalances discussed in this book, sexual harassment is a problem experienced far more often by women than by men.) Today, of the roughly fifteen thousand sexual harassment complaints investigated each year by the agencies of the Equal Opportunity Employment Commission, 89 percent come from women.

Imagine it. You are a sheriff's deputy trying to protect and serve the public, and your superior officer tells you you're "hot" and should wear your uniforms tighter. Then he interrupts a phone conversation you are having with your husband to tell him that he's performing a sexual act on you. You report this to your superiors. Nothing happens—except that you are conspicuously passed over for a job you want. It happened to Elaine Webb-Edwards, a deputy in Orange County, Florida. Her efforts to solve the problem by speaking to her superiors got nowhere until she went public with her complaints and filed a federal suit charging sexual harassment.

You are the head cheerleader for the New York Rangers, out celebrating for the evening with teammates, and somebody from the management of Madison Square Garden sticks his tongue down your throat by force. It is suggested that you and he and his friend should go fool around in the bathroom. When you warn some teammates about these creeps, you are accused of being a "pathological liar" and fired. It happened to Courtney Prince, who according to the Equal Employment Opportunity Commission deserves $800,000 in damages.

These aren't anomalies limited to law enforcement, sports professions, and the occasional midday stroll past a construction site. There's no such thing as a harassment-free profession. From offices to airlines to politics, the culture of "boys will be boys" permeates every professional environment. Sexual harassment is pervasive in our society, creeping around cubicle corners and jumping across streets every day.

In a survey conducted by the American Association of University Women (AAUW) of 1,632 children between the ages of eight and eleven about their experiences with sexual harassment, 85 percent of girls and 76 percent of boys reported having experienced it, with 31 percent of girls and 18 percent of boys saying that it happened "often." Think puberty is the excuse? The AAUW also found that nearly two-thirds of undergraduate college students say they have encountered some type of sexual harassment while in college and more than one-third of female students say the harassment was physical. More than half of the male students admitted to harassing a female in college, a majority of them saying they did so because they thought it was funny.

The law is about respect. Equal respect. For the benefit of both men and women, the important principle of sexual harassment law in the workplace is simple: *If I'm bothered by your actions, I have the right to tell you so and have you stop. If you continue, I have a right to file a com-*

plaint, and if you just don't get it, I have the right to take you to court and make you pay. But what exactly do the courts consider sexual harassment? According to the EEOC, sexual harassment is defined as follows:

> Unwelcome sexual advances, requests for sexual favors, and other verbal or physical conduct of a sexual nature constitutes sexual harassment when submission to or rejection of this conduct explicitly or implicitly affects an individual's employment, unreasonably interferes with an individual's work performance or creates an intimidating, hostile or offensive work environment.

Such behavior is a violation of Title VII of the Civil Rights Act of 1964. Two distinct types of sexual harassment are recognized by the courts. Quid pro quo sexual harassment takes place when a supervisor or boss makes it known that some type of work benefit—a promotion, a raise, a perk, or simply keeping your job—is dependent on sexual favors or continued tolerance of unwelcome advances, verbal or otherwise. Even a single instance of impropriety can be quid pro quo harassment when the stakes are clear: your job, or some benefit of it, is on the line.

Creation of a hostile environment, the second type, need not involve a supervisor or a boss. Ongoing crudeness, unwanted advances, a steady barrage of dirty jokes, or a workplace decorated in sleazy cartoons and *Hustler* pinups can create a hostile environment. Some courts have upheld a "reasonable woman" standard in determining what makes an environment hostile, recognizing that a woman may feel threatened and upset by things that might not bother a man.

Psychiatrists suggest that some men do this as a way of objectifying women and because they can—or think they can—get away with it. Like rape, sexual harassment is more about power than it is about sex. Victims of severe sexual harassment are said to suffer similar emotional aftereffects as victims of rape, and a climate in which sexual harassment is winked at or tolerated blurs the boundaries and paves the way for actual rape. This was acknowledged by the Department of

Defense Task Force on Sexual Harassment and Violence at the Military Service Academies, in a report intended to improve the military's dismal track record of handling these matters. "Harassment is the more prevalent and corrosive problem, creating an environment in which sexual assault is likely to occur," the task force found.

WHAT WE SHOULD DEMAND

Sexual harassment is a nasty thing, which is why our laws are strong and straightforward. Unfortunately, because three out of four federal judges and 95 percent of senior management in this country are men, women are often doubted when they report sexual harassment or, worse, are blackballed or fired. The American Bar Association reports that studies have shown women are often treated differently from men in court proceedings. One such study sponsored by the New York Task Force on Women in the Courts illustrates the recurring theme. The report says, "Cultural stereotypes of women's role in marriage and society daily distort courts' . . . application of substantive law. Women uniquely, disproportionately and with unacceptable frequency must endure a climate of condescension, indifference and hostility." This is particularly vexing, given that less than 1 percent of sexual harassment complaints are false.

Jo-Ann, a former business executive and current full-time mom, said, "I even found another female executive who had had the same experience with my boss. We went to Human Resources together and after an 'investigation' they determined our 'charges' were unfounded. I was left working for the guy. It was highly uncomfortable, so I left the company where I had worked for seventeen years shortly thereafter, and decided to become a full-time mom." Joyce, a forty-three-year-old teacher, recalls: "I was frightened to speak up because he was in the top of the hierarchy of our school district. And when I did it was blamed on his diabetes!"

This type of reaction on the part of people in power may explain why a Harris poll found that 62 percent of adult targets of workplace harassment took no action. Inaction, of course, gives the perpetrator carte blanche to continue this behavior, creating pain in victims that can rise to the level of sleepless nights, relationship problems, and even clinical depression and physical illness. Today, awareness of harassment is greater and the problem may be receiving more attention, but the rights we now have are useful only if we claim them.

Prior to 1991, victims of sexual harassment could claim only back pay and lost wages, and could be reinstated by court order if they had been fired. An amendment to Title VII in that year made it possible for juries to award punitive damages, and to compensate victims for emotional distress, inconvenience, mental anguish, loss of enjoyment of life and the like. That change may explain why, in a 1999 survey conducted by the Society for Human Resource Management, 62 percent of companies offered sexual harassment training to their employees, and fully 97 percent had a written policy.

The EEOC will investigate and initiate legal action on your behalf, though one-third of the cases don't go to trial. Why? There is much pressure to settle, and, as exemplified by the *Jenson v. Eveleth Mines* case, the court system doesn't always treat civil rights plaintiffs with kid gloves. Often, when you've got them dead to rights, EEOC complaints end in negotiation rather than in litigation, resolved by something called a "consent decree." This judicial decree expresses a voluntary agreement between the parties, including an agreement by the defendant to cease activities alleged to be illegal in return for an end to the charges.

Whistle-blowing can be hard and scary—and unfortunately, the Supreme Court recently made it even harder. In *Garcetti v. Ceballos,* the court decided in a 5–4 ruling (with Alito and Roberts in the majority) that the First Amendment does not protect public employees who report misconduct or otherwise try to blow the whistle in the course of doing their official duties. The majority opinion said, however, that public employees would have First Amendment protections if they spoke out as private citizens engaged in what Justice Kennedy called "civic discourse." The upshot is, under this ruling, there could be the strange, if not ridiculous, situation where a whistle-blower would be immune from retaliation if she spoke to a reporter but in jeopardy if she went through official channels.

Before the Garcetti case was handed down, a government employee who was fired because he or she spoke out could file a suit for First Amendment retaliation. But the Supreme Court's ruling in *Garcetti v. Ceballos* effectively took these rights away in many circumstances. Defendants in whistle-blower cases can now argue that the speech at issue is not protected under the First Amendment if one of the plaintiff's duties was to report misconduct to his superiors.

In recent testimony submitted before the House Committee on Government Reform, the chair of the National Whistleblower Center, Stephen M. Kohn, proposed new legislation that would create the first comprehensive national whistle-blower protection law. The legislation, the Protecting Honest Americans on the Job Act, was proposed in order to promptly close the loopholes in whistle-blower protections caused by the Supreme Court's ruling in *Garcetti v. Ceballos.* The Protecting Honest Americans on the Job Act would:

- *Restore whistle-blower rights*
- *Establish an effective administrative and judicial review process for all whistle-blower claims*
- *Provide whistle-blower protections for all employees— including government employees—currently protected under Title VII of the Civil Rights Act*

We must demand that Congress and the president pass this important legislation. As Kohn explained to the House committee, "Without a legislative response to *Garcetti v. Ceballos,* government employees who report valid concerns regarding the violation of federal laws will not have adequate protection. Those who 'speak the truth' and protect the public interest will be at-risk for retaliation. Some will lose their jobs, their careers and their good names simply for disclosing serious misconduct to the wrong person."

The fact is, sometimes whistle-blowing is the only way things ever change. And often the only way to change the culture of a corporation is to hit it where it hurts—right in the pocketbook. Your ultimate success may well mean that the settlement agreement includes conditions that will make the workplace better not just for you, but for every woman working there, now and in the future.

Up-Skirt Down-Blouse Laws

In 1998, Louisiana resident Susan Wilson discovered that her neighbor had set up an elaborate videotaping system in her attic and had drilled small holes in the ceilings throughout her house so that he could secretly watch her and her family. At the time, there were no laws that made this intrusive act illegal. Wilson was shocked, and her case partly inspired a federal law called the Video Voyeurism Prevention Act of 2004, which amended the federal criminal code to prohibit a person from intentionally capturing an image of a private area of an individual without that individual's consent. But there's a big *but*—The law only applies (are you ready for this?) on federal land! So rest easy, ladies, if you're in a national park you won't be videotaped! *Whew!* What a relief, right? And the crime is punishable by a fine of not more than $100,000 or imprisonment for up to one year, or both. That should teach 'em!

So what about Jeffrey Swisher, who was caught using a camera to gaze up the skirts of teenagers at a Virginia mall? What did he get for his crime? Ten days in jail. A loophole in Virginia law prevented prosecutors from convicting him of anything but disorderly conduct. The way the law was written defined a place where someone would expect privacy as "a location where a reasonable person would believe that he could disrobe in privacy without being concerned that his undressing was being viewed, photographed or filmed by another." The judge ruled that a woman would not have an expectation of privacy beneath her skirt because "that location is conceptual, not spatial," the judge wrote, and added, "Enacted in 1998, this statute was not written in anticipation of the cellular telephone/camera." Lawmakers in the state were quick to enact new legislation that addressed that distinction and provides for future advances in technology.

But, unfortunately, on the whole, our laws *aren't* keeping pace with technology, and many states have similar loopholes that prevent them from imposing appropriately harsh—or sometimes any—penalties. Take what happened to Shelley Lebel, a woman who was having dinner at a Baltimore restaurant and was "down-bloused" by a drunken stranger. The man took pictures from an upstairs balcony down her blouse when she bent over to pick up a napkin and then showed her pictures on the Internet. Unfortunately, there was nothing she could do about it. In Maryland there was no law saying that her privacy had been invaded.

In New York, Stephanie Fuller fought back against a system that seemed too easy on a video "peeping Tom." Without her consent or knowledge, her landlord, William Schultz, put a tiny video camera in the smoke-detector that faced her bed. A wire led from the camera into Schultz's apartment where he watched and recorded Stephanie's life. He was only discovered when Stephanie's boyfriend noticed the wire coming out of the smoke detector. Schultz was arrested. *But* New York State's "peeping Tom" laws only covered the use of cameras or other devices peering through a window, so Schultz was charged only with trespassing. His punishment—a $1,468 fine, probation for one to three years, and 280 hours of community service—was the same as if he'd just skipped through Stephanie's apartment.

Stephanie felt victimized twice, and was worried that Schultz had made more tapes than just the ones found in his apartment and that the tapes would end up on the Internet. So she began a campaign for the passage of a more stringent law, one that specifically prohibited video voyeurism. She contacted her elected officials at both the local and state levels and spoke out in the press. She was joined by other women who had been similarly victimized, and the public rallied in her defense. Two of the women, Brenda Thurston and Suzanna Jarzynka, are the mothers of children who were victimized by video voyeurism in 2000. Their daughters were secretly videotaped by their kindergarten teacher, Michael Dorrington, as they changed clothes in a classroom closet. Dorrington was only charged with five misdemeanor counts of endangering the welfare of a child and sentenced to sixty days in jail.

Signed into law in 2003, "Stephanie's Law" makes unlawful surveillance a felony and creates criminal penalties for those who would use a mechanical, digital, or electronic device to capture visual images of another person in a place where that person has a reasonable expectation of privacy and has not given his or her consent. The law went further by creating criminal penalties for those who disseminate, publish, or sell images of the intimate parts of another person's body without their consent. A video voyeur caught using or installing a camera for sexual purposes would be subject to registration with the state's sex offender registry.

The day the law was signed Stephanie Fuller said, "When I discovered I was being videotaped by William Schultz I felt violated, isolated, humiliated, and embarrassed. I suffered a second humiliation when I found out this behavior was not illegal. With the signing of the law no one else will have to suffer this second humiliation. I would love to say that video voyeurism will never happen again; unfortunately we live in a society that cannot guarantee this."

According to the National Center for Victims of Crime, forty-three states now have some type of law that prohibits nonconsensual photography or video recording of persons in a state of undress where the individual has a "reasonable expectation of privacy." Only a handful of states, however, provide protections beyond situations where one would have a reasonable expectation of privacy, such as dressing rooms, bathrooms, and inside one's own home. In other words, covertly shooting up a girl's skirt at the mall is legal, but secretly photographing or recording her in the dressing room isn't.

Unfortunately, in many of these states, the crime is only a misdemeanor, which means even the maximum sentence will get the perpetrator less than a year of a jail time. Shoplifting is a misdemeanor. Traffic violations are misdemeanors. Is secretly taping someone's most private moments comparable to speeding and shoplifting? *No.* These crimes should be classified as felonies, which would mean mandatory jail sentences of at least a year. A year of time seems little punishment for the lifelong psychological torment of the victim, who must live over and over again the pain of knowing that her ultimate privacy was taken away.

Some attorneys argue on behalf of their clients that people in public don't have a right to privacy and that restricting public photography is a violation of First Amendment rights. But when someone is videotaping sexually explicit material, it's assault whether it's in the mall or inside your home. Video voyeurism is a growing problem as technology gets more and more advanced and the recording devices get smaller and smaller. An Internet search on the terms "up-skirt" and "down-blouse" reveals website after website that exposes the intimate parts of women without their consent or even knowledge.

We don't want our daughters videotaped by some pervert as they dangle upside down on the monkey bars at school. And we don't want a camera looking up our skirts whether we're in a national park or in a restaurant, and we have every right to demand to be protected from such violation. It is unconscionable that our laws would allow otherwise. The liberties of a free society do not include having your most intimate moments or body parts caught on tape against your will and used for sexual gratification and/or monetary gain. Period.

We must demand that our legislators pass stricter laws to defend us from these criminal acts and provide harsher penalties for this ultimate invasion of personal privacy. Whether in the workplace or out in public, we all need to understand one simple truth: doing anything to another person that is unwelcome is not okay. And we need to know that if we speak up, we can trust that our laws and our society will help us put an end to the ordeal.

How do we create a new paradigm in which sexual harassment will someday be unthinkable, something that just isn't done? We have to take a good look at the way we educate our children to perceive themselves and each other and the boundaries that exist between acceptable and unacceptable behavior—and the messages we send them through popular culture.

Unfortunately, too many of today's adults—including teachers and school administrators—grew up in an atmosphere where the victim was blamed, shamed, and silenced. We need to come to a mutual understanding that "no" means no, that "stop" means stop, and that we all have our personal levels of what we're comfortable with. This isn't about trying to restrict a person's private thoughts, because it's human nature to notice the attractiveness of others; remember, even Jimmy Carter admitted he had lusted after women in his heart. We're talking *behavior* here—behavior that crosses the line of decency and makes someone feel cornered, uncomfortable, or violated.

It all boils down to one word: permission.

Three Golden Rules

When the Army instituted a hotline that allowed soldiers to anonymously report incidents of sexual harassment or assault, it received more than 4,000 calls within the first nine days. Those calls led to more than 550 investigations. In a 1995 Department of Defense survey, 55 percent of women in the military reported that they had experienced one or more incidents of uninvited sexual attention. In a 2004 Department of Defense survey, 36 percent of female victims of sexual assault at the Military Academy and 26 percent of the female victims at the Naval Academy indicated they did not report the assault because they "feared ostracism, harassment, or ridicule by peers."

The military set up a task force to deal with these alarming statistics and to come up with some good ideas to curb harassment. The task force started with a relatively simple one—besides recommending that the military improve its response to complaints of harassment when they occur, the task force said that there was an insufficient number of women peers and role models in the military and that more women overall—and especially more women in positions of rank and influence—would bring about a change in the overall culture. "A 'critical mass' can make a difference in creating an environment that has a markedly positive effect on the acceptance and integration of women in a mostly male community," the investigators concluded.

So, as more and more women are welcomed in the boardrooms, the mines, and the military, we will see less and less harassment. We have to move for "critical mass," and educate ourselves on how to identify and deal with harassment, as well as provide a safe forum to file complaints without further harassment, ridicule, or threats to our livelihood. When men are made to understand that they are out of bounds and the law has our backs, they will curb harassing behavior.

In a March 2005 article in the *Sacramento Bee,* writers Pamela Martineau and Steve Wiegand interviewed Captain Torrey Hubred, who commands the Sacramento-based 2668th Transportation Company, stationed in Iraq. His unit has been largely free of sexual harassment problems, and he attributes that success to the "three golden rules" under which his troop operates:

1. Treat others the way you want to be treated.
2. Make decisions you wouldn't be ashamed to see in the headlines tomorrow.
3. Ask yourself, "Would I do this if someone I love is watching?"

These are marching orders we should all live by. Sexual harassment *can't* occur if there is *mutual respect.* Just as being paid less than a man is demeaning and demoralizing—wearing you down emotionally and physically and corroding your confidence—so is being harassed. Let's face it: most cases of sexual harassment are not as portrayed in the film *Disclosure.* Most likely, it's not a crazed Demi Moore who has just gotten the big promotion and is out to sexually intimidate and ruin the life of her former lover, Michael Douglas. More often than not, sexual harassment is a *9 to 5* scenario in which a Dabney Coleman sexist, egotistical, lying, hypocritical bigot takes advantage of a subordinate Dolly Parton, verbally harassing her and threatening the safety of her job.

If we feel harassed, we need to use interpersonal communication first, to try to put a stop to the behavior and protect our personal space, but if that doesn't work and the atmosphere is hostile or our job is on the line, we must not be intimidated. As a start, we should collectively demand that workplace sexual harassment training be mandatory and that anonymous tip lines be instituted so that women who are struggling with this issue can be supported.

We must as a society recognize that we each have the right to set boundaries within which we feel comfortable, and we have the right to communicate those boundaries without negative repercussions. Our laws and our courts must support that unequivocally.

CHAPTER 4

PREGNANCY

"I have the right to get pregnant but not get screwed"

When I was pregnant with my first child, my mom gave me the evergreen handbook *What to Expect When You're Expecting.* The list of things to expect was so daunting that if I'd seen it prior to getting pregnant, I might have installed a permanent chastity belt. As I remember it, I was warned that morning sickness could occur at any point during the day and could last from the fourth week until the thirteenth. It predicted that I was going to be tired, as the progesterone created by the pregnancy would act as a sedative. I would have to urinate constantly, as my kidneys were now working for two. (Great news for a prosecutor during tension-filled trials.) I'd have heartburn, headaches, and cramps—but medications were to be avoided. I might faint because of decreased blood flow to my brain. My breasts would ache. My nails would split. My hair would thin. My skin would change.

My husband got no such book and didn't have to worry about a host of potential new physical trials and tribulations. He also didn't have to give much thought to how the baby, after I carried and delivered it, would affect his life. He was never asked how he was going to balance his career and a child, as I was on an almost daily basis by everyone from fellow prosecutors to courtroom judges to a waiter in my favorite Italian restaurant.

One thing that no one was able to tell me was what to expect at work. How would the U.S. Attorney's office react to a pregnant prosecutor? What should I do to make sure my job was safe? When should I tell them? What were my legal rights? I remember very early on in my pregnancy going to lunch with my two best friends at work, Barbara and Cathy, and the issue of pregnancy came up. I almost choked on my salad when they said they "pitied" the first woman in the office who got pregnant. They wondered out loud how our supervisors would take such news. I had no idea. Would they want to get rid of me? Could they? Was I entitled to maternity leave? How long could I be out? Would I still get paid? And what would happen to my position?

THE RIGHTS WE HAVE

We live in a society that punishes women who want to be working mothers. We get pregnant, and our laws and employers render us guilty of the charge of working motherhood. As pregnant women in the United States, our rights are surprisingly limited. We have the right to be treated as though we have a temporary disability—to be given as many allowances for our pregnancies as the guy in shipping who broke his foot at the company bowling outing. We also have the right to twelve weeks unpaid leave and our jobs back as long as a laundry list of caveats is met. Our pregnancies are protected so long as the corporate productivity chart is protected first.

Though we've made progress since the days of our mothers and grandmothers, we still have much further to go to free ourselves from this pervasive form of gender discrimination. In order to do so, every woman in America (pregnant or not) needs to become fully informed about what legal protections we've been granted and those we're lacking and need to demand.

In 1978, in response to years of pressure from women's groups,

Congress amended Title VII of the Civil Rights Act of 1964 to include the Pregnancy Discrimination Act. The PDA was designed to protect a woman's position in the workforce should she choose to become pregnant. Women, the law says, are to be treated in the same manner as other employees or applicants with similar *disabilities* or *limitations*. Now, I don't know about you, but to me that's a red flag from the start. I would never call the wonder of pregnancy and the miracle of birth a "disability" or a "limitation." In fact, it seems to me it's a super-ability and responsibility that we bear and men don't. But let's ignore semantics for a moment and look at the law. What does this law provide for us; what rights are we granted? And how does it protect us from discrimination?

"Can't Be Asked, Don't Have to Tell"

Even though government studies show that 80 percent of working-women are likely to become pregnant during the course of their careers (and of those, more than half return to work within a year of giving birth), women who get pregnant are seen as putting their personal life ahead of work.

"In one interview I was asked point-blank if I have children," Linda, a married attorney, said. "I was interviewing for positions as the in-house legal counsel and the interviewer (a man) put me in a position of trying to convince him that I don't plan on having children in the next several years. I could tell if he thought that I might have children soon, my chances at the position would obviously be compromised."

"I found it interesting that in all of my job interviews," Yvonne, a marketing rep, revealed, "I was asked what my husband does for a living—not just what his profession is, but rather *details* about what he does. The questions that were asked, I think, seemed aimed at determining whether I am the primary breadwinner and therefore less likely to leave if I have children."

The latest studies show that pregnant women are viewed as less competent in the workplace—and the shocker is that both male and female co-workers see them this way. In one study undertaken by the *Journal of Organizational Behavior,* pregnant and nonpregnant women were given tasks that were evaluated by college students, and even though both groups performed with the same proficiency, those who were pregnant were consistently rated lower and viewed as physically limited, irrational, and less committed to their jobs.

The Pregnancy Discrimination Act established that women do not have to reveal their pregnancies to employers and employers do not have the right to ask women if they are pregnant. But let's face it—pregnancy can be concealed only for a while. So if an employer hires you having (illegally) asked that question and you've relied on your right not to tell, your pregnancy (and forced lie) will soon become as apparent as Pinocchio's nose. Then what do you do? Even though it was your right not to disclose your pregnancy, the pregnant pause in the truth may impair your ongoing working relationship.

The *Journal of Business and Psychology* reports that half of the pregnant women interviewed about their experiences in the workplace said their superiors' reactions to their pregnancies were negative. They also reported disturbing comments from fellow workers such as questions about stretch marks and hurtful remarks about big appetites. The law was enacted in 1978, and twenty-five years later women are still experiencing blatant discrimination.

Cindy, an accountant in a very large firm, recounted a story about a senior male partner who had come into a meeting to announce that he had terrible news about a woman who was a senior associate. Someone asked what had happened, and the partner, who was close to hysterical by this point, yelled, "Emily just announced she's pregnant!"

In 1997, Hunter Tylo sued Spelling Entertainment for breach of contract and pregnancy discrimination. Hunter claimed that she was fired from *Melrose Place* because she became pregnant before filming began on her role as the show's sexy vixen, though by law she was not required to inform producers of her pregnancy. Specifically in this case, Hunter charged that after producers of the show discovered she was pregnant, they had gone so far as to suggest, "Why doesn't she just go out and get an abortion? Then she can work." In court, producers argued that they had the legal right to fire her because she couldn't realistically play the seductress while her pregnancy showed. Jurors sided with the actress, saying that she could have still performed the duties of her job, and under the Pregnancy Discrimination Act awarded her $4.9 million.

A woman in New Jersey was fired recently for being pregnant. Though she had been "scared" and "embarrassed" to tell her employer (a major hotel chain) that she was pregnant, she decided it was only fair to tell them because she "didn't want to hide anything." The manager of the hotel told her that he "would have never hired" her if he'd known she was pregnant, and a week later fired her because, according to him, she was unable to fulfill her duties in housekeeping though she had received no complaints or reprimands regarding her work. This isn't just unconscionable; it is illegal according to federal law. She is entitled to and should immediately file a complaint with the local EEOC office.

Working While Pregnant

In 2002, Pan Am flight attendants won a class action lawsuit against their employer's maternity policy after twelve years of struggle and strife. Title VII is very clear in its language: "An employer cannot refuse to hire a woman because of her pregnancy-related condition as long as she is able to perform the major functions of her job." Yet when the flight attendants filed their case in 1990, Pan Am policy required flight attendants to notify their superiors immediately of pregnancy (a clear violation of Title VII, as we've seen) and that all flight attendants take unpaid leaves for the duration of their pregnancies.

By the time this legal battle was settled, many of the women had moved on to different careers and had had to spend countless hours and thousands of dollars to have the court find that it was an invasion of privacy to require flight attendants to disclose their pregnancies immediately. The court also deemed Pan Am's actions discriminatory under Title VII for requiring unpaid leave for the rest of the pregnancy, as there was no evidence offered to prove that a pregnant flight attendant could not perform her duties adequately. The women were awarded monetary damages from $330 to $13,000 based on the amount of time lost from work while on mandatory maternity leave, with one attendant receiving $265,000 for her ten-year fight to be re-instated.

To go back to my own case, when I did finally brave telling my supervisor in the U.S. Attorney's office that I was pregnant, I was armed with the knowledge of what I was allowed by law and already had my plan as to how I could continue my job right up until delivery. After I explained how I could save my sick days and vacation days (I hadn't taken any sick leave in the five years I worked there) to stack up to three months of maternity leave, he took the news fairly well. What else could he say? I knew what I was entitled to by law.

In the last weeks of my pregnancy, my blood pressure skyrocketed, a condition called preeclampsia, and my doctor ordered bed rest. He said I couldn't be on my feet five days a week, and the thought of telling my boss made me a nervous wreck, which I'm sure wasn't great for my blood pressure. After several sleepless nights, I finally waddled into my boss's office and offered a carefully prepared monologue about how I could get the work done. I waddled out still working five days a week, but with approval to work from home one of those days. I spent every Wednesday in bed calling ATF and FBI agents, surrounded by a slew of manila folders filled with case materials.

The Pregnancy Discrimination Act grants us the right to deter-mine for ourselves what exactly we are capable of. This protects us from scenarios such as what happened to teachers in the 1950s, when school boards across the country adopted rules that required teachers to take mandatory maternity leave without pay. The Cleveland, Ohio, Board of Education, for example, required every pregnant teacher to take an unpaid leave, starting five months before the expected birth of the child and continuing until the beginning of the semester after the child had reached the age of three months. Upon her return, the school board did not reinstate the teacher into her classroom; she was merely given priority for reassignment to a position when one became available.

Of course, many women challenged their districts and educational institutions. Insulted by the suggestion she was somehow not capable of working, Inga, an English professor in Washington, found a way around it. "I was in excellent health, loved teaching, and therefore saw no reason to be suspended for the fall quarter without pay, which was the custom of the day," Inga remembers. "A woman so obviously pregnant would be a rare sight in academia at the time—it might give students certain ideas. The issue of whether or not I could stay or would be required to go on leave for the quarter rested with the interpretation of the agreement instructors signed with the college. The decision ultimately turned on the word *shall*, which was open to wider interpretations than would have been the word *must*, as in 'must seek leave of absence.' I went home on Saturday, had my son, and returned to school on Monday with no ill effects. I had spent my two days of 'personal leave' precisely as I had wanted it."

By the early 1970s, women had had enough and started going to courts to demand their rights. The first case to reach the Supreme Court was *Cleveland Board of Education v. LaFleur*, in which three teachers, Jo Carol LaFleur and Ann Elizabeth Nelson from Cleveland, Ohio, and Susan Cohen from Chesterfield, Virginia, argued that mandated maternity leave was an infringement on their constitutional rights.

The school district argued that these policies allowed for educational continuity for the students and protected the "safety" of the students, teachers, and unborn children because some pregnant teachers were too incapacitated to manage their teaching duties. The Supreme Court found the policy unconstitutional, and held that making presumptions that all women who are four months pregnant are physically incompetent was a violation of the due process clause of the Fifth and Fourteenth Amendments.

An endnote in another case that year, *Green v. Waterford Board of Education*, is, to our current thinking, laugh-out-loud funny:

An additional state interest—avoiding "classroom distractions" caused by embarrassed children "pointing, giggling, laughing and making snide remarks" about their teacher's condition—emerges from one of the several cases to which defendants refer. We regard any such interest as almost too trivial to mention; it seems particularly ludicrous, where, as here, plaintiff taught only high school students. Whatever may have been the reaction in Queen Victoria's time, pregnancy is no longer a dirty word.

"Disability" Leave

Title VII states it is a woman's right to decide how long she can safely perform her job, and, though it probably helps employers more than pregnant women, requires employers to treat pregnant women no differently than they treat other "temporarily disabled" employees. For instance, if an employer requires its employees to be able to lift heavy objects, then a pregnant woman may also be required to lift heavy objects (or lose her job) unless the employer provides alternatives to other temporarily disabled employees (such as light duty, alternative assignments, or disability leave). If so, the employer must provide the same alternatives to pregnant women—i.e., it must treat them equally to any other employee with a temporary disability.

Though study after study shows that longer maternity leave helps babies become healthier children, as well as warding off postpartum depression for the mother, the trend is toward shorter and shorter leaves. Specifically, a study by the National Bureau of Economic Research of 1,762 working mothers found that mothers who take at least three months off after childbirth showed 15 percent fewer symptoms of depression after they returned to work than women who take six weeks or less. A new Census Bureau study found that women are returning to work sooner than they did a decade ago, and an Executive Moms survey last year found that some women are taking as little as two weeks off after childbirth.

How long does the law say we can stay home with our baby? According to the Pregnancy Discrimination Act, only as long as our employer allows someone to stay home after a heart attack or broken leg. With my accrued sick leave and vacation time, I was able to take three months after the birth of my son. But any more time and my job (and livelihood) would have been jeopardized. When I returned to my office from maternity leave, I was exhausted, so tired that for weeks during lunch breaks, I would close my office door and sleep on the floor just to get some rest. There was no such thing as flex time for attorneys—we had to be in the office from eight-thirty to five-thirty, no matter what—and I didn't want anyone questioning whether I could do my job.

One thing I noticed about the early months back to work was that my supervisor no longer gave me the big, highly publicized criminal cases. Instead, he asked me to handle a series of low-profile immigration cases that seemed unlikely to build my career. Knowing I was eager for the big cases, was he discriminating? Or, knowing I was a new mother, was he being kind? Regardless, I clawed my way back to the top when a rogue border patrol agent and I turned one of the seemingly small cases into the biggest INS case that year. To this day, I've wondered whether my career would be quite the same if I hadn't had the luck to work on this case.

Sunshine, a single working mother of two, said many of the women she knows have been concerned about their job security during and after pregnancy. "Yes, you are entitled to maternity leave, but your boss also wants an uninterrupted work flow," she said. "And taking any additional maternity leave would mean that not only am I a woman, but now I have to take additional maternity leave and you'll just have to reassign all of my important duties to someone else until I return. Oh, and that someone else should vanish into thin air when I do return so that I can receive the same salary, position, and job responsibilities that I had before I left. It may work on paper, work in your employee manual, but you're still going to get screwed in the end."

Consider the 1987 federal case of Polly Gammon. After informing her supervisor at Precision Engineering Company in Minnesota that she was pregnant, Polly was given her first unsatisfactory performance review and denied a non-merit-based salary adjustment. She was then informed that her receptionist position would be permanently filled when she went on maternity leave, and was, in fact, fired from her job the day before she gave birth. As if this weren't bad enough, her baby was born with hydrocephalus and needed extensive medical care, but her health insurance was also terminated.

When Polly filed suit against her former employer for violating her rights under Title VII, the company fought back, saying her work performance had been poor and that no one's job was guaranteed when returning from a leave of absence. The court found that, in violation of her protections under the Pregnancy Discrimination Act, she had been treated differently than other employees, as the company had allowed a male employee to use accrued vacation time in his recovery from a heart attack and had not terminated his health benefits. The court also found that her company had violated its own policies in her performance reviews. The court awarded her treble back pay, medical expenses, and $10,000 in punitive damages and attorney's fees and costs.

So, taking into consideration Polly's medical needs, does the Pregnancy Discrimination Act protect us in terms of health care coverage? The answer is a resounding "sort of."

The courts have held that pregnancy discrimination is *not* gender discrimination under Title VII when it comes to mandating that public employers pay for health insurance costs associated with pregnancy, nor are those costs covered as a disability—even though, as we've seen, as far as time away from the office is concerned, pregnancy in the United States has been labeled a "disability." In the private sector, the PDA does not mandate health coverage, leaving women to fend for themselves. According to a study by Emory University for the March of Dimes, one out of every eight pregnant women is without health insurance, and the figure is higher among Hispanic and African American women. So if your employer does include it, consider yourself fortunate. If a woman doesn't have coverage, she's got to come up with the money on her own or pay out of her own pocket for special disability insurance that specifically covers pregnancy. The catch-22, of course, is that most insurance plans exclude "preexisting conditions," so you likely won't get coverage if you are pregnant when you apply.

This is a good example of insidious logical thinking gone awry.

The paradigm is "we can't discriminate because of sex," yet women are required to claim pregnancy as a disability, but not a disability like cancer or diabetes since it's something a woman "chooses" to take on (whether or not we can actually make that choice will be discussed later). And therefore we protect men because according to our laws we'd be discriminating against them if we gave special privileges to a woman because of a woman's super-ability to get pregnant.

The Unpaid Dozen

In 1993, the federal government passed the Family and Medical Leave Act (FMLA), granting parents—both women and men—the right to take up to twelve weeks of unpaid time off to care for a child, spouse, or parent with serious health conditions or, for women, if they are sick or unable to work during a pregnancy. Yet again—even though this is an unpaid leave—this law is also rampant with exceptions to the rule. You cannot take the leave if:

1. Your employer has fewer than fifty employees . . . and those must be within a 75-mile radius.
2. You haven't been employed for at least twelve months and worked at least 1,250 hours within those months.
3. Your husband or wife works for the same employer—you're only entitled to twelve weeks between the two of you.
4. You don't give thirty days' notice.

Unfortunately, the loopholes again provide employers with a way out. There are numerous cases in which women take family leave and return to find that their employment situation has changed for the worse—either they've been fired or "downgraded" or part-timed. In some of these situations, the women involved have recourse against their employer; in other situations they do not. The major caveat—you must work in a company with fifty or more employees—means that many women work for companies that have no obligation to hold a job for them once they leave to become mothers.

There's also a more prevalent, often unspoken, factor that keeps new moms on the job even when the Family Leave Act, in theory, is fully applicable. Employers are allowing new moms to take their leave but then putting more and more pressure on them to "volunteer" to return to work early. Consider, for instance, Jessica, who lives in St. Louis and works for a national nonprofit organization. She planned to take the full twelve weeks as granted to her by law when she gave birth to her second child. She didn't take any time off prior to the birth and even went into labor on a Saturday, having worked the previous day. When Jessica arrived at the hospital, she called her boss, Aileen, and left an excited message on her answering machine saying that she was in labor, so she wouldn't be in on Monday and would start taking her leave effective immediately.

While she was in the delivery room, Jessica's cell phone rang; she answered it since she was expecting a call from her mother. It was Aileen calling to ask Jessica whether she could come in later in the week to help out with a new project that needed her expertise.

"By saying that I'd be letting down the team if I couldn't do it," Jessica recalled, "what she did was make me feel guilty. . . . I told her it probably wasn't the time to be talking about it—I was having an epidural!"

Throughout her leave, Aileen called constantly with questions and coercive remarks, trying to get Jessica to return earlier than scheduled. During one call, Jessica suggested to Aileen that she was really enjoying being at home with her daughter and was a little anxious about putting a three-month-old into day care, so she might want to extend her leave using vacation days. Her boss immediately said, "No!" and hung up the phone.

Even though her leave was a right by law, Jessica felt there would be larger repercussions if she didn't help out. She knew that if she didn't "take one for the team," her years of good work and devotion to the company would be forgotten and all that would be remembered was that she took too long on her maternity leave. Jessica juggled her life—she had her sister fly in for a few weeks, her husband took vacation, and she hired a nanny—to accommodate her boss and return to work earlier than scheduled.

Today, Jessica says that she resents missing out on time with her daughter and admits she's become less enthusiastic about a job she once loved. "And what did going back early get me?" she asked. "After paying the nanny, my salary was negligible, and I certainly haven't received any big promotions as a result of my loyalty. In retrospect, I think I should have quit. It would have been a lot easier on everyone in my family, and I would have kept my dignity."

Jessica's plight is shared by many women who, in spite of the legal protections available to them, feel tremendous pressure to go back to work quickly after they give birth. Some women, too, find that their employers' policies specifically compel them to return. Lisa, an admissions director for a small private university in Pennsylvania, told me about a significant legal curveball thrown at adoptive mothers by the university. Though mothers at the university are typically given six weeks of short-term disability (paid leave) followed by the twelve weeks of unpaid leave provided by the Family Medical Leave Act, adoptive mothers are permitted to take only the federally mandated twelve weeks. When Lisa and her husband adopted, there was nothing in place for her to take a leave. "I didn't get any paid time off," she said. "And the cost of adoption is significant. So I had to work." Fortunately, Lisa felt strongly enough about the need to grant adoptive parents paid time off that she met with the vice president of human resources. "I can proudly say that my school now offers four weeks of paid leave for adoptive parents," Lisa added. But most workplaces offer nothing to parents who have children through adoption, since the law, which bases its provisions on the concept of disability, simply does not require it.

Don't "Skirt" the Law

There have already been several notable cases in which wily companies have tried to skirt the law by hiding their pregnancy discrimination behind a clever façade—if they can't fire employees for being pregnant, they'll fire them for the way they look. There are no federal or state laws that directly ban employment discrimination based on appearance, though a few court cases have emerged asserting that employers do not have free rein to base employment decisions on employees' looks. Appearance-based discrimination may be actionable if it is related to sex, race, age, religion, disability, or some other protected category.

Consider, for instance, the 1987 case decided by a federal court in Alabama in which a pregnant desk clerk sued a Howard Johnson's motel after she was fired for refusing her supervisor's instructions to wear makeup when her complexion broke out due to hormonal changes during her pregnancy. The day she told her supervisor she was pregnant, he instituted a new dress code requiring all female employees to wear makeup and lipstick. Given that she had always worked without makeup, the court determined that wearing makeup in order to work at the motel was not a bona fide occupation qualification and was instead a ruse to fire the woman for being pregnant. Just note that the verdict was not about pregnancy.

Okay, we can't be asked if we're pregnant, can't be told if we should or should not work on our swollen ankles, are not supposed to be charged more for our health insurance, and might be able to take an unpaid twelve-week leave of absence. We've got it made, right? Not exactly. Even though the Pregnancy Discrimination Act provides certain protections, there are so many legal loopholes for employers that it's almost every woman for herself. In fact, for every claim made it is estimated there are hundreds that are just dropped or never filed to begin with.

Pregnancy discrimination is difficult to prove. Women are also too busy, too unaware of how to challenge the system, and too plain exhausted to take up the battle. In fact, despite the Pregnancy Discrimination Act, perhaps the most precarious time for a woman professionally is when she's pregnant or during maternity leave. Who has the energy to fight when you're busy mothering? And who has the money? Besides, who wants to be blackballed or stigmatized at work (if you're lucky enough to have your job) as the "troublemaker" if you do win?

According to the National Partnership for Women and Families' analysis of government data, during the decade prior to the passage of the Pregnancy Discrimination Act, more than half of employed women quit their jobs when they became pregnant. After its passage that number dropped to 27 percent of pregnant women, but time and again over the last twenty-five years, women have had to use the law to fight unfair treatment within the workplace. For every woman who has "won," though, there are a thousand others who've suffered and carried the burden of inequality. And pregnant women across the nation continue to claim they've been unfairly fired, denied promotions, and, in extreme cases, even been encouraged to terminate their pregnancies in order to keep their jobs. Why? The law is weak. And state laws are generally of little use, varying widely and often falling below the protections of federal law. Shouldn't we be protected as American women, not simply on the basis of what state we reside in?

RIGHTS WE SHOULD DEMAND

It is apparent that the laws protecting pregnant women today are hardly complete. Even the Supreme Court recognized that when in 1987 it upheld a California law requiring employers to give unpaid pregnancy disability leave of up to four months and guaranteeing employees their jobs upon their return. (California is one of a handful of states with such benefits.) The case involved Lillian Garland, a receptionist at California Federal Savings and Loan who lost her job after taking a three-month pregnancy leave. The court, in an opinion by Justice Thurgood Marshall, rejected arguments by business groups and the Reagan administration that it is discriminatory to require leave for a pregnant worker when an employer doesn't have to provide similar accommodations for workers with other disabilities such as broken arms. Marshall wrote that the Pregnancy Discrimination Act should be considered a "floor beneath which pregnancy disability benefits may not drop—not a ceiling above which they may not rise."

It's high time to go above the ceiling and raise the roof. Some courts have noted that the Pregnancy Discrimination Act is to be used as a shield, not a sword. It's time to create a sword to cut our way through the bureaucratic jungle. It's time for us to go on the offensive. Women should be free to have children without confronting the risk of job loss and economic hardship. And we must fight for that right.

This is a country that limits access to birth control and abortion, yet does little or nothing legally or financially to make it easier for us to have families. While most American women would agree that paid maternity leave should be every woman's right, instead the complete opposite seems to be the norm. We get pregnant, and we get punished. Many women hide their pregnancies from their employers until they are literally about to pop for fear of negative repercussions. Others delay childbirth for fear of discrimination and lost wages. Though they want children, they want to have careers as well, and are concerned that a decision to have a child will indicate to their employers that they have chosen to be "Mommy" rather than a "Senior Vice President" who's also a great mom.

Why is it that women almost always are made to feel they must make some kind of choice between family and work? Remember the hoopla surrounding Massachusetts governor Jane Swift in 2001? She had been lieutenant governor when she became pregnant with twins. Nine months later the governor was appointed as ambassador to Canada, and suddenly Swift was in a difficult position. She had been ordered to take bed rest by her doctor, but due to a rule in the Massachusetts state constitution, as governor she had to meet weekly with a commission to ensure that state employees got paid. Thinking logically, she conducted these meetings by speakerphone. This was met with a lot of resistance, mostly by political foes who used her pregnancy against her, saying she should relinquish governorship.

A case was brought to the state supreme court challenging the constitutionality of holding meetings by speakerphone without the governor being physically present. The controversy flooded the local papers and talk shows for several days, with most people condemning the Governor's Council for taking the ludicrous position. In fact, nine days later, the council voted 8–1 to reverse its earlier decision to ask the Supreme Court whether the speakerphone was legal, attempting to put the whole issue behind it. "We can just move on now," said Councilor Carole Fiola, a Democrat. "I think the sensation is over and we can just get back to normal business."

The one dissenter, Councilor Ed O'Brien, complained, "Nothing in the Constitution says it's appropriate to do this so long as the governor happens to be a girl and happens to be pregnant or happens to be delivering a child." Throughout her term she was accused of being a bad mother for attempting to have a demanding job and be a mother at the same time (even though her husband was a stay-at-home dad). Her political foes used every opportunity to suggest she was abusing her gubernatorial privileges to take care of her family. For example, Swift had made use of a state police helicopter to return home to her sick daughter during a period of heavy Thanksgiving traffic; she had also made requests that state aides pick up her children at day care. In the end, Swift elected not to seek another term as governor. "Having said early on that time with my family was non-negotiable," Swift announced, fighting back tears, "something had to give."

Can you remember the last time a male politician was criticized for his parenting? Or made to feel that he was incapable of doing his job or abusing his privileges because he's a father? And, to stick with the disability argument made by our laws, when was the last time a male politician was considered unfit for a position because of a bad back or stomach ulcer?

There is a blatant disregard for our rights. Perhaps worse are the subversive, subtle, discriminatory acts that aren't fully realized until much later. Some of the discrimination just comes from ignorance, but more comes from employers' strategic, manipulative, and sometimes downright mean acts in pursuit of protecting the bottom line. Even companies that are noted for their generous maternity leave and telecommuting programs have recently come under fire for pregnancy discrimination. Novartis, pharmaceuticals maker and ironically the producer of Gerber baby brands, was picked by *Working Woman* magazine as among the best one hundred companies for women, yet in 2005 a dozen sales representatives filed a $100 million lawsuit contending that the company discriminated against them in pay and promotions, particularly after these employees became pregnant.

Samantha, a thirty-two-year-old attorney, said, "I would love to have the European option of taking several years off without penalty for maternity leave. I think that this country undervalues families." Katie, a twenty-six-year-old producer and editor, agreed: "Great Britain is currently working to reform their laws to encompass six months' paid time off for both mother and father. Now, that's pro-family."

Bodil, a pediatric nurse who lives in Copenhagen, Denmark, says she has always been dumbfounded by the way pregnant women in the United States are treated. "It's like you have the plague," she said. "In Denmark, we are cared for and protected when we get pregnant. We get a paid year off from work, which makes women happy to be able to be with their babies during that first year and makes them better workers when they return. Everybody wins."

According to the International Labor Organization, more than 120 countries currently have laws providing paid maternity leave, and a 2004 Harvard University report showed that, out of 168 countries studied, the United States is one of just five that does not offer some form of paid maternity leave. Most of the countries in the world recognize the need for laws and social policies that protect women of childbearing age in the workplace.

For example, in Canada, when a woman is pregnant, her employer must allow her time off from work to have her child. Canada also provides a second kind of leave, called a "parental leave." This is additional time either parent can take away from work to care for a new baby, and it's also available to parents who have a newly adopted child. In Canada, during your leave, the federal government (not your employer) pays you benefits that partly replace your salary. Your employer cannot lay you off, fire you, or penalize you in any way because you take maternity or parental leave. In addition, while you are on leave, you still accumulate seniority as you did while you were working, and you can also continue to participate in employee pension plans, as well as life and health insurance plans, unless you ask not to. The Canadian federal government will provide up to fifteen weeks of maternity benefits and up to thirty-five weeks of parental benefits. Benefits amount to 55 percent of your regular salary based on your earnings over the last twenty-six weeks, up to a maximum of $413 per week.

In our southern neighbor, Mexico, the constitution, besides guaranteeing equal rights for men and women in Article IV, goes on to say that every person has "the right to decide in a free, responsible and informed way the number and spacing of children." And that's only a start. The Mexican Fair Labor Act entitles pregnant workers to six weeks of paid maternity leave both before and after childbirth, for a total of twelve paid weeks. And, unlike all the exceptions that are made in the United States to the FMLA's twelve weeks of unpaid leave, this law applies to all employers—whether state, federal, or private. Throughout their leave, women are entitled to their full salary and, should they decide they need to extend their leave, they are paid one-half their normal wages for sixty days. Furthermore, women are guaranteed either the same or a similar job if they return within one year of their child's birth, and they continue to accrue seniority while on leave.

Great, right? Well, it is unless you're a woman working the assembly lines for one of Mexico's nearly three thousand maquiladoras, or factories operated under a program to encourage foreign investment in the country by companies such as General Motors, General Electric, Zenith, Panasonic, Sunbeam-Oster, Sanyo, and AT&T. At least 90 percent of the factories are run by American companies, and they get away with subjecting female applicants and employees to mandatory urine testing and invasive questions regarding contraceptive use, menstruation schedule, and sexual habits. Human Rights Watch found that all these companies require pregnancy exams as a condition of employment, subjecting women to different hiring criteria than men;

once hired, if a woman becomes pregnant, she is forced into difficult work situations in an effort to make her resign.

Is this the American way?

We certainly didn't learn from our "mother country," England. There, statutory maternity pay (notice again, nothing about "disability") is paid during the twenty-six weeks of ordinary maternity leave. It's 90 percent of an employee's average earnings for the first six weeks of leave, and then reduced to a flat $195 a week thereafter.

In Sweden there is no specific "maternity leave." Instead, in the interest of true equality, Sweden provides prenatal, childbirth, and postnatal care and a total of eighteen months of paid leave per child for families in which both parents are employed. This leave is available from birth or adoption of a child until the child turns eight years old and may be split between the two parents in any way. During leave, parents are entitled to 90 percent of their gross earnings for the first year and to a reduced rate for the remaining six months. Sweden also has a publicly funded day care program designed to take over where the parental leave program ends. The program is available to children between the ages of eighteen months and twelve years.

Doesn't that sound civilized? The expense is vastly outweighed by long-term employee loyalty, increased productivity, and a positive national morale that such pro-parent policies encourage.

Since it is unlikely that we will be able to implement European-style pregnancy and maternity leave, we should try to get every state in the Union to pass a paid-leave bill. Massachusetts has taken the lead in this arena, with a family-friendly proposal that offers workers in the state (both male and female) up to twelve weeks of paid leave to care for newborns, adopted children, or sick family members. It's also available to care for elderly parents or if you get sick down the line. Here's how the plan works: it's a voluntary program, like disability or life insurance, in which employees would contribute around $2 a week to a state-managed savings plan. When faced with a family emergency, employees would get the time off they need and still get paid up to $750 a week. In addition, the plan ensures job security, making it illegal to fire an employee who takes paid leave under the new policy.

This proposal comes on the heels of recently signed legislation in Massachusetts extending health insurance to nearly every Massachusetts state resident. If the Massachusetts paid-leave bill passes, the plan would cover an additional three million workers in public and private sectors. Critics of the legislation argue that requiring workers to pay a premium could encourage more time off and financially strain already overstretched businesses. While it's true that more people would take leave, research studies show employers actually *benefit*, saving hundreds of millions of dollars when factoring in less turnover and fewer sick days.

The Massachusetts bill is the right law at the right time. It's high time that we caught up with the rest of the world. Massachusetts moms (and dads) will no longer have to choose between caring for their families or supporting them. It's a big step forward for women, and I hope it will serve as a blueprint for the rest of the country. We need to demand to be supported by our country and our employers, not considered a burden because we're also mothers. As one woman said to me, "I had a baby, not a lobotomy!"

CHAPTER 5

AGE AND WEIGHT

"I have the right to get old and fat and not lose my job"

The thought of someone assuming our spot, not because we're incapable of doing our job but because we're old or fat is alarming. But ask any woman who's above the age of forty or forty pounds overweight and you'll see it's a real worry. Women had almost 11 million cosmetic procedures last year in order to improve our appearances and reverse the signs of aging. Given that there are around 110 million women who are older than eighteen in the United States, about one out of every ten of us sought out something—from syringe to scalpel—that would help combat the march of time. Age discrimination claims by women increased 39 percent in the last decade, while claims by men dropped 24 percent.

Why is it that as men age they become "distinguished," but as women age we become just "old"? Or as Rikki Klieman noted, "It has been said that men are afraid of dying and women are afraid of aging. We revere older men and we avoid older women. And anyone who says that appearance does not matter is kidding themselves—we know that taller women get higher salaries."

Women were outraged when Dr. Stanley Title, one of the country's leading weight-loss experts, proclaimed in a 2005 *New York Times* article that it's a man's job in life to make money, but "a woman has to look good." It's hard to know what's more shocking—that he said it or that our society proves it true. Let's face it, not all of us are a size six, and no matter how much Oil of Olay we slather on our skin, we don't remain forever young. Neither do men, but the fact is that the workplace puts a brighter spotlight on a woman's aesthetics than it does a man's. One study by University of Vermont professor Esther Rothblum found that 60 percent of those women considered "fat" and 30 percent of those women considered "moderately fat" had been refused a job based upon their weight. By comparison, only 42 percent of men considered "fat" and none of the men considered "moderately fat" reported similar weight-based discrimination. Another study published in the *New England Journal of Medicine* found that obese women have a 10 percent higher rate of poverty and make, on average, $6,710 less per year than do women who are not overweight. The study found no association between weight and socioeconomic variables for men.

Researchers at New York University found that women's weight gain brings a decrease in their family income and a decline in their status at work. Sociologists Dalton Conley and Rebecca Glauber found that a 1 percent increase in a woman's body mass results in a 0.6 percentage point decrease in her family income and a 0.4 percentage point decrease in occupational prestige. Additionally, the study found that an increase in a woman's body mass directly correlates to her chances of marriage, her *spouse's* occupational prestige, and her *spouse's* earnings. The findings, sponsored by the National Bureau of Economic Research, also confirmed other researchers' findings that men experience no negative effects of body mass on their economic situation.

Women can't catch a break. If we're too fat, we make less money and have less chance of getting married. If we're too sexy, we're considered less smart and studies prove we have a tough time being taken seriously within the corporation. In a study led by Peter Glick, a professor of psychology at Lawrence University in Appleton, Wisconsin, men and women were shown videos of a businesswoman discussing her background and hobbies. In different tests, the same woman played the part of either a receptionist or a manager. In one round she wore professional attire—flat shoes, slacks, and a turtleneck—and in another she wore high heels, a tight skirt, and a low-cut blouse. The subjects rated the businesswoman on competence and guessed at her college GPA and the quality of the college she attended. The sexy outfit didn't affect their assessment if she was a receptionist, but the sexy manager was viewed as less competent.

In the December 2005 issue of *Psychology of Women Quarterly*, the researchers wrote, "A female manager whose appearance emphasized her sexiness elicited less positive emotions, more negative emotions, and perceptions of less competence on a subjective rating scale and less intelligence on an objective scale. Although various media directed toward women . . . encourage women to emphasize their sex appeal, our results suggest that women in high status occupations may have to resist this siren call to obtain respect of their co-workers."

Again, the double standard. We're a society of mixed messages for women—we're too fat, too thin, too tall, too short, too young, too old—underlined by a barrage of sexy bodies wearing youthful clothes in magazine ads and pouty-lipped young models touting diet colas on TV. It's bad enough that we have to deal with this undue competition in our personal lives, but these images are being projected into the workplace like understudies waiting in the wings until we gain one pound too many or age one year too old.

You may remember the story of Christine Craft, a news anchor who filed a federal case challenging the sexist practices of the television news industry. After starting her career in the mid-1970s as a weather reporter and substitute sportscaster at a small station in Salinas, California, she was hired by CBS to host the "Women in Sports" portion of the network television program *CBS Sports Spectacular*. At the request of the network, she cut her hair short and bleached it blond, and she was required to use black eyebrow pencil, dark red lipstick, and heavy makeup for each appearance. After thirty weeks, the show was canceled, but KMBC in Kansas City was looking to "soften" its news presentation with a new female co-anchor.

When she met with the news director, she made it clear that she was bothered by her unpleasant experience at CBS and that she was not interested in the job if the station intended to make over her appearance. Though she was assured they planned no changes to her appearance, after accepting the job she was asked to meet with media consultants who immediately began expressing concerns about various aspects of her appearance. She was provided with a copy of the book *Women's Dress for Success* and KMBC arranged for Macy's to provide clothing to Craft in exchange for advertising time.

In the spring of 1981, Media Associates conducted four focus groups, which found their response to Craft's appearance was "overwhelmingly negative." A "clothing calendar" was instituted that detailed exactly which blazer, blouse, and skirt, or occasionally slacks, Craft was to wear on a given day, including whether the appropriate accessory would be either a single string of pearls or a single gold chain. As further research, Media Associates conducted a telephone survey that asked participants to rank Craft in comparison with the female co-anchors at KMBC's competitors in response to some fourteen statements, four of which dealt with "good looks" or the dress or image of a "professional anchorwoman." Craft came out trailing in almost every category. Media Associates' report on the results suggested that Craft was adversely affecting KMBC's acceptance among Kansas City viewers and recommended that she be replaced.

The next day Craft was told by her news director that the results of the research was "devastating and unprecedented in the history of the consultants of Media Associates," and that she was being reassigned to the position of reporter at no loss of pay or contractual benefits. Craft alleged her boss told her that she was being reassigned because the audience perceived her as "too old, too unattractive, and not deferential enough to men."

Craft refused to be reassigned, and when further negotiation failed to resolve the matter, she returned to her old job in California and filed suit against KMBC. The news director denied making any of the statements Craft alleged, and the district court believed his version of the conversation. The district court held that KMBC required both male and female on-air personnel to maintain professional, businesslike appearances "consistent with community standards" and that the station enforced the requirement in an evenhanded, nondiscriminatory manner. Any greater attention to Craft's appearance was "tailored to fit her individual needs" and was necessary because of her "below-average aptitude" in matters of clothing and makeup. Can you believe that? "Below-average aptitude" from a court?

Despite Craft's argument that women were subjected to greater scrutiny and held to stricter standards, the district court concluded that KMBC had at different times taken issue with many male on-air personnel's appearances and that there was one woman who had never been told to do anything different regarding her appearance. This was sufficient, in the court's view, to show that KMBC sought to modify the appearance of on-air personnel in an individualized manner and not based upon sex.

The fact that KMBC placed a greater emphasis on appearance for women than men, as evidenced by the fact that the survey regarding Craft contained numerous questions about her appearance while a survey regarding her male co-anchor did not, was not proof that the sexes were treated unequally in this respect. This was because the survey was based specifically on Craft's shortcomings as discovered in the focus groups. The survey regarding her co-anchor and a number of other male newscasters placed a greater emphasis on personality and demeanor, which were supposedly their weaknesses as revealed in other focus groups.

Craft further argued that even if KMBC provided "individualized" attention to personnel, the "standards" were based on stereotypical notions of gender that fostered sexism. The court disagreed, holding that because television news was clearly a visual medium, KMBC could take into account looks in running its business and could compel its employees to conform to the image that viewers desired, even if that image reinforced stereotypical notions of gender.

The Court of Appeals stated that Craft was essentially asking it to review *factual* determinations made by the lower court. (That she was ugly, with "below-average aptitude" as a clotheshorse?) While the appeals court speculated that some of the evidence offered by Craft tended to support her claims, it said it would not be appropriate for a higher court to reexamine a lower court's findings of fact unless they were clearly erroneous, which the appeals court concluded was not the case. Thus, the court of appeals upheld the ruling of the lower court against Craft.

Craft's story provides not only disturbing evidence about what matters most in television but also sad proof of our society's emphasis on a woman's looks over all else no matter what the profession. Women certainly should not be unkempt, unclean, unshowered people, but this case does illustrate the emphasis that is placed on women's looks. Women are subjected to sexism, ageism, and weightism, and men, once again, get off easy in each of these arenas. So what laws, if any, are there to protect us from such flagrant discrimination?

THE LAWS WE HAVE

Anti-discrimination laws have expanded and evolved significantly since the mid-1960s, when Congress passed the Civil Rights Act of 1964, the law that outlawed employment discrimination on the basis of race, national origin, sex, or religion. The Age Discrimination in Employment Act of 1967 prohibits employment discrimination against people forty years of age or older. Federal laws provide no prohibition against discrimination based on an employee's weight—at least not explicitly. The Americans with Disabilities Act (ADA), passed by Congress in 1990, comes the closest by prohibiting employers from discriminating against employees based on physical disabilities, which in some circumstances prohibits discrimination based on an employee's weight or other elements of her physical appearance. Let's examine each of these laws in action.

Age

Bringing a claim of age discrimination is by no means *easy*, but the path to litigation is at least clearly established. For example, Elizabeth Banks had an impressive résumé: a BA in English and a master's in education, as well as a certificate in technical writing and corporate publications. Impressed by her education and her work experience as an English teacher and a computer marketing representative, Travelers Company hired Elizabeth in 1986 as a technical writer. Soon she received a promotion and distinguished herself through her superior performance reviews, awards, and experience. Ten years later, when Travelers wanted to make cuts, Elizabeth was replaced by Cindy Dvorachek, a woman twenty years her junior.

Evidence showed that while the company put up a façade of following a methodical process of meetings and evaluations to determine which of the two women to promote and which to fire, the process was in fact illusionary: regardless of the quality of the women's work or qualifications, the managers had already made their decision, and they knew that they wanted to fire Elizabeth.

Because Elizabeth was forty-nine at the time of her termination, however, the Age Discrimination in Employment Act protected her from discriminatory treatment based on her age. Convinced that the firing was illegitimate, she brought suit in federal court. In 1998, a jury found that Travelers did, in fact, base its employment decisions on the fact that Elizabeth was nearly twice Cindy's age, and awarded Elizabeth close to $80,000 in damages.

Our statutes prohibiting age discrimination derive their force from what has become a well-established, clear area of law. As a result, these prohibitions generally provide potential plaintiffs with protections and guidance.

Weight

Some employees have managed to succeed with weight discrimination claims when they are coupled with other claims of discrimination. For example, some plaintiffs have prevailed in sex discrimination claims that allege that their employers have adopted certain weight standards but require only women to adhere to them. In 2003, United Airlines agreed to pay $36 million to female flight attendants who sued for being held to a different standard than men. From 1980 to

1994, using the Metropolitan Life weight charts as its standard, United allowed male flight attendants to reach the maximum weights of large body frames, but limited female flight attendants to the weight requirements for medium-framed women. Failure of the female flight attendants to maintain weight below the standard resulted in discipline, including suspension without pay and termination of employment.

When a group of United's flight attendants filed a class action suit in 1992 to challenge these requirements, they contended that by adopting this discriminatory weight policy United discriminated against women and older flight attendants in violation of Title VII of the Civil Rights Act of 1964, the Age Discrimination in Employment Act, the Americans with Disabilities Act, and the California Fair Employment and Housing Act.

During the 1960s and early 1970s, you may remember, it was standard practice for the airlines to hire only women as flight attendants. The airlines required their flight attendants to remain unmarried, to refrain from having children, to meet weight and appearance criteria, and to retire by the age of thirty-five. After the airlines began hiring male flight attendants, United required female flight attendants to weigh between fourteen and twenty-five pounds less than their male colleagues of the same height and age.

The plaintiff flight attendants attempted to lose weight by various means, including strict diets, use of diuretics, and purging, but ultimately were disciplined or fired for failing to meet the weight requirements. Shortly after the class action suit was certified, United suspended its weight policy "until further notice" and returned to service all attendants who were being held out of service for improper weight. On August 16, 1994, United eliminated the weight policy entirely and by 1995 was offering to reinstate many of the fired women.

In December 2002, U.S. District Court judge Martin Jenkins ruled that the weight requirement would be legal only if trim physiques were a "bona fide occupational qualification"—meaning that unless flight attendants' weight restricted them from doing their job, it wasn't legal. There was nothing to show that having a thinner female flight attendant was necessary for the job, and the court approved a $36.5 million settlement between United and its female flight attendants. In that same month United filed for bankruptcy. When United emerged from bankruptcy, the court approved the sale of the class bankruptcy claim to an investment bank for 16.5 percent of the value of the claim. The women fought (and waited) for fourteen years only to get screwed in the end by receiving compensation that was 84 percent less than they had actually won.

Looks

Even when women perform extraordinarily well, we are judged on our looks. For example, Elysa Yanowitz had been employed by L'Oréal as a regional sales manager for California and the Pacific Northwest since 1986, when she was promoted from sales representative. During her first ten years as a regional sales manager, her performance was consistently reviewed as "above expectation" and in some instances fell just short of "outstanding," (the highest possible rating one could receive). In 1997, Yanowitz was named L'Oréal's regional sales manager of the year, and received a Cartier watch and a congratulatory note complimenting her on her ability to inspire team spirit and her demonstration of leadership, loyalty, and motivation. When Yanowitz's division merged with Ralph Lauren in 1997, many regional sales managers were laid off. Yanowitz, however, kept her job and was given full responsibility for marketing Ralph Lauren fragrances in her region.

Shortly after the merger, Jack Wiswall, general manager for the new designer fragrance division, and Yanowitz toured the Ralph Lauren installation at a Macy's store in San Jose. After the tour, Wiswall told Yanowitz there needed to be "a change" because the female sales associate he saw working the counter was "not good-looking enough." Wiswall instructed Yanowitz to fire the associate and directed her to "get me someone hot."

On a return trip to the store, Wiswall discovered that the sales associate had not been fired as he had instructed. He again ordered

Yanowitz to fire the associate. On his way out, he passed "a young attractive blonde girl" at another counter who was "very sexy." He turned to Yanowitz and said "God damn it, get me one that looks like that."

Yanowitz refused to fire the young associate despite Wiswall's repeated instructions to do so, and would simply reply to his demands by asking for an adequate justification to dismiss her. In 1998, Yanowitz found out Wiswall had initiated a campaign to have Yanowitz herself fired for disobeying his instructions even though the young sales associate had become one of the top sellers of men's fragrances at the Macy's where she worked.

Wiswall sought out others at L'Oréal who "had issues" with Yanowitz and began to compile and document a list of such grievances. In May 1998, Yanowitz was summoned to New York and verbally attacked for her "poor performance" and "dictatorial" management style. Her job was threatened. Then, a few months later, she met with Wiswall, who screamed at her and said he was tired of all her "fuck-ups."

Finally, Yanowitz received a memo from Wiswall that criticized her handling of several recent product promotions and called her ineffective. She was required to reply to the memo within a week and to change her behavior immediately. Yanowitz believed the memo to be a mere pretext for firing her in the near future. At the next meeting, Wiswall berated her with questions about the accusations in his memo until she broke down in tears. She went on disability leave two weeks later due to the stressfulness of the situation and was replaced shortly thereafter.

Yanowitz sued L'Oréal for unlawful retaliation for her refusal to follow Wiswall's unreasonable and illegal order to fire one of their top sales associates because he didn't find her sexually attractive. The Appellate Court of California agreed with Yanowitz that her superiors accused her of poor performance and solicited complaints from employees who worked for her as a pretext to fire her when the real reason was her refusal to fire an employee who was not considered "hot" or attractive. Her refusal to fire the associate was protected conduct under Title VII because the supervisor's instruction was essentially an order to commit sex discrimination.

The court stated that "the notion that an employer may not insist on only attractive women employees has long been established. . . . Nor is it permissible to hire both men and women, but then subject women to more severe and burdensome appearance standards." The Supreme Court ruled that Yanowitz could sue L'Oréal for damages, and her case is still in the courts.

RIGHTS WE SHOULD DEMAND

A handful of American states and city governments have passed ordinances prohibiting discrimination based on height, weight, or other physical characteristics. The intent of these laws is clear: to protect women from discrimination as they age, gain weight, and otherwise grow out of their youth in ways that are irrelevant to the quality of their work.

In 1992, Santa Cruz passed what the media was quick to call "the most far-reaching anti-discrimination law in the country"—more graphically, the "ugly ordinance." The ordinance prohibits discrimination on the basis of "sex, gender, sexual orientation, height, weight and personal appearance." Several other cities, such as Urbana, Illinois, and Madison, Wisconsin, have passed ordinances similarly prohibiting discrimination based on appearance. San Francisco has adopted a statute, the "short and fat law," that explicitly prohibits discrimination on the basis of height or weight. These nicknames are an indication of how far we as a society still need to go to eliminate baseless discrimination.

The District of Columbia recently passed the District of Columbia Human Rights Act, which specifically makes it illegal for employers to discriminate on the basis of "personal appearance," defined in the law to include everything from hairstyle and dress to bodily condition. This law operates very similarly to Title VII but seeks to widen the scope of protected classes and provide protection to more victims of discrimination not covered under Title VII. Of course, the D.C. law also provides exceptions to employers who can show that there is a legitimate business purpose for a certain standard, as long as that standard is applied evenly.

Santa Cruz's law goes even further, protecting against discrimination based on physical characteristics that are derived from birth, accident, or disease. The law seeks to protect against employment discrimination based on so-called immutable traits—those that are not under the direct control of the individual. Title VII protects exclusively such immutable characteristics as race and gender, but Santa Cruz has recognized that aspects of one's physical appearance that exist because of no action or fault on the part of the individual are immutable traits as well. The Santa Cruz ordinance also has a "legitimate business purpose" exception.

Protect the Class

The National Association to Advance Fat Acceptance has organized a media campaign and numerous protests in order to raise awareness of the problems that overweight people face in the workplace. Some recent lawsuits have argued that obesity should be seen as an impairment under the Americans with Disabilities Act, but it is nearly impossible to win a weight discrimination suit under the Americans with Disabilities Act, leaving people who are moderately obese—or even merely overweight—to suffer employment discrimination based on their weight.

These legal complications are extremely frustrating for litigants because they are all based on how overweight and thereby "disabled" a given individual is. It's a tough road for overweight people, particularly overweight women. The argument itself seems to perpetuate negative stereotypes and messages about obesity—deeming it a "disability"—and focusing the case on the problems of excess weight, deviations from "ideal body weights," and perceptions that an employee is unable to perform because she's fat.

Grace Hazeldine and her employer at Beverage Media, a small publisher of magazines for the wine and spirit trade, agreed on at least one thing: Grace's weight never interfered with her ability to do her work at the company. Hired in 1980 as a part-time proofreader, Grace weighed 150 pounds when she first walked through Beverage Media's doors. Over the next ten years, she gradually gained weight, reaching 290 pounds. Yet, as Grace would later testify, she worked harder and longer hours than most people at Beverage Media, and her work product was strong.

Grace received several promotions—although she did not receive those promotions as readily as other employees did. On November 24, 1992, however, Grace faced what no employee ever wants to encounter: a boss informing her that while she was an "excellent employee," she was nevertheless being fired on account of "financial considerations." According to Grace, she offered to take a pay cut, but her boss refused, quipping that "the company was moving to smaller offices," and that since she was a "big girl," there was "no room for her there."

When Grace sued in a federal court in Manhattan, alleging, among other things, weight discrimination in violation of the Americans with Disabilities Act, her boss denied everything—he denied that he fired her due to her weight, denied that there were any financial considerations about her weight, and denied making the "big girl" comment. Yet none of these denials were even necessary, because the judge threw out Grace's weight discrimination claim without so much as considering the truthfulness of her assertions. There were no grounds upon which she could prevail, the judge concluded, because the American with Disabilities Act only protects those who suffer from "a physical or mental impairment that substantially limits one or more . . . major life activities" or, alternatively, those that are "regarded" by their employer "as having such an impairment." Ironically, Grace's success in adjusting to her weight—her inability to think of a single "physical activity that she could not perform because of her obesity"—was what ensured her downfall in court. The judge found that Grace had not presented "sufficient evidence for a reasonable jury to find that she is disabled under the ADA, either because her obesity substantially limits a major life activity or because Beverage Media regarded her as disabled." As a consequence, he dismissed her claim.

Not all plaintiffs attempting to invoke the ADA are rebuffed so summarily. Bonnie Cook, for example, filed a claim against her employer, the Rhode Island Department of Mental Health, Retardation, and Hospitals, for weight discrimination. She was able to convince a court that the ADA protected her from discrimination based on weight because her employer *perceived* her size—at five feet two inches tall and more than 320 pounds—to be a disability, despite a finding by that same employer that her weight would not affect her ability to do the job. The court recognized the negative stereotypes that American society associates with the obese are evidence that society perceives obesity as a disability.

Bonnie and Grace fell into the same medical classification of weight: "morbidly obese," a technical description of an individual that is based either on body mass index or weight in pounds in relation to some "ideal body weight." Courts, already hesitant to entertain any ADA claim brought on the grounds of weight, tend to draw the line at recognizing a weight-based disability afflicting anyone besides the morbidly obese.

The occasional success of weight-discrimination plaintiffs under the ADA is cold comfort for any employee facing discrimination based on her weight, since the inconsistent treatment by the courts makes it nearly impossible to predict whether it is worth lodging a complaint. In Grace Hazeldine's case, she was a great employee at Beverage Media, and her weight did not in any sense hold her back. Yet once she realized that her employer was discriminating against her based on her size, she was stuck. She either had to accept that the termination had nothing to do with performance, since she was willing and able to do all that was asked of her, and find a new job in silence, or attempt to fight that termination in court, and have to convince a judge that her weight significantly interfered with her ability to work, perform everyday tasks, and take care of herself the way a woman of "normal" weight would. Either route is humiliating, and the choice itself reveals the limitations of applying the ADA to weight-discrimination claims.

Barbara Lamoria, a registered nurse since 1959, was fired after working as a nurse for nearly two decades at Sun Valley Manor

Retirement Home in Michigan. She worked hard at her job until July 7, 1994, when her employer terminated her. At the time, Barbara was fifty-five years old, stood five feet seven inches tall, and weighed about 240 pounds. Her new administrator, Marilyn Martin, had made her views about "fat people" clear: she didn't like them, she thought that they undermined the company's image, she thought that there were too many employed at Sun Valley, and she wanted them fired.

Martin and the regional manager soon began alluding to a "hit list" of employees whom they wanted to fire and even targeted a few to build a case for termination or force to resign. These targeted employees included several women that Marilyn had identified to be, by her standards, overweight. At the same time, though, Barbara was receiving excellent feedback about her work. She received a promotion in 1991, and her last evaluation before the termination, in the fall of 1994, remarked upon her "demonstrated loyalty" to the company and her potential for further promotion. A co-worker, later asked to testify, confirmed her excellence: "I respect her. She has good standards. She's honest and credible and trustworthy. She expressed and demonstrated a lot of behaviors that are consistent with a high degree of caring. I would describe her as dedicated." Yet with Martin at the helm, all Barbara's hard work produced one regrettable result: a termination. Barbara's experience was certainly traumatic. Fortunately, however, she lived in Michigan, which allowed her to sue her employer directly for discriminating against her on the basis of weight. She didn't need to force the ADA to cover this form of discrimination, and she didn't need to rely upon a hybrid claim.

The forward-thinking legislature in Michigan thereby allowed Barbara a remedy where she would not otherwise have had one. This hasn't opened the doors for all of Michigan's aggrieved employees to attack their former employers in court without cause as the opposition had argued it would, but has caused most companies to revise their policies and increased the number of weight discrimination settlements. In crafting the law, Michigan's legislature provided a broad exception for employers who can show that a certain height or weight is a bona fide occupational qualification for the position being offered.

Michigan stands as an optimistic model of how to successfully implement a prohibition against weight discrimination. Laws there specifically place height and weight considerations out of bounds to employers when making hiring decisions, thus designating those not of ideal height or weight as a protected class. Unfortunately, jurisdictions such as Michigan are currently few and far between. It is time for more cities and states—and the federal government—to adopt similarly protective policies.

Stop "Lookism"

Local and state laws, providing protection to women who have been discriminated against on the basis of appearance through legislation, are unfortunately far from common. Federal Title VII law should be extended to cover appearance discrimination, with state law providing the model for such an expansion.

As it stands now, Title VII, which protects against gender and racial discrimination, does not cover appearance discrimination, nor does it recognize "appearance-challenged" individuals as a protected group. Title VII has been interpreted by the courts to allow employers to discriminate on the basis of appearance so long as they apply standards evenly to both men and women. The courts have held that as long as attractiveness criteria are applied to different classes of people equally and do not result in disparate impact, the practice is not actionable.

Moreover, as was the case for Christine Craft, if an employer who requires both men and women to meet appearance standards can show that there is a legitimate business purpose for them, the employer will not be liable, even when the standards are not applied evenly and more of an emphasis is placed on the appearance of female employees.

Title VII really affords no protection to women who are discriminated against on the basis of their attractiveness unless they can show that the employer has no legitimate reason to apply appearance standards or that legitimate appearance criteria are being applied unequally to men and women. And even then a woman who has been the victim of discrimination still may not prevail because Title VII protections in this area are so weak.

In "The Prevalence of 'Look'ism in Hiring Decisions: How Federal Law Should Be Amended to Prevent Appearance Discrimination in the Workplace," which appeared in the *University of Pennsylvania Journal of Labor and Employment Law*, Karen Zakrzewski argues that Title VII should be expanded to recognize the "appearance-challenged" as a protected class. She disagrees with those who say that amending Title VII in such a way would be futile and that the states should be left to deal with this issue on their own, because, she argues, such an approach will not yield uniform results and women who are discriminated against in states without such protections will be powerless to fight it.

Critics of expanding Title VII protection argue that appearance is fundamentally different from other classes protected by Title VII, such as gender or race, and point out that the "appearance-challenged" or unattractive are a diverse group that is difficult to define. If they do constitute a class, it is one that has not had to deal with the type of discrimination faced by racial minorities or women.

Zakrzewski counters that the unattractive have long faced widespread discrimination of a systematic nature, pointing to the "ugly laws" once enforced in many cities that prevented disabled, physically maimed, or just very ugly people from appearing in public as the most extreme example, and to the discrimination that still goes on in hiring practices today. She also argues that dissimilar classes are already protected under Title VII, as race is clearly different from gender in that there are actual biological differences between the sexes, while there are none between the races. Title VII accounts for such differences by extending the proper amount of protection to each, as exemplified by the prohibition on race being a bona fide occupational qualification in employment but not gender. Thus, appearance should not be unprotected simply because it is different from other classes that are already protected.

Zakrzewski proposes that Title VII be expanded to include the immutable characteristics of appearance but not those that relate to self-expression or are clearly mutable, such as provocative or inappropriate dress. This would limit such protection to the purpose for which Title VII was created: to protect individuals with no control over some trait possessed by them that has no bearing on their qualifications for employment.

The problem of proving that one is in the protected class of "appearance-challenged" people at first may seem daunting because attractiveness is a subjective determination, unlike race or gender. However, courts are required to make subjective determinations frequently, for instance, in the context of the "reasonable person" standard in a tort action, or determining consumer confusion in an action for trademark infringement. In many cases, proving membership in a protected class may not even be an issue if the employer admits that attractiveness was a factor in its hiring decision by asserting that it is a bona fide occupational qualification for the position. Then, the employer must show that this qualification is truly a necessity for the particular line of work, such as modeling or acting.

For example, if a clothing store applies the outwardly neutral employment practice of requiring all employees to wear that store's products during working hours (as do the Gap, Abercrombie & Fitch, and nearly all other stores that sell their own brand of clothing) but does not make clothes that fit a large segment of the population, the seemingly innocuous policy actually has the effect of preventing many people from being employed there. The employer would have to prove that the appearance requirement of wearing its brand of clothes during working hours was a business necessity. A showing by the employer that this practice was merely good for business would not be sufficient to meet its burden.

While it would be impossible for Title VII protections against appearance discrimination to completely eliminate the problem, just as Title VII protections for race and gender have not totally prevented discrimination on those grounds, it is a significant step in the right direction. Protections for appearance should, like other Title VII protections, compel employers to recognize that although certain differences exist, these differences do not constitute sufficient grounds on which to base hiring decisions. Amending Title VII to protect against appearance discrimination also has the benefit of providing uniformity to this area of the law and protecting all those who suffer appearance discrimination throughout the country—not just the most extreme cases.

Discrimination law is a complicated and difficult subject. Women suing under these protections face an arduous road, as litigation is expensive and one's prospects of winning are generally not high. What is more, the process itself is time-consuming and emotionally and financially draining—things that anyone who has just suffered through the humiliating experience of losing a job or a promotion generally hopes to avoid.

But the laws regulating discrimination in the workplace are underdeveloped. Certain areas of the law, such as those governing sex and age discrimination, are relatively fleshed out. Employers have paid more than $200 million in legal awards and settlements in age discrimination lawsuits since 1996. (About 20 percent of all discrimination charges filed by the EEOC are for age discrimination and—employers beware—the settlements are much higher than the settlements for sex discrimination and disability cases.) Despite these numbers, in this youth-oriented culture most age discrimination goes unreported, either because the process intimidates people or because the cases get thrown out of court because of a lack of evidence. (It's your word against theirs.) And, sadly, even when the suit is successful it doesn't bring back the career, provide the advantages of years spent climbing the corporate ladder, or repair damaged self-esteem.

Other areas of discrimination such as weight and appearance are still in their vestigial stages, so individuals suffering such discrimination often face a nearly impossible task in trying to be heard in court in order to protect their rights—or what *should* be their rights.

The first thing we need to do before passing these laws is work toward a shift in our thought processes as a society. Did you see *Shallow Hal*, the movie about a guy whose shallowness is cured by hypnosis such that he can only see a woman's inner beauty? Under his spell, Hal falls in love with the generous and kindhearted, 300-pound

Rosemary (Gwyneth Paltrow, who donned a fat suit for the movie) because he sees her as a gorgeous, thin blonde. While filming the movie, Gwyneth decided to go out in public in her fat suit to see how the public actually responds to an obese person. "No one recognized me at all," she told the TV show *Entertainment Tonight*. "Nobody would make eye contact. It was disturbing and sad." She said that she had entirely new respect for overweight people and society's judgment of them: "It's so much more important who you are and how you conduct yourself as opposed to how you look." If only we could all walk in a fat suit, we might understand.

We all aren't overweight, but we all do age, and it seems that, once again, it is women who bear the brunt of being examined under society's magnifying glass. When I was a young prosecutor and a new professor, people recommended I wear glasses and pull my hair back to make myself look older, more authoritative, more "in charge." Now that I'm older, it seems I'm joined by many other women in a constant battle to look younger, I suppose to prove that I'm neither "too old" nor a "has-been." (I also recently found my diary from when I was in high school complaining I was "so fat." Yeah, right. I'd love to be that weight again, but I'm not.)

It is, admittedly, extremely difficult to address and legislate appearance discrimination in the workplace. Our looks and others' judgments of whether our appearance is good or bad are private and complicated, but the writing and enforcement of a statute or ordinance is impersonal and abstract. As the last forty years of legislation, litigation, and changes in the workplace have shown, however, laws prohibiting discrimination are necessary if we are to work toward a society where certain groups—particularly those who have historically been subordinated and stigmatized—are treated with fairness at their place of employment, rather than discriminated against on the basis of some characteristic—such as pant size, number on a scale, or hair color—that has little or no relationship to the individual's ability to contribute in the workplace.

Catherine Malarkey had worked as a secretary for Texaco for more than seventeen years. During that time, it became increasingly clear to

Malarkey that the more senior secretarial positions at Texaco seemed to go disproportionately to younger, more attractive women, regardless of whether those women were the best-qualified candidates for the job. She brought a suit against Texaco alleging that the company promoted women "on the basis of their physical attractiveness" and that "younger women are viewed by management as being more attractive than older women." Malarkey, while equally if not better qualified than younger women at the company, had not fared as well as them in job opportunities, and argued that Texaco's policy constituted unlawful discrimination under Title VII.

The court dismissed her claim, stating that "nowhere does plaintiff allege that she was denied a promotion in favor of a male, and nowhere does she allege that she has at any time been in competition with a male. She has been in competition only with younger women, and for allegedly no justifiable reasons, has lost out to them. The complaint permits no other construction. If these allegations are true, defendant's behavior is abhorrent. But it is not behavior falling within the proscriptions of Title VII . . . because the complaint alleges that only women were promoted to the positions in question, the ultimate choice of which women to hire could not have been based on discrimination between men and women."

As we've seen, current law will, in certain circumstances, protect women and older people from such discrimination, but our laws must go further to protect women from discrimination as we age, gain weight, and otherwise grow out of our youth in ways that are irrelevant to the quality of our work. A federal law explicitly prohibiting weight discrimination would provide effective and uniform legal protection to overweight people facing employment discrimination. It is time to expand these legal protections, for the purpose of allowing women the opportunity to age and grow gracefully in a more welcoming and productive society. Once we've jumped the hurdles to get here, we won't allow ourselves to be put out to pasture.

CHAPTER 6

MARRIAGE

"I have the right to be married—or not"

You've heard the statistics: each year in the United States there are more than two million marriages, and more than a million divorces. That's 7.5 marriages and 3.8 divorces per 1,000 people. No matter how you do the math, more than 50 percent of marriages end in divorce.

Marriage, at its most basic, practical level, is a contract. And, as any lawyer worth her salt will tell you, what contracts do is prevent troubles before they happen. You wouldn't hire a contractor without working out the details of what he was going to do, right? How much is it going to cost? When will it be finished? Who is going to buy the paint? Unfortunately, we tend to approach marriage wide-eyed, often forgetting to ask the fundamental questions that are basic to most legally binding agreements.

There's an old joke: "There are two times men don't understand women—before the marriage and after the marriage." That may be true, but it doesn't have to be. Given that we have the opportunity to get to know each other before we get married, we should learn enough about each other to solve any future difficulties after our marriage. Even TV shows such as *The Bachelorette* (sort of modern-day arranged marriages, I guess) make the potential spouses get to know each other's wants and needs.

Dear Abby, the disseminator of commonsense advice, offered in a column a few questions she thought a young lady and her fiancé needed to discuss and agree upon in order for them to have a greater chance for a successful marriage. They included:

- *Are you ready for a monogamous relationship?*
- *Are you both self-supporting and capable of supporting each other and any children that come along?*
- *Are your philosophies about child-rearing and discipline similar?*
- *Are your career goals compatible?*

Those are a great start, but a pastor who provides premarital counseling to couples considering marriage wrote in to say Dear Abby had missed that it's not the questions you ask but how you listen to each other that is most important. He said, "It is the lack of ability to openly and honestly communicate about a variety of subjects, and the inability or unwillingness to really listen and hear each other, that causes marital discord."

Psychiatrist Scott Haltzman, author of *The Secrets of Happily Married Men,* says that conventional marital therapy that tries to get men to be more like women by talking about their feelings and their wives' feelings and being more touchy-feely is doomed to failure because men and women are "wired differently." Though he says there are certainly exceptions, learning to listen does not come naturally to males. They are inclined by nature to act, to cull the savannah for food, while women are inclined to maintain. Women communicate; men fix. He suggests viewing marriage "as a job" and learning to listen as if at work—where there's no TV, where you look directly at each other while talking, and seek clarification where needed.

There are, in fact, numerous books—from *The Marital Compatibility Test: Hundreds of Questions for Couples to Answer Together* to *Getting Ready for Marriage Workbook: How to Really Get to Know the Person You're Going to Marry* to *1001 Questions to Ask Before You Get Married,* geared toward learning what each partner expects in the relationship. In *1001 Questions,* author Monica Mendez Leahy says that "love can be bliss, but marriage takes work," and she puts on the table issues that can arise in any marriage, so that you and your betrothed can explore fundamental questions and come to terms with marital expectations. For example, "Is it OK to cheat on your taxes?" and "Is there such a thing as innocent flirting?"

There are the simpler but still difficult questions, such as: *Should we have a big wedding and spend a lot of money or should we save our money and do something more intimate?* And then there are the difficult questions: *Should I sign a prenup? Are we putting both our names on the deed of the house? Are we going to have separate checking accounts? Will we take the same last name?* For example, did you know that assuming your husband's last name is a social custom and not a legal requirement? If you *want* to change your name, the laws of your state will control how this is done. The *New York Times* reporter formerly known as Jodi Wilgoren and her husband made up a new moniker by which they'd both be known in a "commitment to equality, with a nod to family history and a dash of out-of-the-box creativity." They combined his last name, Ruderman, with hers and are now known as Gary and Jodi Rudoren, giving a nod to both sets of patrilineal ancestors. Now, that's a compromise!

Just speaking these questions aloud can present certain discomforts, but, in order to squelch problems before they occur, these questions must be asked and answered. As every marriage counselor, psychiatrist, and lawyer will tell you, when you think through, talk through, and work through these issues *before* you say "I do," your marriage will be stronger and, hopefully, will prevent you from having to draw on your legal rights later. Above all, the goal is to make a marriage work, to keep it together. With that said, let's address the laws that are in place to prevent and deal with marital woes.

THE RIGHTS WE HAVE

Every state imposes some rules for getting married, and as we've witnessed in the gay marriage debate, states differ in marriage laws.

Typically, in order to be legally married, consenting adults above the age of eighteen obtain a marriage license from the county clerk and have a formal ceremony of some type performed by a person authorized by the state to do so. In most states, this includes judges, ordained clergy of recognized religions, and, in some states, justices of the peace and even notaries.

Though very few states allow it, there is also common-law marriage. A common-law marriage comes about when a man and a woman live together for a certain period of time, holding themselves out to others as husband and wife. The legal ramifications of common-law marriages (in the states that recognize them) can be similar to those of the more common type.

Besides being a symbolic joining of two hearts, marriage is a contract that places legal obligations on both parties. There is a mutual obligation to support each other and provide financial sustenance for any children that the pair has. States have varying rules for how property is handled in a marriage, but generally, property acquired during the marriage is considered the marital property of both parties. Property owned before a marriage remains separate property unless legally converted into marital property.

It is important to note that in most states when one spouse dies, any real property owned "jointly with right of survivorship" or in a "tenancy by entireties" by husband and wife automatically goes to the survivor. But be sure to check your deed and the law, as many women assume they are on the deed and discover they are not. Do you know if your name is physically recorded on the deed of your home? When Eileen's husband died, she discovered her husband's first wife now owned the house Eileen had called home for eleven years!

On the flip side of assets are debts. Debts incurred during a marriage are generally the responsibility of both parties. So if your husband loses $25,000 gambling in Atlantic City, in most states you're a loser too. Scary, huh? If you share joint credit cards and know that your marriage is ending, you should immediately cancel the cards to ensure that the balance does not increase any further. Karen discovered she was paying half of her ex-husband's gifts of expensive jewelry and a trip to Paris for his girlfriend!

How do we prevent this? And why do women often get a divorce settlement that they are happy with only to learn later that it wasn't as they expected? Why do women lose in courtrooms around the country every day? Should women sign a prenuptial agreement? What's the difference between an uncontested divorce and a contested one? What's a no-fault divorce and why do religious organizations blame them for the increase in the divorce rate? And what about the kids? Who pays child support and what are the laws concerning deadbeat dads? How do you know if you're entitled to alimony?

The Prenup

Sally, a woman in Florida, recently sued her husband for fraud after learning he had secretly divorced her two years earlier by getting a judge to grant a default judgment in his favor, and continuing to live with her as husband and wife. Even more bizarre than the secret divorce were the terms of their prenup: "Sally will cook breakfast a minimum of three times during the weekdays, and one time per weekend. In return, Renzie will not wake Sally up on her off days. Renzie will rub Sally's back/neck three times during the weekdays, and one time per weekend for a minimum of five minutes. Each time Sally . . . uses the 'F' word, she agrees to do one hour of yard work within the next seven days."

Now, that's a couple who talked *everything* through!

Because of past uncertainty whether courts could enforce prenuptial agreements, a uniform treatment of prenuptial agreements was approved by the National Conference of Commissioners on Uniform State Laws in 1983. (The NCCUSL is a group of lawyers, judges, and professors of law generally appointed to the commission by state governors that make recommendations, which may be written into law by individual states at their option.) The Uniform Pre-Marital Agreement Act provides legal guidelines for people who wish to make agreements prior to marriage regarding ownership, management, and control of property; property disposition on separation, divorce, and death; alimony; wills; and life insurance beneficiaries.

Twenty-seven states and the District of Columbia recognize premarital agreements. (Refer to the Women's Toolbox in the back of the book for the complete list.) Several states that haven't adopted the act have other laws, which often differ from the act in only minor ways. One important difference is that a few states, including California, do not allow premarital agreements to modify or eliminate the right of a spouse to receive court-ordered alimony at divorce. In every state, whether covered by the act or not, couples are prohibited from making binding provisions about child support payments.

But prenups are an extremely sensitive and personal subject that makes both parties lay their cards on the table. Let's take Barbie and Ken, for example. They've dated for years (forty-three, to be exact) and after a recent separation (two years while Ken "revamped his life—mind, body and soul"), Ken has announced he wants to win back his longtime love so that they can rekindle their decades-long romance—or at least that is what their PR representative at Mattel has told the media. Anyway, their assets are a little dissimilar, to say the least.

Barbie has the exquisitely furnished Dream House, the Fashion Plaza, the three-story building "with working elevator," the bake shop and café, and the hair salon, not to mention the carnival. She designs and markets her own clothing line, and receives millions of dollars a year in talent and licensing fees from her numerous product endorsements. She also has a fleet of cars—from a pink Jeep to a purple Corvette Stingray. In short, she's loaded.

And what does Ken have? Several changes of clothes, a Jeep he borrowed from G.I. Joe, and good hair.

So, what should Barbie do? Ask for a prenup? How could she? They are in *love*!

Just the option of being able to obtain a pre- or postnuptial agreement is a breakthrough for women. Women were once looked at as chattel, the property of the husband, and were not able to enter into any type of contract with anyone, especially her husband, because it was the equivalent of the man entering into a legal agreement with himself. Marital contracts are a relatively recent legal development. Until about fifty years ago, spouses were either prohibited from entering into contracts with each other or could do so only through trustees.

Prenuptial agreements are notoriously sticky situations, and there are two schools of thought: (1) "Absolutely!" and (2) "How dare you!" David Latko, a certified divorce financial analyst and author of *Everybody Wants Your Money*, advises his clients, "If you have more assets than your intended when you enter into a marriage, you *definitely* need a prenup. And if your future spouse has more, . . . well, gosh, . . . why sign something that reduces love to a matter of dollars and cents?"

Exactly. "Why would we want to keep *anything* separate?" Ken asks. "I mean, we're in love." Understood. But there *are* reasons to sign a prenup, even if you're 100 percent sure you'll be together till death do you part.

Kiplinger Financial, the creator of the nation's first personal finance magazine, recommends a prenup if:

1. You and your spouse-to-be each has accumulated assets of your own, such as real estate, investment portfolios, or even inheritances that you *want to keep separate*. (This is often the case with older couples.)
2. You have been divorced. (Especially if either spouse has children from a previous marriage. There will have been prior legal and financial commitments made if there are children, and most likely even if there weren't.)
3. You own a business.
4. One spouse has considerably more wealth than the other.
5. You think it may make negotiations or the paperwork more pleasant should your marriage end.

Perhaps #5 is the one that makes prenups such a touchy subject, followed in touchiness by #4, then #3, #2, and #1.

No one will dispute the logic that older couples might see wisdom in a prenup because of the mess they'll bequeath to those they leave behind if they don't have one. The only reason this might not make sense is if they both have no children, no relatives, no friends, and no one else who would be affected by their estate, *and* if the two lovebirds have the same nonprofit benefactor they are leaving their money to.

If one or both of you have children, then there's college tuition, child support, and prior financial and legal settlements that have been made that should be acknowledged in a prenup.

And if one or both of you owns a business, it is easy to see that a prenup might ensure stability within the business and enable its operations to continue running smoothly.

But no one wants to think that the person he or she is marrying is either greedy or, worse, in it just for the money, right? Isn't that basically it? And no one wants to jinx a special relationship by the ominous signing of a prenup. After all, this is the most special relationship of all time, the one that will never end! Unfortunately, as a fact of life, relationships always end. This does not necessarily mean they end in divorce. But all relationships, even the ones that last sixty years, end at some point when one or the other spouse dies. (Consult the Women's Toolbox in the back of the book for advice on estate planning and wills.)

Can prenups be challenged in court? Absolutely. When Jack Welch, retired chairman of General Electric, filed for divorce from Jane Beasley in 2002, she was initially offered a settlement of $15 million. But, she argued, his fortune had grown substantially over their thirteen-year marriage and she maintained that she had helped it grow (not to mention that he had been caught cheating on her). Besides, the prenup that he had had her sign expired after ten years of marriage. Jane received more than $100 million.

In recent years, the states and courts have held to the terms of prenuptial agreements. In 1990, in *Simeone v. Simeone,* the Pennsylvania Supreme Court upheld an agreement that severely limited Ms. Simeone's rights to support payments, even though the older, wealthier man had presented the prenup to his wife-to-be on the eve of their wedding and she had signed it without the benefit of counsel. In a strongly worded opinion, the court underlined the fact that a prenuptial agreement is a valid legal contract "and should be evaluated under the same criteria as are applicable to other types of contracts. Absent fraud, misrepresentation, or duress, spouses should be bound by the terms of their agreements." The court further stated that arguments regarding prenuptials should not land in court and that whether they are reasonable or not should not be decided by the court after they are signed. For that reason, in some states a prenup must be validated by the court; in other states a prenup must still be fair when the couple splits up. In Maine, a prenup is automatically void by state law eighteen months after the couple has a child, unless it is renewed in writing.

What should you do if you are signing a prenuptial agreement and you want it done right? First, each spouse should be represented by a different lawyer, so that it's clear that each one signed the agreement voluntarily. Some prenups are even videotaped so that the couples are shown signing of their own free will. (Overkill?) Second, sign the agreement well before the wedding, so that it's not a shotgun prenup. Third, be fair. The greedier a spouse is, the more likely a judge will be tempted to throw out the agreement later.

Some couples, surprisingly, do not speak about their financial situation prior to marriage, which can prove disastrous once over the threshold. Would you buy a car without asking the price or start a job without asking about the salary? About 5 percent of first marriages and 20 percent of second marriages have a prenup in place. Does a prenup make sense for you? That's really for you and your betrothed to discuss and decide. Just know that in most states the law mandates that the assets of a marriage are split equally between the couple in the case of divorce. Prenups aren't for everyone, but the legal option is there (like a blood test), so know your rights and think it through *before* you sign. A prenup is for a couple that does not want to rely on a court to distribute their assets in the event of death or divorce, but would rather set their own terms.

The "D" Word

According to the National Center for Health Statistics, 43 percent of first marriages in the United States end in divorce or separation within the first fifteen years. Many states term this "dissolution" because, besides death or annulment, it is the legal means of ending a marriage contract. Each state has its own procedural requirements for granting a divorce, and you must follow the requirements of the state in which you are requesting a divorce. You do not, however, have to get a divorce in the same state in which you were married.

The U.S. Constitution requires each state to give "full faith and credit" to the laws of other states by, among other things, recognizing marriages and divorces made across state lines, for example. Without this provision, a divorce recognized as legal in one state might not be recognized as such in another. In one 1948 case, *Sherrer v. Sherrer,* a woman who had been living in Massachusetts received a divorce in Florida after complying with that state's relatively short ninety-day residency requirement. She then remarried and returned to Massachusetts. Although her first husband contested the divorce proceedings, the Supreme Court held that Massachusetts had to recognize the Florida divorce according to the full-faith-and-credit provision.

According to the U.S. Census Bureau, the fastest-growing marital status category is "divorced persons." Why? Prior to the 1960s, social, religious, and moral pressures made divorce relatively uncommon. Societal mores held the courts and legal standards to a strict scrutiny over circumstances surrounding divorce. Until the 1960s and 1970s, divorce typically required grounds and a standard that were severe: adultery, desertion, abuse, insanity, or imprisonment of a spouse.

Today, most courts will accept "irreconcilable differences" as sufficient grounds for the dissolution of a marriage. Yes, some might consider this reason frivolous, but this protects both parties from remaining in an unhappy marriage or, worse, a marriage that involves one of the more severe grounds. Many women, for example, choose not to reveal their husband's dalliances to protect their children. Others air their dirty laundry for all to see. In the case of one feuding couple the man hung a banner from a bridge: "Wendy, I want a divorce. Ted." A few days later, another banner appeared: "No way! You're the cheat! Wendy."

There are two types of divorce, fault and no-fault, and either of these types can be contested or uncontested.

The difference between a contested and uncontested divorce is that contested divorces are those in which either party disputes any issue in the case—the divorce itself, the property division, child custody, and/or alimony. Uncontested divorces fall into two categories: consent divorces, where the parties agree on all major issues, and default divorces, where one of the parties fails to appear to contest the divorce or any issue in it, either because he or she chooses not to oppose it or because he or she cannot be located.

Fault is the traditional type of divorce, which requires one spouse to prove that the other spouse was legally at fault (or to blame) in order to obtain a divorce. The "innocent" spouse is then granted a divorce from the "guilty" spouse. The most frequently used traditional fault ground is cruelty (inflicting unnecessary emotional or physical pain). As noted earlier, other reasons include adultery, desertion, confinement in prison, and incurable insanity. The physical inability to engage in sexual intercourse (if it was not disclosed before marriage) is grounds for a fault divorce in a dozen states.

Today, thirty-five states still allow a spouse to allege fault in obtaining a divorce, but the requirements vary from state to state. Some states, such as Arkansas and Idaho, provide the ground of conviction of a felony; others require substantial prison sentences, and some require that a significant portion of a sentence be served before divorce can be granted. Only two states recognize an attempt on the petitioning spouse's life through poison or other means as grounds for divorce, and only Illinois allows fault divorce if "the respondent has infected the other with a sexually transmitted disease." New Jersey provides "deviant sexual conduct voluntarily performed by the defendant without consent of the plaintiff," and Alabama allows "the commission of the crime against nature, whether with mankind or beast, either before or after marriage."

Why would you choose a fault divorce? Some people don't want to wait out the period of separation required by their state's law for a no-fault divorce. And in some states, a spouse who proves the other's fault may receive a greater share of the marital property or more alimony. Years ago, if both parties were at fault, *neither* was entitled to a divorce. The absurdity of this result gave rise to the concept of "comparative rectitude," to grant the spouse *least* at fault a divorce when both parties have shown grounds for divorce.

No-fault divorce describes any divorce where the spouse suing for divorce does not have to prove that the other spouse did something wrong. All states allow divorces regardless of who is at fault. To get a no-fault divorce, one spouse must simply state a reason recognized by the state. In most states, it's enough to declare that the couple cannot get along (this goes by such names as "incompatibility," "irreconcilable differences," or "irremediable breakdown of the marriage"). Many states require that the couple live apart for a designated period of time in order to obtain a no-fault divorce.

With the advent of no-fault divorce, blame is no longer an issue; this simplifies the divorce process, reducing conflict and cost. Critics argue that no-fault divorce has driven up the divorce rate and shifted acrimony from the battle over who is to blame for ruining the marriage to battles over child support, visitation, and custody. Conservatives feel that no-fault divorce has caused the divorce rate to rise and has weakened the institution of marriage. According to them, it has become much too easy to obtain a divorce, thus making marriage vows meaningless. They also claim that divorces are bad for children, as children raised in single-parent homes are lacking "traditional family values."

No-fault divorce wasn't widely instituted until the 1970s. Before no-fault divorce, a judge (rather than the spouses) would decide whether the marriage was viable. A judge could order that a marriage stay intact! Battered-women's groups and feminist organizations fought for the change in law, claiming that the lack of no-fault divorce left many women trapped in abusive and unstable marriages.

Recent studies show that they were right. Stanford Graduate School of Business professor Justin Wolfers and Harvard-trained economist Betsey Stevenson studied the female suicide rate and claims of domestic violence. They found a drop of almost 20 percent in the female suicide rate after the implementation of no-fault divorce, and also found that spousal violence declined in states that implemented no-fault divorce while it increased in states without it. The researchers also noted that divorce rates rose sharply immediately after the implementation of no-fault law but either returned to normal or went down within ten years. The researchers credit that spike to a pent-up demand for divorce.

"If you're looking for the 'smoking gun' to explain the decline in the traditional American family," Wolfers said about the findings, "it's not the no-fault divorce laws. Rather than looking on them as the *cause* of family ills, these laws may actually provide a safety valve for the pressures of family life."

RIGHTS WE SHOULD DEMAND

Convoluted as all this is, we must always remember to be thankful for the freedoms we have as American women. Many women in poorer countries don't have the opportunity to weigh the differences between fault and no-fault divorce, because they simply can't get a divorce. Divorce in Chile finally became legal in 2006. Until then, a woman's only option to get out of a bad marriage was annulment, which meant that the marriage never existed in the eyes of the law, leaving women with no protections or support payments for her or her children.

Even though many women simply left abusive, dysfunctional marriages, they were still considered their husbands' property and could not make any financial decisions on their own, such as applying for a mortgage, starting a business, or remarrying. One of the consequences of this long-term ban on divorce was a sharp drop in the marriage rate. Many young people did not want to make an agreement they couldn't get out of. This is something to think about as conservatives try to make divorce harder and harder to obtain—the harder it is to leave the marriage, the fewer the people who want to commit to marriage.

President Bush has earmarked $200 million for programs that "develop innovative approaches to promote healthy marriages." Some states have implemented a new type of marriage, called a "covenant marriage," in which couples express their intention to remain married for life and agree to both premarital counseling and further counseling by a member of the clergy or marriage counselor before filing for divorce. Covenant marriage also restricts them to a handful of legal grounds for divorce: adultery, felony conviction, one year of abandonment, or sexual or physical abuse. It's been enacted in Louisiana, Arizona, and Arkansas. Proponents are recruiting as many pastors as possible to allow only covenant marriages in their churches. No one would argue in favor of more divorces, but making divorce more difficult seems to potentially hurt the children of dysfunctional families.

No-fault divorce is so important that we women must demand it remain an option. It allows women (who often lack resources) to skip the long and expensive process of arbitrating who was at fault. Before no-fault divorce it was mostly the man's decision whether or not to get a divorce because he was the one with the money to hire a lawyer. This left many women, especially low-income women, trapped. Now, women can leave a man as easily as a man can leave a woman. In fact, women now file for more than two-thirds of all divorces, sometimes against the wishes (and demands) of their husbands.

Remove the Roadblock

After twenty-six years of marriage, Cathy and Robert Jacob divorced in January 2003, but Robert was unhappy with the financial terms imposed by the court and appealed the decision. The appellate court reviewed the decision and decided that neither of the Jacobs had shown proper grounds for divorce in New York State; it ruled that, after four years of being separated, the Jacobses were still married. Divorce denied.

According to a 2004 article in the *New York Times,* the Jacobs' case is not an anomaly in New York. A supreme court justice on Staten Island, for example, denied a divorce to a couple after ruling that a wife had failed to prove "that she repeatedly requested a resumption of sexual relations," and acting supreme court justice Jeffrey Lebowitz denied a divorce to a teacher who sought to end her thirty-year marriage on the grounds of cruel and inhumane treatment because the judge wanted to send a message to the state legislature that the law must change. Even though he expressed sympathy for the woman, he said her complaint (which included her husband's threats to cut up the couch with a chain saw) weren't severe enough by state divorce law for the couple not to continue living together.

New York is the only state that does not recognize no-fault divorces, requiring one spouse to lay blame on the other for such offenses as adultery, abandonment, and cruel and inhumane treatment. No doubt we all want to promote the preservation of healthy families, but long, acrimonious divorces do nothing to protect the children or preserve the family. In fact, no-fault divorces have been proven to *lessen* the hostility because there's less finger-pointing.

Take It to the Bank

Unfortunately, despite the legal right to file for divorce, women still suffer financially from divorce. Studies show that men have an overall rise in income after divorce while women have an overall fall in income. In fact, after a divorce, the average annual income for a household with the custodial mother drops about 30 percent while the husband's finances rise by 10 percent. Why?

According to David Latko, a certified divorce financial analyst, the biggest problem is that 95 percent of women, lawyers, and judges don't know anything about money, so everything they do is structured toward getting half. But "equal" is not the same as "equitable." Women typically enter the divorce proceedings with the goal of getting to keep the house and custody of the kids, and the half they end up with is, in essence, dead assets—that is, assets such as the house, which consumes the woman's financial resources. Women end up scraping by as long as they can, depending on support money or alimony they discover is not enough, and ultimately even that lifeline runs out. Where are they then? Stuck. And where are the ex-husbands? They've started anew. He's shed all his liabilities, his pension continues to grow, and he's not worried about the boiler breaking, taxes, and the electric bill. He's out there making more money, while the ex-wife is trying to keep her world from collapsing.

"In general the one common denominator in all divorces," Latko explains, "is that the women involved are under tremendous pressures to settle for what is almost always the most awful terms possible, financially speaking." They often can't endure the emotional and financial pressures of a long court battle and so settle for getting what they can.

In his book, *Everybody Wants Your Money,* Latko explains how many women end up taking a divorce settlement that at first looks good, but, in fact, is actually financially ruinous. He advises women to determine how their soon-to-be-ex-husband's finances will look five, ten or twenty years down the road, so that the settlement is indeed fair.

He tells of one woman who came to him for advice on how to invest the proceeds from the settlement she was just about to accept. "When we tallied up the marital assets," he explains, "the total came to about $243,400. Her lawyer, as many do, had a single-minded goal—get the assets split straight down the middle, give or take a few dollars. I had the unpleasant task of showing her that, under the plan she was about to sign she would have been *dead broke* in eleven years. But using the same provisions of the settlement, her ex-husband would accumulate a net worth of $477,000!"

It doesn't take a financial genius to see the inequality in a plan that impoverishes one partner while ensuring the prosperity of the other. Yet it happens every day. Most women leave the divorce thinking they got half, when in fact they end up with much less than half. In this case, Latko points out that she would have been spending $17,052 more in the first year than she was taking in. Six months into her newfound freedom from a bad marriage, she would have been forced to sell her home and/or borrow against the house in order to survive.

The courts try to make up for this inequality with alimony payments, also called spousal support payments. Unfortunately, there is no concrete way that judges award alimony. It is completely up to the court's discretion. The courts look at a variety of factors, including length of marriage, the ability of each of the parties to earn money, their respective age and health, the property involved, and the conduct of the parties. Usually, courts award alimony only if one party has been financially dependent on the other for most of a lengthy marriage. This leaves many women out in the cold. It also leads to much frustration in both women and men because alimony payments are often seemingly arbitrarily applied. Because alimony awards are solely up to the discretion of the judge, the couple up the street, your coworker, and you might all have drastically different alimony awards, despite similar circumstances.

Take the example of Beth, who works as a teacher and makes very little money; her ex-husband is a doctor, making a healthy salary. Her husband proposed an agreement for an equal division of property and no alimony. When she tried to protest, her husband tied her up in court proceedings involving her financial past and credit rating for months; she couldn't pay her lawyer for all the time necessary, so she accepted the agreement, in spite of its unfairness, simply to be done with the whole process.

Because of the time and money necessary for lawyers and court proceedings, what happened to Beth is not unusual; in fact, our court system is heavily skewed toward the party with the most money. As we have seen, women usually make much less than men and are often responsible for the care of the children. The combination of these factors leads many women to accept unfair arrangements simply because they lack resources.

What should we do? Besides hiring an attorney, women should seek out a financial adviser and demand our fair share. These provisions in state law establish that there are certain factors that must be considered by a court in determining the fair distribution of marital assets, including the "contributions and services as a spouse, parent, wage earner and homemaker, and to the career or career potential of the other party" of the spouse who does not hold title to the property. In English, that means that the spouse who takes care of the children and the home so that the other spouse can pursue a career should share in the property and value acquired by the breadwinner. Or if one spouse works while the other spouse obtains a degree, the one who supported the other during his or her time as a student should share in the value of the degree bestowed on the other and the higher earnings potential that comes with it.

This gets to the nature of a marital partnership. Is it an equal partnership, or is the wife a junior partner if she's the primary caregiver? "What she needs to live on" is quite different from a "50/50 partner." This typically comes into play in big-money cases, such as *Wendt v. Wendt*, after a thirty-two-year marriage in which Lorna Wendt served as mother, homemaker, and corporate wife, her husband had climbed to be chief executive officer of GE Capital Services, General Electric's most profitable division. The Superior Court awarded approximately half of all marital assets to Lorna. Gary Wendt was shocked because his fortune was so big. But why should it make any difference whether he's wealthy or working as a used-car salesman?

The Children

Custody battles are often the longest and most drawn-out of any divorce proceeding. It has been shown that judges seem to favor women for custody because usually they have been chief caretaker during the marriage and the courts like to maintain as much continuity as possible in reference to children. For this reason, women also often end up with the house because the judge doesn't want to force the children to move.

Of course, this is a double-edged sword: as much as most women want to be the caretakers of their children, being a single mother is extraordinarily hard. Not only are you chief chauffeur, nurse, and referee, you are also responsible for ensuring that the bills are paid. This includes making sure that the child support payments that are due to you are received. An astonishing number of women have to fight tooth and nail to get the fathers of their children to pay their fair share of the costs of raising kids.

The trend in law has been to replace the terms *custody* and *visitation* with *parenting times*. It is degrading to give one parent "custody" and the other parent "visitation," regardless of who spends the most amount of time caring for the child. The blurring of the line between custody and visitation has also led to a modern phenomenon called "shared physical custody." This means that the children will spend equal time during the week with each parent. The theory in support of shared physical custody is that fathers have as much rights to their children as do mothers, the children have rights to a full relationship with both parents, and the children are better off when they spend equal amounts of time with each parent. The results are that the child is shipped back and forth between two households, usually several times during the week.

"In some cases this arrangement works," says Connecticut family lawyer Cindy Hartwell, "but for the most part, it injures the stay-at-home mother, whose primary job has always been to rear the children and run the household. Orders for shared physical custody can be a real blow to the woman's self-esteem. She has lost her 'job' and she is left with the additional feeling that she has lost her children. She still has the same full-time concerns as a parent, but she is only given a part-time schedule with less money and resources to fulfill her parenting goals."

Unfortunately, some women withhold access to the children as a "punishment" for their husband's wrongdoings. It is important to understand that your children are not yours alone, and using them in this way is destructive to their well-being. (On the other hand, it is important that you pay attention to any signs of abuse or financial irresponsibility on the part of their father.)

For the last twelve years Maria's ex-husband had been dictating to her what he would and wouldn't pay, constantly micromanaging her financial decisions about redecorating, medical care, sports, and even where she should have telephones in her house. She was embarrassed that he continued to hold such power over her, but she put up with it. Had he stopped there, it's possible she never would have resisted. But when he started deducting from child support for Christmas gifts he provided to the children, she had had enough. She had to take him to court and wage a whole new custody battle, spending thousands of dollars in new legal fees in order to get him to live up to his end of the agreement.

As if collecting from ex-husbands wasn't hard enough, there was a setback for women as a result of the new bankruptcy law passed in 2006 by the Bush administration. Under the previous laws spousal and child support payments had priority status, meaning they were to be paid before credit card and other debt. Under the new rules, support and debt repayment have the same priority, and given the fierceness of credit card debt collection, it looks like support payments will fall by the wayside. The one upside to this law is that the support recipient is automatically notified of the debtor's bankruptcy as well as his or her address and the name and address of his or her employer. This is helpful in cases of disappearing spouses. But does it seem fair that our lawmakers are protecting credit card companies' bottom lines before protecting women and children? Or does this once again reek of corporate interests over the interests of women?

Deadbeat Dads

In 1992, the passage of the Child Support Recovery Act allowed for vigorous prosecution of egregious offenders, but they could only be charged with misdemeanors. The problem still flourished and in 1998, the Deadbeat Parents Punishment Act created two new categories of federal felonies for the worst child support violators.

Today, a child support violator can be prosecuted under federal law if the violator willfully failed to pay a known child support obligation that has remained unpaid for longer than a year or is greater than

$5,000 (misdemeanor) or has remained unpaid for longer than two years or is greater than $10,000 (felony). According to the Federal Office of Child Support, in 2003, 68 percent of child support cases were in arrears, and an astounding $96 billion in accumulated unpaid support was due to children.

Why do we still have almost $100 billion in unpaid child support? Because federal law applies only if the child resides in another state from the nonpayer.

Unfortunately, many women find themselves too broke for another court battle, so they are forced to hire child support collection services. Sasha, a woman with two kids, two jobs, and a deadbeat ex-husband, hired a collection service after her ex disappeared, cutting off all contact and payments. These agencies are extremely effective; they have specialists for locating people as well as some strong-arm tactics. However, they charge a hefty percentage of collected child support, usually a whopping 25–33 percent. But as Sasha said, "It was better than nothing."

The other option is to go through social services; it is free but often takes a long time, as local social service agencies are severely understaffed and underfunded.

Fortunately, some states have passed legislation so that we don't have to continue to fight in order to receive payments due. Many states will suspend driver's licenses, business licenses, or contractor licenses if an individual owes significant support payments or has a record of not consistently paying support. In 2000, for example, the state of Tennessee revoked the driver's licenses of 1,372 people who owed more than $13 million in child support. In Texas noncustodial parents behind more than three months in their payments can have court-ordered payments deducted from their wages, tax refunds, or lottery winnings; have their assets seized; and have their licenses revoked (even hunting and fishing licenses). A Kentucky family court judge has gone so far as to sentence offenders who owe more than $10,000 in child support and have children with more than three women to either thirty days in jail or a vasectomy. States have also adopted uniform seizure laws for delinquent parents, making it much easier to pursue a parent across state lines, and the federal Child Support Enforcement Agency has developed a database of delinquent parents with constant updates about new hires at companies.

The efforts by our lawmakers to crack down on this insidious form of child abuse are positive, but the fight is not done. We must demand that our lawmakers—on both the state and federal levels—ensure that nonpayment is not tolerated. We must demand that all states pass legislation to freeze bank accounts or garner wages if court-ordered payments are not made.

That so many women are left worse off after divorce is often a result of the adverse effects of time off for pregnancy and child care on our careers. Then, when our marriages don't work, the courts and the laws of this land add insult to injury by doing little to support us in receiving child support payments. Even after we win such payments in a court of law, we are often left as the chief enforcer and collector of child support payments owed to us.

We women have spent a long time fighting for equal rights, and one of the most important is not to be left floundering after divorce. Fair marriage and divorce laws are of utmost importance to us in this struggle. Women should not be left destitute if our marriages end, and we should not feel trapped in bad marriages simply because of bad laws or economic factors.

CHAPTER 7

VIOLENCE AGAINST WOMEN

"I have the right to be safe, whether at home or in public"

Where do you think the most dangerous place for a woman is in the United States? Mall parking lots? Seedy neighborhoods? Parks after dark? The most dangerous place for a woman in the United States is her own home. It may be hard to believe, but domestic violence is the single biggest threat of injury to women in America—more than heart attacks, cancer, strokes, car wrecks, muggings, and rapes *combined*. Every day in the United States, an average of four women *die* as a result of domestic violence.

O. J. Simpson, Scott Peterson, Mark Hacking, Neil Entwistle—they are all names that have come to be emblematic of domestic violence and send shivers down our spines. Perhaps the reason that these cases caught the attention of the nation (and even the world) is that the atrocities that happened to these women could happen to *any one of us*. The thought is chilling—from the outside these were "typical" marriages and these were "normal" men, all functioning in society like regular Joes, who committed the unthinkable.

Scott Peterson, the handsome fertilizer salesman, was living two lives leading up to his wife's murder. To his beautiful wife, Laci, and her family, he was a devoted husband, excitedly awaiting the birth of their son. To Amber Frey, his girlfriend, he was a world-traveling bachelor who was head over heels in love with the single mom and her daughter. The story of the investigation and murder trial caught the nation's attention: The wife in a young, attractive couple disappears. Her husband acts suspiciously, selling her car and preparing to sell the house before the police discover her body. We ask ourselves, as we stare across the dinner table at our own husbands: *How did she not know he would kill her?*

Hospital orderly Mark Hacking, who lied to his wife about getting into medical school, had an argument with her after she found out. She went to bed and he stayed up for an hour playing video games. Then he went and got his deer rifle and, according to his guilty plea to first-degree murder, "I intentionally shot Lori Hacking in the head with a .22 rifle," threw her body into a Dumpster, and reported her missing. He was sentenced to *six years* to life in prison, the maximum sentence allowed under Utah law. Does a story like this make us have momentary second thoughts about going to bed angry?

Neil Entwistle, a man sinking deeper and deeper into debt, was charged with murdering his wife, Rachel, and their nine-month-old daughter, Lillian, as mother and daughter slept side by side in their Boston home. A search warrant revealed that he had searched the Internet for information on how to kill someone. Authorities say he may have been planning to commit suicide after the murders, but instead he fled to his native England. Rachel's family issued a statement that they were "deeply saddened" by the arrest and that "Rachel and Lilly loved Neil very much. Neil was a trusted husband and father, and it is incomprehensible how that love and trust was betrayed in the ultimate act of violence." Love and trust?

Violence against women has become a national epidemic. Once a private issue, domestic abuse gained attention during the women's movement of the 1960s and '70s. When the National Women's Conference met in Houston in 1977 and issued their National Plan of Action, they stated that "the President and Congress should declare the elimination of violence to be a national goal." Thirty years later, the statistics are bleak and the laws that protect us from violence are far from adequate. According to the Department of Justice, an estimated two million wives are beaten by their husbands each year, an average of one every sixteen seconds. How can our laws curb these crimes? Protect us? Help us feel confident to reach out for help? How can our government support us and provide safe havens against abuse? What do we do if we're abused? Where do we go?

THE RIGHTS WE (SORT OF) HAVE

Historically, incidents of domestic violence went unpunished and uncompensated because of the "interspousal immunity" derived from common law. Women were the property of their husbands, and when married, husband and wife were one person under the law. Her existence was suspended and incorporated into her husband's. So what went on within a marriage was only between the two of them. Defense attorney Mickey Sherman remembers a man who stood before a judge many years ago after having been arrested for giving his girlfriend a black eye. "I would never hit a woman I wasn't married to!" the man declared indignantly. As late as 1981, Pennsylvania still had a law on the books saying that it was illegal for a man to beat his wife after 10:00 P.M. and on Sundays!

It is not surprising that legal folklore suggests the phrase "rule of thumb" had its birth in a supposed pronouncement by British judge Sir Francis Buller that a man was allowed to hit his wife with a switch no thicker than the width of his thumb. British common law had long held that it was legal for a man to discipline his wife as long as it was done in moderation. Perhaps this sort of thinking is why many men who beat their wives don't think there's anything wrong with it.

Domestic abuse involves a vicious cycle of behaviors. It may start with a slap across the face or namecalling and then turn more physical—pushing, punching, shoving, confinement, sexual molestation. But it can also be emotional—stripping the victim of her control over finances, using the children as a means to threaten the victim, breaking her connections with friends and family, mental abuse, and threats. Often the physical or emotional abuse does not occur until after the marriage, frequently beginning during a woman's pregnancy. One study indicated that one out of every six infants is born into a home where the mother was abused during the pregnancy.

Domestic violence can turn to murder. According to the Federal Bureau of Investigation, about three of every ten female murder victims are killed by their husbands or boyfriends. Given the statistics, it is not surprising that when a woman is killed the first person on the suspect list is the husband or boyfriend. These murders often occur after years of battering or stalking and may include efforts by the victims to leave the relationship.

IT'S NOT A "FAMILY MATTER"

Nicole Simpson had called the police to her house no less than eight times prior to her murder. Why was something not done? During the football legend's trial, the prosecution laid out their theory that O. J. Simpson, unable to move on after their divorce, snapped after being rejected by Nicole at their daughter's dance recital and decided to kill her. The murder of Nicole, according to the prosecution, was the final act in an abusive seventeen-year relationship. At his trial, we heard chilling 911 tapes:

> NICOLE: Could you get somebody over here now,
> to . . . Gretna Green. He's back. Please?
> DISPATCHER: What does he look like?
> NICOLE: He's O. J. Simpson. I think you know his record.
> Could you just send somebody over here?
> DISPATCHER: What is he doing there?
> NICOLE: He just drove up again. *(She begins to cry)* Could
> you just send somebody over?
> DISPATCHER: Wait a minute. What kind of car is he in?

NICOLE: He's in a white Bronco, but first of all he broke the back door down to get in.

DISPATCHER: Wait a minute. What's your name?

NICOLE: Nicole Simpson.

DISPATCHER: Okay, is he the sportscaster or whatever?

NICOLE: Yeah. Thank you.

DISPATCHER: Wait a minute, we're sending police. What is he doing? Is he threatening you?

NICOLE: He's (*expletive*) going nuts. *(Sobs)*

DISPATCHER: Has he threatened you in any way or is he just harassing you?

NICOLE: *(Sighs)* You're going to hear him in a minute. He's about to come in again.

DISPATCHER: Okay, just stay on the line . . .

NICOLE: I don't want to stay on the line. He's going to beat the (*expletive*) out of me.

DISPATCHER: Wait a minute, just stay on the line so we can know what's going on until the police get there, Okay? Okay, Nicole?

NICOLE: Uh-huh.

DISPATCHER: Just a moment. Does he have any weapons?

NICOLE: I don't know. He went home and he came back. The kids are up there sleeping and I don't want anything to happen.

Police detective John Edwards, who responded to that 911 call, testified at trial that a severely beaten Nicole Brown Simpson ran from the bushes, grabbed hold of the police officer, and screamed, "He's going to kill me, he's going to kill me!" referring to O. J. Simpson. Her face was badly beaten, with a cut lip, swollen and blackened left eye, and swollen cheek; the policeman could see a hand imprint on her neck.

Eight times the police came, and what did O.J. tell them? He'd come to the door and tell the officers: "This is a family matter. Why do you want to make a big deal of it?" Hundreds of thousands of times this line is repeated by men meeting police at the door. That worked in years past, as police officers, prosecutors, and judges are hesitant about stepping over the threshold into what has been traditionally a private realm.

The "family matter" approach worked for O.J. at least seven of the times when police were called to the Simpson home. On one occasion, in 1989, prosecutors requested that O.J. be made to serve thirty days in jail and go through a yearlong counseling program for wife-beaters, but instead he received no jail time and was allowed to phone in his counseling sessions with a therapist of his own choice because of his busy schedule.

In what came to be known as "O.J.'s suicide letter," discovered shortly before his televised Bronco ride and arrest, he wrote:

> Nicole and I had a good life together. All this press talk about a rocky relationship was no more than what every long-term relationship experiences. All her friends will confirm that I have been totally loving and understanding of what she's been going through. At times I have felt like a battered husband or boyfriend but I loved her, make that clear to everyone. And I would take whatever it took to make it work.

According to abuse counselors, men who commit violence against women often think their relationship is normal, and, if anything, that she's the problem, that she's "asking for it," and he is entitled, as her husband, to put her in her place.

In a June 30, 1994, letter to the editor in the *New York Times*, a woman wrote about suffering at the hands of her husband and how she was treated by the system. After years of being beaten at the hands of her abusive husband, the woman escaped her situation only to be stalked by her husband for years. She changed her name. She lived like a fugitive. And each time she called the police and recounted her husband's threat to kill her or kidnap her children, she was told it was a family matter and to "call back when a crime has been committed."

If there is a gift Nicole Simpson left to women, it is that her death raised the country's awareness of the domestic violence crisis. Her 911 calls were bone-chilling. After her death, domestic violence hotlines across the country reported large increases in the number of calls, and numerous shelters for abused women received additional funding and governmental attention. But what about the law? If calling authorities only further riles an abusive husband by bringing unempowered police to the scene, why would these women risk asking for help?

For decades, police would make arrests; courts would slap the abuser on the wrist and release him. Or courts would issue protective orders and the police would respond to a call, only to let the man go because no violence had yet occurred. The law began to change in the 1980s, when states began to pass legislation making domestic violence a crime and encouraging law enforcement agencies to work together.

Today, even though there are protective laws in place, there are still women who think the abuse is their fault and blame themselves. There are others who in spite of the abuse feel they'd be betraying their marriage or relationship if they turn their spouse or boyfriend in. One abuse victim said, "For so long, I thought, 'I can't have my own husband arrested.' I got over that when his fist put me in the hospital." And certainly there are women who provide excuses for their abuser's behavior: "He was drunk," "It was just a one-time thing," "He didn't mean it."

Let's be on the same page: *no one* has a right to hit us, for any reason. Abusers must be held accountable first by their victims, and then supported by our laws, the police, and our courts. Period.

PROTECTIVE ORDERS

Until about ten years ago, many states still had laws that required an officer to witness an assault before making an arrest. Today, in most states, if abuse is obvious, the abuser is taken to jail and the victim can file for a protective order. If there is an "immediate and present" danger, the officer may be able to issue an emergency protective order on the spot. Protective orders (also known as restraining orders or temporary protection orders) are issued by the court according to state law and are a civil action (not criminal) ordering the abuser to stay away from you, your home, your workplace, and your child's school and not to contact you. Most states have "cease abuse" provisions, as well as "no contact" provisions, allowing the victim to decide if any contact (telephone, fax, e-mail, or even delivery of flowers) is allowed.

Research shows that almost *half* of the perpetrators re-abused their victims after the issuance of a protective order. How can they get away with this? Police officers frequently view protective orders as a civil matter associated with divorce or custody rather than a criminal matter. Yet violations of the order are a criminal matter and often a signal that something worse is about to happen. How much weight does a protective order actually hold? You're armed with just a piece of paper; it doesn't come with a set of handcuffs. Does it really guarantee protection?

In 1985, the case of Tracey Thurman in Connecticut caught national attention and helped change attitudes in police departments and courtrooms across the country. Tracey Thurman would call the police each time her husband, Buck, beat her to within an inch of her life. Protective orders and judges' threats did little to dissuade Buck's actions. He'd break an order, and the police and judges would wag their fingers at him and issue another order.

One day, when Tracy called the police, Buck began slashing her face with a knife. The responding officer from the local police department, apparently tired of responding, took his time getting to the house. By the time he arrived, Tracy Thurman's injuries were life-threatening, but the officer still didn't arrest Buck. Attorney Burt Weinstein sued the city of Torrington in federal court on Tracy's behalf. The jury found that seventeen police officers lied about the incident, the history of the family's abuse, and the policies of the city's police department. Tracy was awarded several million dollars and Buck was sent to jail.

In 1999, a court granted Jessica Gonzales a protective order barring her estranged husband, Simon, from having contact with her and her three daughters, ages seven, nine, and ten. The court order also required the police to enforce its terms by arresting her husband if he violated the order.

Simon abducted the young girls a month after the court order was issued. Jessica immediately called the police only to be told there was nothing they could do and that she should "call back after 10 P.M." if the girls did not turn up. Jessica called Castle Rock police again that night and eventually drove to the police station to plead for help in person. The police refused to enforce the court order and help her find her children.

Later that night, at 3:20 A.M., after the Castle Rock police had ignored five requests from Jessica, Jessica's husband drove up to the police station and opened fire with a gun he had purchased that day. After he was killed in a gun battle with police, the dead bodies of Jessica's three daughters were found in his truck.

Jessica made it her mission to help other women in her situation, and sued the town for failing to enforce a domestic violence restraining order. The Supreme Court eventually heard her case after the Denver-based U.S. Court of Appeals for the Tenth Circuit ruled that the Colorado statute had mandated the enforcement of protective orders. The Supreme Court, in a shocking 7–2 ruling, declared that the police cannot be sued for refusing to enforce a domestic violence restraining order.

If protective orders aren't going to be enforced, then what's the point? "This is a truly outrageous decision," said Kim Gandy, president of the National Organization for Women. "The U.S. Supreme Court just hung a 'Shoot Here' sign around the necks of battered women and their children all across the country." With this ruling, the Supreme Court effectively gave law enforcement a green light to ignore restraining orders.

There have been great strides in bringing *attention* to the horrors of domestic violence, but we still have a long way to go to develop a system that *eradicates* these horrors. If our courts aren't going to support the arrests, then what protection do women have? Abusers *often* defy the order, placing victims at high risk. According to the book *Do Arrests and Restraining Orders Work?* by Eve and Carl Buzawa, there are many calls to police reporting violations of protection orders, but arrests are rare. In one study, 60 percent of those obtaining protection orders reported violations within one year. In another study, nearly half of the victims who obtained a protection order were re-abused within two years.

When Ronyale White's husband showed up at her Chicago home on May 3, 2002, she had an order of protection against him, so the thirty-one-year-old mother of three called 911:

> WHITE: Can you send a squad car to 10611 South LaSalle please?
> 911: This is a house, an apartment, or on the street?
> WHITE: This is a house.
> 911: And what's going on?
> WHITE: My husband is here. He's under an order of protection. He's not supposed to be here.

White's husband, Drexel, could be heard shouting in the background while the 911 operator asked whether there were children present, whether he had a gun, what he looked like, and how he had gotten into the house.

> WHITE: He came in with a key.
> 911: All right, watch for the police, ma'am.

Three minutes after her call, the police are dispatched. Their drive time would be no more than five minutes, but five minutes later, at 11:45 P.M., when the police hadn't shown, White called 911 again, more panicked:

> WHITE: Yes, I just called the police from 10611 South LaSalle. My husband is threatening me.
> *(Unintelligible)*

WHITE: He has a gun. He's left the house—back of the
house. He's clubbed my tires on my truck.
(Scream)

DREXEL: You dead!

Another five minutes pass. At 11:50 P.M., White, hiding in her bedroom, calls 911 again. This time, the call is her last.

911: Chicago emergency, O'Connor.

WHITE: Where are you?

911: Hello?

WHITE: Where are you?

911: You need the police and fire department?

WHITE: Yes. 10611 South LaSalle.

911: 10611 South LaSalle. What's wrong?

WHITE: My husband has a gun and he's trying to kill me.

911: Okay. You already called a few minutes ago, right?

The door was broken in, and Drexel shot his wife three times, killing her. Fifteen minutes after they were first dispatched, a squad car finally arrived—too late. The officers initially claimed that they were held up because of mandatory pre-shift checks on their squad car, but it was revealed in court proceedings that one of the officers made a personal call that lasted a minute, and then spent two minutes retrieving his cell phone voice mail messages, before responding to the call. Chicago settled with the woman's family for $4.2 million and Drexel is serving life in prison. Ronyale White is still dead.

So, what can we do? How do we prevent this lack of urgency? How can we ensure that if we need help, we're going to get it? According to Lenora Lapidus, the director of the Women's Rights Project for the American Civil Liberties Union, we have to make it a state issue. "Three state courts have interpreted sovereign immunity law to allow people to sue police when they fail to carry out their duty. So, in the wake of this decision, we're working to ensure that state legislation is in place. Forty-seven states to go."

In Reno, Nevada, with the help of a state grant to fight violence against women, the Reno Municipal Court has hired a full-time marshal to make certain that domestic violence offenders comply with their sentences. According to judges across the country, jail time for first-time offenders is often suspended if they agree to certain conditions such as fines, counseling, community service, parenting classes, or drug and alcohol rehabilitation. Unfortunately, the offenders often fail to follow through, and even though contempt-of-court orders are issued, batterers have been getting away by disappearing into society. Having an enforcement officer has been very effective in Reno. He has the power to track offenders down—on the golf course, at a restaurant, and even at work—and haul them off. The result is that the rulings of the Reno Municipal Court are being followed.

"I really believe that the courts and prosecutors have had their consciousness raised considerably," defense attorney Mickey Sherman says, "and are now asking for astronomically high bail bonds when people violate these orders. What frustrates them is the high percentage of victims who sit in the front row asking that their husband/spouse/partner be treated leniently because they want to patch things up. The system cannot deal too well with victims who—for whatever reasons: good, bad, or absurd—want to continue to be victims.

"My only real criticism of the direction these cases have taken is that the courts too often try to use a 'one size fits all' approach to these cases. The boyfriend who gave his girlfriend a black eye after having too much beer is not the same as the guy who threw a Ritz cracker at his wife at breakfast when they argued over who should control the TV clicker!"

We must treat these cases—both defendants and victims—more individually. Experts say there are positive results when protection order violations are reviewed on a case-by-case basis. Orange County, Florida, gets it right. It methodically tracks protective order violators, viewing all cases as potential homicides. As a result, they've seen a 13 percent decline in the number of domestic abuse homicides from 1998 to 2003.

Unless we hold perpetrators accountable for their violence, victims will never be safe. One of the efforts under way is to dispense tougher penalties for protective order violations. Oklahoma state representative Ron Peters wrote and sponsored a bill that requires counseling, mandates follow-up hearings, and makes attempted strangulation a felony.

Most states now provide training for a range of personnel—from law enforcement to prosecutors to family court judges. Law enforcement and criminal justice response to domestic violence has improved dramatically. These calls are no longer considered "nuisance" calls; they are taken seriously, and procedural requirements in most states require that some type of a "domestic incident report" be filled out whenever an officer responds to any domestic incident, regardless of whether an arrest is made.

The New York State Office for the Prevention of Domestic Violence instituted a system called RADAR (Respond, Ask, Document, Access, Review) for officers answering domestic incident calls.

- *Respond.* Recognizing that domestic incidents are often the most dangerous situations for officers, officers are ordered to respond to the scene as if it were a potential crime. Safety is the top priority for both the officer and the victim. It is the duty of the officer to stabilize the situation, determine probable cause, and make an arrest if required.
- *Ask.* In order to obtain a detailed statement, the officer interviews the victim and witnesses, asking direct questions:

  - "Someone called for our help. What happened?"
  - "I can see a cut on your forehead and a bruise on your neck. Who did this to you?"
  - "Has anything like this ever happened before?" "When?" "Did you tell anyone about it, or call the police?"
  - "Are you afraid?" "Of what?" "Has your partner threatened you in any way?" "Have your children been harmed or threatened?"

- "Did your partner use or threaten to use a weapon against you?"

- *Document.* The officer documents the call, describing observable injuries in detail, recording admissions and statements in exact words, and collecting and preserving any evidence. It is also important that the officer indicate why he or she did or did not have probable cause to make an arrest.
- *Assess.* The officer evaluates whether the victim will be safe once the police leave the scene and whether or not to obtain an order of protection.
- *Review.* The officer informs the victim of her legal options, makes referrals, and informs her of victim's rights.

What happens after an arrest? It depends on the circumstances surrounding the arrest. For example, how seriously was the victim injured? Were others involved? Has this ever happened before? In most states, the abuser could be put on probation and required to attend counseling if it's a first offense and the injuries minor. More severe cases and repeat offenders are charged criminally.

Some states have moved in the right direction by ordering the abuser to pay temporary support, continue home payments, pay medical costs, and even grant the victimized wife sole use of the car. Some courts are also enabled by state statute to require the abuser to relinquish firearms, attend counseling, or have drug testing. When the abuser does something that the court ordered him not to do, the court determines the penalty. Depending on the law, the court charges the offender with a civil or criminal offense, which results in a fine or imprisonment, or both.

STALKING

Every state now prohibits stalking, and in 1996 Congress passed the Interstate Stalking Punishment and Prevention Act, making it a fed-

eral offense to cross state lines "with the intent to injure or harass another person . . . or place that person in reasonable fear of death or serious bodily injury." Given that more than a half million women are
stalked each year, it's obvious the laws are often sporadically enforced.
In order to prosecute someone on charges of stalking, most states require proof that the perpetrator willfully, maliciously, and repeatedly
followed or harassed another person. Prior to the enactment of anti-
stalking laws, police had no means of intervening until *after* violence
had occurred. Today, police are empowered to make arrests based on a
pattern of harassment, and, depending on the state and circumstances,
can charge either a misdemeanor or a felony.

California was the first state to institute anti-stalking laws after
the stalking and murder of actress Rebecca Schaeffer, the star of the
television series *My Sister Sam,* by a crazed fan who had staked out
her home. Though there have been many high-profile cases of
celebrities being stalked by strangers, the majority of stalking victims
are ordinary people who are being pursued by someone with whom
they've had a prior relationship. Stalking by former husbands and
boyfriends accounts for 80 percent of all stalking cases.

In California, a stalker is defined as someone who willfully, maliciously, and repeatedly follows or harasses another and who makes a
credible threat with the intent to place the victim or the victim's immediate family in fear for their safety. The victim does not have to
prove that the stalker ever intended to carry out the threat. The criminal penalty for stalking in California is imprisonment for up to a year
and/or a fine of up to $1,000. The victim may also bring a civil lawsuit
against the stalker and recover money damages.

In addition to the Interstate Stalking Punishment and Prevention
Act, there are other federal laws that address this issue. There's a law
that requires training for judges to ensure that when they issue orders, they have access to criminal history and other pertinent information from state and federal sources. Two laws authorize grants to
improve databases of stalkers on the local, state, and national levels
and for law enforcement agencies to develop programs dealing with
stalking. The attorney general is charged with compiling and re-

porting data on stalking as part of the National Incident-Based Reporting System.

But the system is still a long way from ensuring the safety of women. Some anti-stalking statutes still require that a stalker overtly threaten his victim. For example, Colorado's anti-stalking statute provides that a person commits stalking if he makes "a credible threat to another person and, in connection with that threat," either "repeatedly follows that person or a member of that person's immediate family" or "repeatedly makes any form of communication with that person or a member of that person's family, whether or not a conversation ensues." The problem here is that many suspects don't make overt threats. Their threats are much more insidious. What constitutes a "credible" threat is incredibly unclear. States such as Colorado should change their laws to require either an overt threat or conduct that implies a threat.

The World Wide Web allows stalkers easy access to personal information about their victims. Perpetrators can anonymously post their victims' personal contact information in chat rooms and on websites, encouraging third parties to harass or threaten them. There have been several cases in which global positioning satellite systems were secretly installed on cars, allowing stalkers to track their victims' every move, and computer programs have enabled stalkers to capture victims' documents and monitor Internet sites they visited.

Roughly one-third of the states have incorporated electronic stalking into their stalking statutes, and a handful of states have enacted separate cyberstalking laws. We need to insert the phrase "including, but not limited to" before a list of current technological examples to ensure our laws apply to all newly developed forms of communication. We must demand our legislatures and courts keep laws current with the times.

RAPE

Do you remember the William Kennedy Smith rape trial? The woman in that case was known as the "blue dot." While there were cameras in the courtroom, in deference to her the TV networks didn't show her face; they literally put a blue dot in its place, even though her name had already been released to the public by the media without her consent.

There have been halfhearted attempts to ensure rape victims' protection since Michigan passed the first rape shield law in 1974. Rape shield laws are supposed to protect the integrity and reputation of a rape victim by limiting the introduction of evidence about a victim's sexual history, reputation, or past conduct. These laws prevent jurors from making decisions based on stereotypes. Before rape shield laws were passed, it was everyday practice for defense lawyers to attack rape victims on the stand by painting them as promiscuous liars. They did this by asking questions about a victim's past sexual history solely for the purpose of exposing to the jury some past dalliance that would make her claim of rape less credible. But what relevance, really, is a victim's prior sexual history to the question of whether she was raped? None.

The law says that evidence of the victim's specific sexual conduct is irrelevant unless it's direct evidence of the source of injury, semen, pregnancy, or disease that's at issue in the rape case. Every state now has some variation of a rape shield law, but in case after case women who report a rape still lose their privacy and anonymity. In some states, rape shield laws ban testimony about what a woman was wearing at the time of the alleged rape. All states should include such provisions.

Rape shield laws were created, in part, so that victims would be more likely to come forward to report rapes. Fewer victims will report rapes if they know their sexual and personal histories will be fodder for aggressive defense lawyers. But the law only protects victims from the introduction of such evidence during trial. And in recent years we've seen the limitations of these laws.

The judge in the Kobe Bryant case, for example, had allowed the victim to use a pseudonym and ordered attorneys to protect her identity. But the same judge mistakenly released her name on the Internet and accidentally e-mailed court documents about her sexual behavior to the media! Websites soon published her name, photos, e-mail address and home address. Soon after the release of this information, the victim dropped the charges and the judge dismissed the case against Bryant. Did she drop the case because she wasn't raped or because she didn't want to be "raped" all over again?

In 2006, a judge in Naperville, Illinois, went so far as to threaten an alleged rape victim with jail because she didn't want to view a video of her rape at her trial. She said she was unconscious during the rape, because she'd had too much to drink. One of her four assailants had videotaped the rape, but she had no memory of it. Showing her the video would have been completely irrelevant to her testimony. She simply had no recollection.

How did she know she was raped? She woke up the next morning, naked from the waist down and with vulgar words written on her legs with marker. It may be appropriate for the jury to look at the videotape to decide if the sex was consensual, but does the victim need to see it?

Rape, like child molestation, is different from almost any other crime. While being robbed, having our home broken into, or even having our property vandalized is a form of invasion, rape is an invasion of our body, soul, and spirit. The courts' and criminal justice system's growing indifference to the victims of these crimes is alarming.

RIGHTS WE SHOULD DEMAND

Studies have shown that women who come forward and speak up about domestic violence are three times less likely to end up dead, as it curbs the abuser's power. Because of the nature of violence against women, we must create a culture and environment in which a woman can be heard, protected, and given the ability to free herself from the abusive relationship.

The right to safety should be fundamental law. We will not be beaten in our homes or anywhere else. Our laws need to allow for each case to be carefully analyzed, as each situation is different. The only common thing is the violence. Our judges and prosecutors need further education in the area of domestic violence so that they can be more compassionate and understanding of the volatility women feel when faced with these situations. Unfortunately, many judges (the vast majority of whom are male) still don't seem to think that men are capable of doing such horrible things to their families—until it is too late.

Jay Silverman, assistant professor of society, human development, and health and director of violence prevention programs at the Harvard School of Public Health, has discovered an alarming pattern. Repeatedly, judges have ignored documented evidence of male partners' prior abuse, failing to consider police reports, restraining orders, and social workers' evaluations. Flouting state law, these judges award unsupervised visits and even sole physical and legal custody of children to abusive men, giving them new opportunities to victimize their families. "U.S. courts remain incredibly reluctant to punish men for crimes against their families," Silverman observes. "In this country, family violence is still seen as a private matter."

Yet there remains much debate on the effectiveness of actions by both the judiciary and law enforcement agencies. One thing that's certain is that if one link in the chain—from the 911 operator to the judge—is weak, the system gives way and women are left without effective protection. We must ensure that law enforcement officers make arrests, that prosecutors do their job to get convictions, and that courts follow through by enforcing orders and imposing strict sanctions. Batterers must get the message from society that their actions will not be tolerated and that our criminal justice system will make sure abusers are stopped in their tracks.

Unless we have a system to hold perpetrators accountable, the victims lose faith in the system. Knowing that the perpetrators will be hunted down and face consequences if they ignore their sentences is an appropriate first step. In addition, we need societal and governmental support. We need more financial assistance for agencies that help women in these situations and their children. "We have made significant progress in this country to draw attention to and eliminate domestic terrorism—violence against women and children—but we need to do more," singer Michael Bolton, who started a charity for children and women at risk, says. "We need more phone lines and additional people to handle the volume of calls, more programs to which we can refer victims, more shelters to accommodate those whose lives are threatened, and more long-term solutions."

Strengthen the Violence Against Women Act

In 1994, Congress passed the Violence Against Women Act (VAWA) to deal with the inadequacies of state judicial systems that often regarded sex offenses as unworthy of serious attention. The act was included in the larger Omnibus Crime Control Act after studies confirmed that women seeking relief after being assaulted faced many obstacles. The statute provided funding to states for criminal law enforcement against perpetrators of violence.

A key aspect of the bill—Title III—was a civil rights provision that made violence against women a violation of the rights guaranteed by the Constitution and gave female victims of violence access to federal courts. Title III had the potential to become a powerful tool by creating a civil rights category of action for women who become the object of violence motivated by gender and providing a remedy for female victims of violence analogous to civil rights suits for injury motivated by race.

The civil rights section of the VAWA came before the Supreme Court in 1999 in a rape case brought by Christy Brzonkala, who was raped in her dormitory room at Virginia Polytechnic Institute shortly after the start of her freshman year. Her two attackers, varsity football players Antonio Morrison and James Crawford, allegedly raped her twice within the first thirty minutes after meeting her. After filing a complaint with the school, she learned that the college was taking no action against one of the boys and gave the other a deferred suspension so that he could continue playing varsity football. She withdrew from school and filed suit.

The federal appeals court in Richmond, Virginia, dismissed her suit. She appealed, and in 2000 the Supreme Court upheld the appeals court. In a 5-to-4 decision, they declared that "the Constitution requires a distinction between what is truly national and what is truly local," and struck down the civil remedy provision of the 1994 Violence Against Women Act, invalidating the provision of the federal law that allowed victims of rape, domestic violence, and other crimes "motivated by gender" to sue their attackers in federal court. The majority ruled that the right did not fall under the equal protection guarantee of the Fourteenth Amendment or as a valid regulation of interstate commerce. Since federal courts can award much more money on constitutional grounds and claims in state courts sometimes take years, this is, bluntly, a deliberate strike against women.

Kathryn Rogers, then executive director of the NOW Legal Defense and Education Fund, criticized the decision, saying: "The Rehnquist Court's ruling in *U.S. v. Morrison* is a setback for women's rights and a triumph for those who seek to roll back thirty years of federal civil rights law under the guise of states' rights. The Court has slammed shut the courthouse door, wished women good luck, and sent us back to the states for justice."

When Congress approved and President Bush signed the reauthorization of the Violence Against Women Act 2005 into law, the act contained some important additions. It authorizes funding for programs that provide services (such as counseling, rape survival kits, legal assistance, and medical aid) for victims of sexual assault, and provides grant money to train health care professionals on how to deal with abuse victims. The act also established that landlords can't evict tenants who call the police to report abuse, expands transitional housing options, and ensures victim confidentiality within the homeless-services system.

While these are positive additions, we need to have stricter laws requiring mandatory jail time and counseling for abusers in all states. Without teeth, laws intended to protect us do come down to being "just a piece of paper."

Enforce Financial Penalties

While most states permit victims of assault to seek damages against their attackers, most courts require the abuser's conduct to be "extreme and outrageous." How extreme does it need to be? Let's take a look at *Hakkila v. Hakkila* as an example. The New Mexico trial court discovered that the husband's abuse included assault and battery, locking his wife out of the residence in the middle of winter, prohibiting her from pursuing outside activities, blaming his sexual inadequacies on his wife, and refusing to have sexual relations with her.

The trial court ruled that the husband had intentionally inflicted severe emotional distress upon his wife and his acts were "so outrageous in character and so extreme in degree as to be beyond all possible bounds of decency and were atrocious and intolerable." The appellate court, in overruling the decision, cited a 1936 law review article that said, "It would be unfortunate if the law closed all the safety valves through which irascible tempers might legally blow off steam." Since when is assault and battery a safety valve? Adding insult to injury, the appellate court went further, suggesting that the trial court had infringed upon the *husband's* rights, stating: "Many, if not all, of us need some freedom to vent emotions in order to maintain our mental health." Freedom, I suppose, to slam your wife's head against the wall.

We must not raise the bar so high that the wife needs to be brought into the courtroom in a coffin in order to have courts recognize abuse. Abuse, whether "venting" or not, is abuse and will not be tolerated in our society. As in personal injury cases, in which victims are compensated for their pain and suffering, victims of domestic violence too should be allowed compensation for the abuse.

Given that women generally take a bigger financial hit than men when they divorce, women are often faced with a conundrum when it comes to abuse. In many states, if they don't leave their abusive spouse, the court may later view them to be at fault for putting up with the abuse. But the courts refuse to consider abusive behavior of one spouse against the other in distributing marital assets during a divorce. New York, for example, does not have in place a method of compensating the victims of domestic violence. There is something intrinsically wrong with a physically abusive spouse receiving half (or more) of the assets acquired during a marriage in which he physically and emotionally damaged his spouse.

Women must know that they will have a financial remedy if they flee an abusive marriage. Our laws should apportion marital property in a way that compensates abused women for their injuries. If we want to send a clear message that abuse will not be tolerated in our marriages, we will enact laws to ensure that a victim of domestic violence receives a greater share of marital property.

Positive Corporate Action

Victims of domestic abuse miss nearly eight million days of paid work each year—the equivalent of more than thirty-two thousand full-time jobs—with an estimated annual loss in productivity worth as much as thirty-six billion dollars to the corporate world. It's hard for businesses to ignore the impact on both the individual and on the bottom line. The American Institute on Domestic Violence reports these workplace statistics:

- 68 percent of senior executives surveyed agreed that their company's financial performance would benefit from addressing the issue of domestic violence among its employees.
- 94 percent of corporate security directors rank domestic violence as a high security risk.
- 78 percent of human resource directors identify domestic violence as a substantial employee problem.
- 56 percent of corporate leaders are personally aware of specific employees who are affected by domestic violence.
- 60 percent of senior executives said that domestic violence has a harmful effect on their company's productivity.
- Homicide is the leading cause of death for women in the workplace. Partners and boyfriends commit thirteen thousand acts of violence against women in the workplace every year.

According to a 1998 report by the U.S. General Accounting Office, as many as 52 percent of domestic violence victims have lost their jobs because of the resulting absenteeism, poor work performance, and workplace violence. Oftentimes, that's exactly what the batterer wants—because it makes the victim's further dependence on him even more likely. In fact, studies suggest that economic security is the primary reason battered women return to their abusers.

When a business chooses to deal with the problem of domestic violence by blaming the victim, it has only helped the batterer gain more power over his victim. Violence has a direct impact on the work environment: 74 percent of employed battered women are harassed at work. According to the Institute on Domestic Violence, partners and boyfriends commit thirteen thousand acts of violence against women in the workplace every year. Historically, employers, fearing for the safety of other workers, often found it necessary to get the victim out of the office; organizations were able to terminate abuse victims without any worry of legal action. Today, because of provisions in the Occupational Safety and Health Act, employers are responsible for maintaining safety in the workplace. If a company has received notice that someone has harmed or threatened harm to an employee, it has a duty to protect the employee.

The Polaroid Corporation, according to an article in *Human Resources Magazine,* was one of the first companies in the country to establish a program to assist employees who were experiencing domestic abuse. In 1984, a supervisor at the Polaroid Corporation asked a battered female employee why she had not come forward and sought assistance; the employee responded, "How could I tell you that I was a nobody at home when I'm a somebody at work?" The corporation then established a support group for six female employees who were victims of battering, and began funding shelters for battered women.

Ten years later, the company had to deal with a situation that every company fears: five employees were taken hostage by the husband of a battered employee. Though the hostages were rescued unharmed, the corporation made multiple changes in its policies, including developing educational programs with community organizations to teach employees how to recognize abuse, offering assistance, instituting improvements in plant security, and drafting a corporate code of conduct that specifically addresses domestic violence.

Many other businesses are developing innovative strategies to help. For example, in 1991 Liz Claiborne, in an effort to end domestic violence instituted a program called "Love Is Not Abuse" (www .loveisnotabuse.com). The company provides information and tools that men, women, children, teens, and corporate executives can use (whether they work in the company or not) to learn more about the issue of domestic violence and find out how they can help end this epidemic. "As a company, we do what we can to accommodate employees victimized by domestic violence," Jane Randel, Vice President of Liz Claiborne, explains. "This includes allowing time off so that employees can seek safety and protection, attend court appearances, arrange for new housing, or take care of other matters." The company also arranges for flexible hours, short-term paid leaves of absence, and extended leaves without pay.

The company has five to ten cases annually of abusive husbands trying to access victims at work, and has come up with excellent programs to create a supportive environment. Many of the ideas are simple and should be standard operating procedure at every workplace in this country: screening out unwanted telephone calls, removing an employee's name from automated telephone directories, escorting people to and from their cars, and hiring counselors who can provide support and referrals.

If every corporation in America took these actions, it would positively impact the lives of thousands of workingwomen who experience violence in their home every day. It would show these women that they have a support network, and it would help put an end to the abuse. Unfortunately, human resource departments are slow to catch on that by implementing programs such as these, all employees benefit. Companies can't afford not to deal with the issue of domestic abuse. With three out of every ten women having been abused by their husbands, this is a problem that is not going away.

Every day there are news stories of women who are suffering at the hands of their abusive boyfriends or husbands. In New York City alone calls to domestic violence hotlines have increased an astonishing 70 percent since 1998. There have been nearly a quarter of a million desperate pleas for help over the past six years. Nearly 40 percent of women killed in New York City die at the hands of overbearing men, causing the city Health Department to coin a new term—"femicide."

On the national level, one in three teenage girls is physically, sexually, emotionally, or verbally assaulted by a dating partner each year. And, according to the Bureau of Justice Statistics, more than half a million American women became victims of nonfatal violence committed by an intimate partner in 2001.

Domestic violence is much like rape; women are afraid to come forward because they feel they are partly to blame, or at least that society will blame them. We must promote further legislation to provide protection for women—from enforcement of protective orders to stringent rape shield laws—and, as a society, let abused women know that they can come forward and be supported. We are *not* powerless, and we must demand laws that support our safety—whether at home, on the Internet, or out in public.

CHAPTER 8

MY BODY

"I have the right to decide what goes into or comes out of my body"

We've come to a great moral impasse in this country. Both sides of the abortion argument are vehement about their position. As a result, this is not a chapter about a right that we all want to have. It can't be divided into "rights we should have" and "rights we should demand" because, in the end, this issue is much more complicated. Before our argument even gets to the question of whether abortion is right or wrong, though, we must educate women and men to prevent unwanted pregnancies.

The numbers speak for themselves: the 7 percent of American women who do not use contraception account for 53 percent of all unintended pregnancies. Why do you think that is? Could it be that they weren't properly educated? Or maybe they didn't have access to proper contraception? Surely it wasn't that they were *planning* on having an abortion.

SEX EDUCATION

Ready for some frightening numbers? One million teenage girls become pregnant every year. Seventy-eight percent of those pregnancies are unintended. Whether we like to think about it or not, four out of five young people have sex as teenagers. The vast majority of us support sex education for teenagers. According to the Sexuality Information and Education Council of the United States, 93 percent of Americans believe sex education should be taught in high school, and 84 percent believe it should be taught in middle schools.

In a 2005 editorial in the *New York Times*, Nicholas D. Kristof reminded us that in times of yore, the mere mention of sex sent social conservatives into a tailspin. In fact, when the *Ladies' Home Journal* published articles about venereal disease in 1906, seventy-five thousand readers canceled their subscriptions.

Today, an influential minority is promoting abstinence-only, medically inaccurate sex education in schools across this country. Eighty percent of schools that currently teach sexuality education are promoting abstinence as the preferred or only option for adolescents. President Bush has sunk millions of dollars into programs that teach abstinence-only education and fail to include other ways to avoid sexually transmitted diseases and pregnancy. During the president's first term in office, White House spokesperson Ari Fleischer went so far as asserting that "abstinence is more than sound science, it's a sound practice. . . . Abstinence has a proven track record of working." The truth is, abstinence-only programs fail to delay the onset of intercourse. In fact, the National Campaign to Prevent Teen Pregnancy released a report on its research findings with this blunt statement: "There do not currently exist any abstinence-only programs with reasonably strong evidence that they actually delay the initiation of sex or reduce its frequency."

In 2002, President Bush appointed Dr. Joe McIlhaney, the founder of the Medical Institute for Sexual Health, a Texas-based proabstinence think tank, to be his representative on the Presidential Advisory Council on HIV/AIDS and on the advisory committee to the director of the Centers for Disease Control (CDC) and Prevention. The former OB-GYN worked with President Bush in Texas, where he was reprimanded by the Texas Department of Health for spreading false information about sexually transmitted diseases and the ineffectiveness of condoms. During President Bush's tenure as governor of Texas, from 1995 to 2000, his multimillion-dollar abstinence-only programs resulted in Texas's being dead last in the nation in the decline of teen birth rates among fifteen- to seventeen-year-olds. While the rest of the nation experienced dramatic declines in teen pregnancy, Texas had one of the highest rates of unplanned teen pregnancy in the United States (exceeded by only four other states) and the highest number of uninsured in the country. Not a very stellar record.

That's why it was surprising to hear George W. Bush in his 2006 State of the Union address claim that his abstinence policies had led to the lowest rate of abortion in the United States in three decades. The reality is that he was quoting figures from 2002, the most recent data available, reflecting the final year of the initiatives instituted by President Clinton. He was taking credit for the results of his predecessor's policies, which were profoundly different from his own. During President Clinton's leadership, our nation's first pro-choice president, the abortion rate experienced the most dramatic decline in recorded history—the rate of abortions declined 12 percent between 1992 and 1996 and another 5 percent from 1996 to 2000.

President Clinton's approach was prevention. It's an approach his wife, Senator Hillary Rodham Clinton, is arguing for today: education, access to birth control, and new contraceptive technology. She says, "We should all be able to agree that we want every child born in this country and around the world to be wanted, cherished, and loved. The best way to get there is do more to educate the public about reproductive health, about how to prevent unsafe and unwanted pregnancies."

It's simple, really—preventing unwanted pregnancies decreases the need for abortion. Until President Bush came into office, the Centers for Disease Control disseminated information on its website about sex education programs that have been proven effective. Up until 2002, none of the five "Programs That Work" was "abstinence-only"; instead, they provided comprehensive sex education to teenagers. When the initiative was discontinued by the Bush administration, the information was pulled from the website and replaced with the statement that the CDC is "considering a new process that is more responsive to changing needs and concerns of state and local education and health agencies and community organizations."

What about other countries? Are they more or less successful in their approaches to this quandary? According to a report prepared for Advocates for Youth by Linda Berne and Barbara Huberman, entitled "European Approaches to Adolescent Sexual Behavior and Responsibility," the Netherlands begins sexuality education in preschool and integrates it into all levels of schooling. It boasts the lowest teen birthrate in the world—a rate eight times lower than in the United States—and the teenage abortion rate is more than three times lower than that of the United States. Germany targets its sex education to the reading and developmental needs of its students. Its teenage birthrate is four times lower than that of the United States and its overall AIDS rate is 11.5 times lower. France mandates sexuality education for every student beginning at age thirteen and prohibits parents from withdrawing their teens from the program. France's teenage birthrate is six times lower than that of the United States and its teenage abortion rate is more than two times lower.

So what are we teaching our teenagers? According to a report by California representative Henry Waxman, entitled "Federally Funded Abstinence-Only Programs Teach False and Misleading Information," our programs use curricula that distort information about the effectiveness of contraceptives, misrepresent the risks of abortion, blur religion and science, treat stereotypes about girls and boys as scientific fact, and contain basic scientific errors.

Want some examples? The report found errors or misrepresentations in more than 80 percent of the thirteen curricula used by the schools, hospitals, and community groups that received federal funding from the Community-Based Abstinence Education initiative. The lesson plans included false information about the lack of effectiveness of contraception (i.e., "14 percent of the women who use condoms scrupulously for birth control become pregnant within a year" when in fact, when used correctly and consistently, only 2 percent of couples who rely on the latex condom as their form of contraception experience unintended pregnancy), pregnancy ("pregnancy can result from touching another person's genitals"), and the risks of abortion ("studies show that 5 to 10 percent of women will never again be pregnant after having a legal abortion," when in fact medical textbooks state fertility is not affected by having an elective abortion). The lesson plans also relied on religious beliefs instead of scientific fact.

One course presented as scientific fact the idea that men find happiness through "admiration" and "sexual fulfillment," while women require "financial support." Another text used in the program included a story about a knight who rejected a princess in favor of a village maiden because the princess offered him "too much advice" about how to slay a dragon. "Moral of the story," the ending reads, "occasional suggestions and assistance may be all right, but too much of it will lessen a man's confidence or even turn him away from his princess." These curricula all seem intent on saying to women: *Admire your man and he'll provide for you, but don't speak, and for gosh sakes don't be sexual!*

Planned Parenthood points out how these federally supported curricula trickle down to the states. In California, Pennsylvania, Alabama, and many other states, schools regularly host chastity pledges and rallies on school premises during school hours. Students who don't participate are often spurned by those who do pledge "to God" that they will remain abstinent until they marry.

In Texas, the State Board of Education approved the purchase of new health textbooks that promote abstinence exclusively. Because the state is the second-largest buyer of textbooks in the United States, it is likely the same books will be used throughout the nation. The school board in Franklin County, North Carolina, ordered three chapters literally cut out of a ninth-grade health textbook because the material did not adhere to state law mandating abstinence-only education. The chapters covered AIDS and other sexually transmitted infections, marriage and partnering, and contraception. In Belton, Missouri, a seventh-grade health teacher was suspended when a parent complained that she had discussed "inappropriate" sexual matters in class. The teacher had answered a student's query about oral sex.

Comprehensive, medically accurate sexuality education is becoming the exception rather than the rule. What is wrong with us? Just because we don't talk about the purple elephant in the room doesn't mean it's not standing there. We can't afford *not* to talk to our children about these issues, to educate them about sexuality, contraception, and the consequences of pregnancy. If we fail to talk to them about it, we can't be shocked when they get the hormonal itch, get pregnant, and then face the toughest decision a woman should never have to make. All because they just "didn't know."

It has been proven around the world that sexuality education, in its most honest form—untainted by our religious and moral vehemence—is the most successful approach to preventing unwanted pregnancies. Organizations such as the American Medical Association, the American Academy of Pediatrics, and the American Public Health Association have raised objections to the abstinence-only education movement. They say that teens need comprehensive information regarding pregnancy prevention and STDs in order to make mature choices. Despite all this, our federal government continues to increase funding for abstinence-only education. In a culture as sexualized as ours, to knowingly not give our youth information that could save their lives and health is a catastrophe. We women should insist that our tax dollars are used in a way that benefits our daughters (and sons) instead of putting them at risk.

We must give our children the truth. Yes, we *hope* for abstinence, but we must make them aware of options and the results that occur if they don't choose to protect themselves.

CONTRACEPTION

As late as 1960, the American legal system was still keeping women from making decisions as to whether or not to get pregnant. Thirty states had statutes prohibiting or restricting the sale and advertisement of contraception. It started in 1872, when Anthony Comstock set off to Washington with an anti-obscenity bill that he had drafted himself. He thought contraceptives promoted lust and lewdness and allowed women to be promiscuous.

The following year, the Comstock Act was passed by Congress. It defined contraceptives as obscene and illicit, making it a federal offense to disseminate birth control through the mail or across state lines. It was the first statute of its kind in the Western world, and soon after its passage, twenty-four states enacted their own versions of the law to restrict contraceptives on a state level. In Connecticut, for example, married couples could be arrested and put in prison for a year for using birth control in the privacy of their bedrooms.

One woman made it her mission to challenge the Comstock Act. Named by *Time* magazine as one of the most important people of the twentieth century, Margaret Sanger started a crusade to end this injustice. Motivated by her mother's death after eighteen pregnancies and eleven live births, Sanger worked as a nurse and midwife in the poorest neighborhoods of New York City. She witnessed these women being deprived of health, sexuality, and the ability to care for their children. She felt that denying contraception was a means that enabled politicians and business leaders to ensure a cheap workforce. Children born to women in poverty would probably remain in poverty their entire lives.

Margaret Sanger was jailed in 1916 for selling a birth control pamphlet to an undercover policewoman. The case that grew out of her court battle resulted in the 1918 Crane decision, which allowed women to use birth control for therapeutic purposes. She began distributing her journal, *The Woman Rebel,* with the aim of stimulating women to think for themselves and "build up a conscious fighting character." She proclaimed, "A woman's body belongs to herself alone" and posed the question, "Is there any reason why women should not receive clean, harmless, scientific knowledge on how to prevent conception? . . . As is well known, a law exists forbidding the imparting of information on this subject, the penalty being several years' imprisonment. Is it not time to defy this law?"

In 1936, Sanger once again decided to challenge the law. She ordered a new type of diaphragm from a Japanese physician and had it shipped to her in the United States. It was seized and confiscated under the Tariff Act of 1930, which included the anti-contraceptive provisions of the Comstock Act. In 1936 she was again in court. Sanger won, but the government appealed. The appellate court affirmed and Judge August Hand removed the federal ban on birth control, ending the use of the Comstock Act to target birth control information and devices. While this decision didn't eliminate the problem of "chastity laws" on the state level, it was a crucial ruling. Physicians could legally mail birth control devices and information throughout the country, paving the way for the legitimization of birth control.

Yet these laws didn't begin to be struck down officially until the 1960s. In 1965, the Supreme Court ruled in *Griswold v. Connecticut* that the right to contraceptives was protected by the Constitution, based on the idea that people have a right to privacy. While this right is not explicitly written into the Constitution it was decided that it is implicit within the First, Third, Fourth, Fifth, Ninth, and Fourteenth amendments. This case was the genesis of the officially recognized right to privacy and decreed that a marriage was a personal contract and the government had no right to interfere with a married couple's private decisions about bearing children.

A second case, *Eisenstadt v. Baird* (1972), struck down a Massachusetts law making it a crime for anyone to distribute contraceptives, other than doctors and pharmacists prescribing them to married persons. This case established that people have a right to privacy not just within a marital contract but as individuals. A law that applies only to married people violates the equal protection clause by discriminating against those who are not married. The opinion of the court stated, "If the right of privacy means anything, it is the right of the individual, married or single, to be free from unwarranted government intrusion into matters so fundamentally affecting a person as the decision whether to bear or beget a child."

It is no surprise that these decisions launched a new era in the lives of women, both personally and professionally. To have control of your reproductive life is extremely powerful, as it means you are no longer a slave to your fertility—where sex before marriage could easily end up in an unplanned pregnancy and a child stigmatized by having been born illegitimate, where you were limited in your professional choices because of the burden of bearing unwanted children. Access to contraceptives means that we can decide when and if to have children and still have a sex life.

And yet there are still roadblocks in the way of women who want contraceptives. Our access to them is often limited by regulations, moral opponents, and insurance providers that refuse to include oral contraceptives in their prescription plans. Even though the most common forms of contraception have been available for more than forty years, only 15 percent of large group plans cover all five of the most common methods of reversible contraception: oral contraceptives, diaphragms, Depo-Provera, IUDs, and Norplant. In 1998, two months after Viagra entered the U.S. market, a *Business and Health* report found that insurers were paying for Viagra three times as often as they paid for oral contraceptives. This lack of coverage results in women of reproductive age spending approximately 68 percent more than men in out-of-pocket health care costs.

Jennifer Erickson, a young pharmacist, not only had to foot the bill for her own birth control but also had to explain to other women why this prescription was not covered by insurance. Fed up, in 2001 she sued her employer, Bartell Drug Company, charging that the company was discriminating against women. Bartell self-insured its health plan, which, like many health plans, covered numerous prescription drugs while excluding certain ones, including contraceptives. The plan also excluded coverage for, among other things, drugs prescribed for weight reduction, infertility, and smoking cessation.

Under Title VII, it is unlawful for an employer to "discriminate against any individual with respect to his compensation, terms, conditions, or privileges of employment because of such individual's race, color, religion, sex, or national origin." The Pregnancy Discrimination Act amended Title VII in 1978 to define discrimination "on the basis of sex" to include discrimination "on the basis of pregnancy, childbirth or related medical conditions." In *Erickson v. Bartell*, the parties agreed that fringe benefits, such as a prescription plan, are part of an employee's "compensation, terms, conditions, or privileges of employment." They disputed whether excluding coverage of prescription contraceptives was discrimination on the basis of sex. In ruling on the case, Judge Robert S. Lasnik adopted the Equal Employment Opportunity Commission's position and announced in June 2001 that excluding coverage of prescription contraceptives is a violation of Title VII. He ordered Bartell to include contraceptives in its health plan.

The court found that prescription contraceptives are "a fundamental and immediate health care need," and the exclusion of woman-only prescription benefits from a generally comprehensive prescription plan is sex discrimination under Title VII. The court's holding turned on the fact that prescription contraceptives are "used only by women" due to "unique sex-based characteristics." The court said that Title VII requires that benefit plans provide "equally comprehensive coverage for both sexes." The court ordered Bartell to "cover each of the available options for prescription contraception to the same extent, and on the same terms, that it covers other drugs, devices, and preventative care" and to "offer coverage for contraception-related services, including the initial visit to the prescribing physician and any follow-up visits or outpatient services, to the same extent, and on the same terms, as it offers coverage for other outpatient services."

Bartell had argued that the plan excluded prescription contraceptives from coverage because they are voluntary and preventative and because they do not treat or prevent an illness or disease. The court noted, however, that Bartell's plan covered other preventative drugs, such as blood-pressure and cholesterol-lowering drugs. In response to Bartell's argument that pregnancy is not an "illness or disease," the court stated that "being pregnant, though natural, is not a state that is desired by all women or at all points in a woman's life. Prescription contraceptives, like all other preventative drugs, help the recipient avoid unwanted physical changes." The court, citing a high percentage of unintended pregnancies, opined that "the availability of affordable and effective contraceptives is of great importance to the health of women and children because it can help to prevent a litany of physical, emotional, economic, and social consequences."

Other courts have ruled similarly. In *Maudlin v. Wal-Mart*, Lisa Smith Maudlin sued Wal-Mart, claiming that the retail chain discriminated against women by refusing to provide health insurance coverage for prescription contraceptives. The court granted class status to those women who actually used prescription contraceptives.

EEOC v. United Parcel Service was a class action suit alleging that UPS's failure to provide prescription coverage for an oral contraceptive (that in this instance was used for treating female hormonal disorders) violated Title VII because the defendant provided prescription coverage for the treatment of male hormonal disorders. Plaintiff's motions to dismiss were denied.

Two female employees from Kansas City have added their voices to the national debate over whether company health plans should include contraceptive coverage. They recently filed a class action against the AT&T Corporation, alleging that its health insurance plans cover sex-related prescription drugs such as Viagra and Cialis for men but not prescription contraceptives for women. This class action will include tens of thousands of women.

Since the Equity in Prescription Insurance and Contraceptive Coverage Act (EPICC) was first introduced in 1997, twenty states (Arizona, California, Connecticut, Delaware, Georgia, Hawaii, Iowa, Maryland, Massachusetts, Maine, Missouri, North Carolina, New Hampshire, New Mexico, Nevada, New York, Rhode Island, Texas, Vermont, and Washington) have adopted laws and/or regulations requiring coverage of contraceptives. Despite these gains and the recent rulings confirming women's right to coverage for contraception, employers and regulators have been slow to respond.

In 1998, Congress voted to ensure access to contraceptive coverage for all participants in the Federal Employees Health Benefits Program, and has renewed this coverage every year. Yet while Congress has considered legislation explicitly requiring all health plans to cover contraceptives, nothing has happened. Many women nationwide are still faced with a choice of either paying high prices for oral contraceptives or taking a risk and going without them—even though the drug they are seeking is necessary to avoid pregnancy, relieve menstrual cramping, regulate menstrual cycles, and clear up skin breakouts. On the contrary, men are totally supported when looking for coverage of the popular drug Viagra, which helps men achieve and maintain an erection. Used only for pleasure, this drug is covered by most insurance plans.

Although Senators Harry Reid and Hillary Rodham Clinton introduced legislation in 2005 to require insurance companies to cover contraceptives, the legislation is currently stuck in committee. Getting insurance coverage for contraception is not the only hurdle we face. There are other, more insidious ways in which our right to contraceptives is limited. There is a growing movement among pharmacists and OB-GYNs who are refusing to prescribe or distribute contraceptives on moral grounds. They argue that hormonal contraceptives do not always stop eggs from being released. If those eggs become fertilized, the hormonally altered uterine wall will not allow the fertilized egg to implant; they call this a "chemical abortion." That the pill has never been proven to prevent implantation or that most doctors do not consider a fertilized egg to be an established pregnancy (about half of all fertilized eggs don't implant, for a variety of reasons) does not sway their argument. They say it is their right to refuse to prescribe or distribute contraceptives they morally disagree with.

This might not seem like a big deal to women who live in cities or urban areas, but it is critical to women in rural areas. Imagine if the only pharmacy in a fifty-mile radius won't distribute your birth control pills, or if the only local OB-GYN won't prescribe them. Does a woman's right to birth control override a pharmacist's right to his or her moral beliefs?

The American Pharmacists Association has a two-part policy on this subject: (1) The pharmacist has a right to conscience and the patient has the right to legally prescribed medication. The pharmacist must tell his or her employer if he cannot perform the task. (2) If one pharmacist refuses to fill a prescription on the grounds of conscience, another pharmacist must do it. The idea behind the policy is that neither the pharmacist nor the patient should be embarrassed or penalized for taking advantage of their rights.

Spurred by the rising influence of the religious right in our politics, many states are considering enacting laws that would protect pharmacists and doctors from being sued for refusal to distribute contraceptives on moral grounds. Twenty-six states have introduced bills allowing pharmacists to refuse to fill birth control prescriptions. Eight are considering whether to implement "conscience clauses" to protect pharmacists who refuse. Four states are considering laws that would actually require pharmacists to fill the prescriptions, despite their beliefs.

In a big reversal of policy, Wal-Mart recently began stocking Plan B contraceptives (commonly referred to as the "morning-after pill") in all of its pharmacies after initially refusing to carry them. Ron Chomiuk, vice president of pharmacy operations for Wal-Mart, said, "We expected more states to require us to sell emergency contraceptives in the months ahead. Because of this, and the fact that this is an FDA-approved product, we feel it is difficult to justify being the country's only major pharmacy chain not selling it. The company will, however, maintain its conscientious objection policy, which allows employees who don't feel comfortable dispensing a prescription to refer customers to another pharmacist or pharmacy."

Illinois governor Rod Blagojevich recently approved an emergency rule requiring pharmacies to fill birth control prescriptions quickly. As Blagojevich said, "Our regulation says that if a woman goes to a pharmacy with a prescription for birth control, the pharmacy or the pharmacist is not allowed to discriminate or to choose who he sells it to. . . . No delays. No hassles. No lectures." A judge in Wisconsin recently recommended that a pharmacist be reprimanded and required to attend ethics classes after the pharmacist refused to fill a woman's prescription for birth control pills.

Almost 95 percent of women use contraceptives at some point in their lives. The decision to use contraceptives should be between a woman and her doctor, and, if she's married, with her husband. A pharmacist's beliefs should not come into play in such an intensely personal decision.

In another stunning blow to women's health, religious and political extremists are opposing a vaccine that would eliminate most cases of cervical cancer. Why? This type of cancer is caused by a sexually transmitted virus known as the human papillomavirus (HPV). Though the vaccine is effective in preventing 70 percent of all cases of cervical cancer, opponents claim that making it a regular part of children's vaccine protocol would encourage young women to be more sexually active.

"I lost my grandmother to cervical cancer and have two daughters who might be spared that fate with this vaccine," says National Organization for Women president Kim Gandy. "Opposing an effective vaccine that would save hundreds of thousands of women's lives with the vacuous assertion that it would lead to promiscuity is inexcusable."

How the vaccine will be used will largely be determined by the Centers for Disease Control's Advisory Committee on Immunization Practices. One member of the panel, Dr. Reginald Finger, a Bush appointee and former medical analyst for the conservative group Focus on the Family, suggests that the vaccine may send a message to teens that they are expected to be sexually active. The Christian Medical and Dental Association reported that parents are calling to say the vaccine "will sabotage our abstinence message."

One question: if this was a vaccine to prevent prostate cancer, would we even be having this discussion?

ABORTION

The aspect of women's health care that is ever-present in the headlines is abortion. There is no easy way around this debate because it is difficult to find common ground. There are genuine religious convictions on the pro-life side of the argument, and as a matter of conscience, their adamant position that "all abortion is wrong" is understandable. Yet statistics show that almost no one takes the decision to terminate a pregnancy lightly. One woman who had an abortion before having her daughter told me that "every day I think, *What if.*" She constantly marks the anniversaries of the baby that would have been: "My baby would have been five, ten, twelve years old." But, she says, "it was a *choice* I had to make at the time." A recent survey by the Pew Research Center for the People and the Press indicates that while a consistent majority of Americans (65 percent) are opposed to overturning *Roe v. Wade,* most Americans also favor some restrictions on abortion. For example, 73 percent favor requiring women under the age of eighteen to get parental consent before being allowed to have an abortion.

Abortion is always an awful thing, but the right to legal abortion is crucial. Here's why: the ability for a woman to have dominion over what happens to her own body is fundamental in a free society. The government's ownership of women's bodies is the deepest imaginable contradiction to the freedoms guaranteed by our Constitution.

There are many legal cases and battles (in the past, in the present, and in the future) that examine the complexity of this issue. Whether or not you think abortion is morally correct, in a free society we cannot force women into back alleys for their health care options. Illegal abortion accounts for an estimated seventy-eight thousand deaths worldwide each year, or about one in seven pregnancy-related deaths. In some African countries, illegal abortion may result in as many as 50 percent of pregnancy-related deaths. In Romania, where abortion was outlawed from 1966 to 1989, an estimated 86 percent of pregnancy-related deaths were caused by illegal abortions. In countries where abortion is legal, less than 1 percent of pregnancy-related deaths are caused by abortion. Here in the United States, we need to ensure that our citizens have full and safe access to health care whether or not we agree with their decision making.

The modern debate over abortion stems back to the landmark 1973 case *Roe v. Wade.* In this decision the Supreme Court struck down a Texas law banning abortion except when the life of the mother was at risk. This decision effectively nullified the abortion laws of almost every other state. The court ruled that abortion was a constitutional right that the states could abridge only after the first six months of pregnancy. More specifically, the court held that the right to privacy includes the right to abortion; since abortion is a fundamental right, state regulation must meet the "strict scrutiny" standard, which means the state must show it has a "compelling interest" in any law that attempts to circumvent the Constitutional right.

Justice Blackmun's famous opinion went on to say that the word *person* in the Fourteenth Amendment does not apply to the unborn. The state has an important interest in both preserving the health of a pregnant woman and protecting fetal life, but this latter interest becomes compelling only at viability—six months. The state may not regulate abortion at all during the first trimester; the state may regulate abortion during the second trimester if the aim of the law has to do with the mother's health; the state may regulate or ban abortion during the third trimester to protect fetal life.

Although from the moment the decision in *Roe v. Wade* was announced people have been trying to limit and even overturn this ruling, over the next sixteen years subsequent rulings expanded the protections first granted in the revolutionary 1973 decision. In 1976, in *Planned Parenthood of Central Missouri v. Danforth*, the court struck down Missouri laws that mandated written spousal consent for elective abortions, parental consent for minors, the requirement that late-term abortions be performed in a manner that best permits a viable child's survival, and a law that banned second-trimester saline abortions as a danger to maternal health.

In 1986, in *Thornburg v. American College of Obstetricians and Gynecologists*, the Court struck down provisions of a Pennsylvania state law that required a woman to receive information on abortion alternatives, human development in utero, and the possible health dangers of abortion; that the state keep detailed statistical records of abortions; that post-viability abortions be performed in such a way as to allow a child to survive the procedure, unless this would significantly increase risk to the woman; and that a second physician be present at post-viability abortions to care for a child who survives the procedure. The Court held that these provisions invaded the privacy of the woman and her doctor and were an attempt by the Pennsylvania legislature to "intimidate" women and try to dissuade them from having abortions. These rules impermissibly put the lives of viable fetuses over the health concerns of women.

The turning point came in 1989, with *Webster v. Reproductive Health Services*. Abortion law would never be the same after the Court let stand a Missouri statute stating that human life began at conception, barring use of state property for abortions, and requiring viability tests for advanced pregnancies. The Court's opinion was that the state has a compelling interest in fetal life throughout pregnancy and that the trimester framework of *Roe* and its viability line ought to be discarded. In this decision the Court could have almost completely overturned *Roe v. Wade*, but instead it merely upheld the legislation. The decision left abortion law in flux—not expressly overturning *Roe*, but not following it either. A number of legislatures took the cue and began to pass new abortion restrictions.

In 1990, the Supreme Court held in *Hodgson v. Minnesota* that in cases of underage girls seeking abortion, the Fourteenth Amendment allows a judge to order that parents don't need to be notified, thereby bypassing parental notification statutes mandating parental notice to both parents. Yet in 1992's *Planned Parenthood of Southeastern Pennsylvania v. Casey* the court upheld a Pennsylvania statute's twenty-four-hour waiting period, informed consent requirement, parental consent provision for minors, and record-keeping requirement while striking down the spousal notice requirement. This decision is often considered a pragmatic compromise, allowing limited (and politically popular) state regulation of abortion with a floating viability line as long as those restrictions did not impose "an undue burden" on women, yet effectively preserving the general access to abortion that was the goal of *Roe*. This decision has replaced *Roe v. Wade* as the dominant precedent on abortion in this country.

The attempts at doing away with *Roe v. Wade* right by right continued. In 1996 the Congress enacted a bill banning the practice of late-term abortions. President Clinton vetoed the law because it failed to permit use of the procedure when a fetus displays severe abnormalities or when carrying a pregnancy to term presents a serious threat to a woman's health or life. Yet during the 1990s, more than thirty states passed laws banning use of the procedure. In June 2000, in *Stenberg v. Carhart,* the Supreme Court struck down a Nebraska ban on late-term abortion. The court stated that the ban was an unconstitutional violation of both *Roe v. Wade* and *Planned Parenthood of Southeastern Pennsylvania v. Casey.* The critical issue has been that most of these laws don't include any reference to preserving the health of the mother, which renders them unconstitutional.

Yet our lawmakers are continuing to attempt to enact further restrictions on late-term abortions, often by outlawing the specific procedures that are used. In 2003, President Bush signed the Partial-Birth Abortion Ban Act, and shortly after the signing, four doctors in New York, Virginia, Nebraska, and Iowa who perform late-term abortions filed suit against the attorney general seeking to stop enforcement of the act. On September 8, 2004, U.S. District Court judge Richard Kopf sided with the doctors and ruled that while the law provided an exception for saving the woman's life, there was not an exception for preserving her health when her life was not immediately threatened. On appeal, the three-judge panel of the Eighth Circuit Court of Appeals agreed unanimously to uphold Kopf's ruling. Judge Kermit Bye wrote, "We believe when a lack of consensus exists in the medical community, the Constitution requires legislatures to err on the side of protecting women's health by including a health exception."

Though it was passed and signed in 2003, the law has never been enforced because of these rulings. But that all may be about to change.

Piece by Piece, State by State

It is not coincidental that after the confirmation of President Bush's two new appointments to the Supreme Court, John Roberts and Samuel Alito, there has been an instant onslaught of states passing or proposing legislation that bans abortion outright or extremely limits it. On Alito's first day on the bench, the Supreme Court decided it would rule on whether the controversial late-term abortion ban is legal.

Both of these justices went through confirmation hearings that tiptoed around the issue of whether *Roe v. Wade* would stand as legal precedent or be overturned. The fancy verbal acrobatics these two men performed during hearings left us all betwixt and between as to how they would rule. Alito said that *Roe* must be treated with respect because it has been reaffirmed by the high court several times in the past three decades, but when Illinois Senator Richard J. Durbin asked Alito if he considered it "settled law," Alito responded: "If 'settled' means that it can't be reexamined, then that's one thing. If 'settled' means that it is a precedent that is entitled to respect . . . then it is a precedent that is protected, entitled to respect under the doctrine of *stare decisis*" (Latin, meaning "to stand by that which is decided"). Alito refused to distance himself from a statement he wrote while working in the Reagan administration in 1985 in which he said, "The Constitution does not protect a right to abortion." Alito told senators, "That was a correct expression of what I thought in 1985."

During his confirmation hearings for the post of chief justice, John Roberts said there was no room for ideologues on the Supreme Court and declared an "obligation to the Constitution." Senator Dianne Feinstein, the only woman on the Senate Judiciary Committee, said the decision by Judge Roberts in one of his first rulings to join a dissent from the Court decision that upheld Oregon's assisted suicide law bodes ill for the future considering that during his hearings he "told us that he had the view that the federal government should not enter this arena." About Alito, she declared, "If one is pro-choice in this day and age, in this structure, one can't vote for Judge Alito. It is simply that simple."

Up until 2006, Supreme Court rulings allowed individual states to regulate abortion in the following ways:

- Banning elective abortions after viability
- Requiring parental consent or notice before a minor can ob-

tain an abortion, although usually a judicial bypass option must be made available. (Judicial bypass allows a young woman to explain to a judge if circumstances such as incest preclude her getting parental consent.)

• Requiring waiting periods before an abortion may be performed. (Usually twenty-four to forty-eight hours.)

• Requiring that informed consent or counseling be obtained before an abortion. (States often mandate what information must be presented.)

• Requiring certain kinds of record keeping

Immediately after these justices were sworn in, the dominoes began to fall. South Dakota's legislature passed a law banning all abortions, except when necessary to save a woman's life, and threatens doctors who perform abortions with a five-year prison term and a $5,000 fine. Proposed amendments to the law to create exceptions in cases of rape or incest were voted down. Five states have proposed similar bans.

Louisiana governor Kathleen Blanco, a Democrat, recently signed a bill banning abortion that has no exception for rape or incest victims. It allows abortion only in cases where the woman's life is in danger or when childbirth would permanently harm her health. The law will go into effect only if the Supreme Court overturns *Roe v. Wade*. Several other states have similar laws.

Mississippi already has some of the strictest abortion laws in the nation, requiring parental consent and a twenty-four-hour waiting period for the state's one and only abortion clinic, but in March 2006, Mississippi joined the "ban wagon" when a Mississippi state house committee voted to ban abortion in the state with the only exception being if the life of the pregnant woman was endangered. No exceptions for rape or incest. Public Health Committee chairman Steve Holland persuaded his committee to put the abortion ban into a state senate bill that was originally written to require that sonograms be performed early in pregnancy so that a woman could hear a fetal heartbeat. "I have a strong dilemma within myself on this," Holland said. "I can only impregnate; I can't get pregnant myself." Exactly.

That same week in Atlanta, a Georgia state senate committee approved Bill 429, requiring abortion providers to perform a sonogram or ultrasound on women seeking abortion. The woman would then be given a choice about whether to view the images, with an exception for women whose pregnancy was the result of rape or incest. The next step, of course, is *requiring* women seeking abortion to study a sonogram before getting an abortion so they'll be further haunted by the decision and perhaps change their minds.

At the most extreme end of the spectrum, Ohio Republican state senator Tom Brinkman has proposed a bill that would outlaw all abortion in the state, without any exceptions, including when a woman's life is at stake—and would also make it a felony for anyone to take a woman out of Ohio to obtain an abortion in another state.

Fetal Rights

The anti-abortion coalition is also trying to create legal precedents that may help overturn the right to abortion by giving an unborn fetus victim status in prosecuting crimes. Though on its surface this sounds logical and protective, these laws are in fact stealthy maneuvers to give a fetus personhood and thereby move closer to eradicating the rights of *Roe v. Wade*.

In 2004, the Unborn Victims of Violence Act, also known as Laci and Conner's Law, was signed into law by President Bush. This law makes it a separate offense when an unborn child (fetus) suffers death or injury as a result of a violent crime. The punishment for this offense is the same as the law would provide for any other victim. Under this law there is no requirement that the person who commits the crime know that the woman is pregnant or intends to cause death or injury to the child. This law exempts any person performing an abortion with the consent of the pregnant woman herself.

On the issue of abortion we are the Divided States of America. People have very strong moral opinions about women's bodies, especially when it comes to our reproductive health, and this issue highlights the gap between two very different views. These views ought to be re-spected, but not above the sanctity and privacy of a woman's body. The decision to have an abortion is never easy. What we as a society need to do is make sure abortion is safe and legal, but also make sure it is a last resort. That starts with accurate information about and ac-cess to contraceptives—proven as the best way to dramatically reduce the number of abortions. If you oppose abortion, you can't then op-pose sex education and federally funded contraceptive programs that have been proven to make abortion less necessary. But in a free soci-ety, keeping abortion legal is in itself a defining part of that freedom.

Josie, now in her thirties, was raped at knifepoint during a party at her Catholic college two decades ago. At the hospital, she was given the morning-after pill in order to prevent any pregnancy, and to this day, twenty years later, she says, "I feel guilty." But imagine if she were your daughter at a school governed by an abortion law like the one proposed in South Dakota and had no choice but to carry the child of her rapist to term. And then, once her rapist got out of jail, he had parental rights?

Sarah now has an adorable child, but in order to become pregnant, she went through lengthy in vitro fertilization treatments. She, like many women who struggle with pregnancy and become pregnant through in vitro fertilization, was carrying three fetuses. The chances of perinatal morbidity and mortality and maternal morbidity increases with each fetus, creating the potential for very serious problems. There are, of course, ethical considerations, but in order to increase the chances of survival of one child (and herself) she followed her doctor's recommendations and went through a process called "selec-tive termination." During the procedure, the doctor picks the embryo with the strongest chance of survival. If abortion is outlawed, this pro-cedure might be outlawed as well, leaving many women who want to have children deciding in vitro is not worth the risk.

Whether we are pro-choice or not, all women should be afraid that this "new" Supreme Court will pick apart *Roe v. Wade* piece by piece and turn abortion into a states' rights issue. It will be less about abortion and more about states becoming self-ruling, which in the end hurts poor women in those states that do outlaw abortion. Why? Much like the contraception issue in the 1900s, wealthy women will still have access to abortion by being able to travel to other states. Poor women will either have to carry to term (presenting the baby as an instant welfare recipient) or have a back-alley abortion, which really can involve a coat hanger.

There is some irony in the fact that in 2006 the Colombian government not only moved to legalize abortions in that South American country but also did so on the basis that the right to abortion is based in a woman's right to health, life, and equality—not, as we have it, in our constitutional right to privacy. A country in South America, a bastion of male chauvinism, is ensuring women's equality, while the "progressive" United States is moving to eradicate it.

There is nothing pretty about abortion. But we women must have autonomy over the decisions involving our bodies. Our government should not legislate morality; it should ensure its citizens' freedom and self-determination. Our bodies are not public property and must not be used for political gain—on either side. Men would never accept anything less. Neither should we.

CHAPTER 9

THE SOCIAL COMPACT

"I have an equal right to have it all"

Legal rules are basically a mirror of societal values. Social inequities spur legal reform, but until the injustice is recognized, it's hard to get legal rights. The seventeenth-century English philosopher Thomas Hobbes theorized that when scarcity and congestion reach a critical mass, the self-interested motivation of individuals convinces them to come together and reach a consensus—a social compact. Perhaps that is where we are today, at critical mass, and what we need between the sexes, among each other, and within ourselves individually is to come to an understanding, a consensus to correct the inequities in the law that affect our lives as women—and then go out and fight for change. We can also make changes in our own lives that will help each of us redefine some part of the social compact.

HOME

A study by the website salary.com suggested that if stay-at-home moms were paid for all the work they do, they'd be earning a six-figure income for the estimated 91.6 hours a week they work. Workingwomen don't see our jobs as a reason to do less at home.

Instead, we attempt to overcompensate. We juggle work, the kids, the social obligations, the pets, and the house, and even try to toss a few more balls in the air because we're asked to join the PTA or organize a charity auction or take care of a sick relative. . . .

Recently a friend recounted a conversation he had with his grandmother. She was most upset that his brother's wife had failed to send a birthday card to *his* mother. "But Grandma," my friend asked, "why should *she* have to remember to send a birthday card to someone who isn't her mother?!" "Because," his grandmother replied with indignation, "it has always been the responsibility of the women in this family to send the birthday cards!"

Is there a law that says a woman has to send birthday cards? Certainly not. These responsibilities have fallen into our laps, and we've accepted them. Some years ago, when my son was about two, a neighbor was looking over my fence into my yard on Bainbridge Island and heard me bemoaning the many weeds that had overtaken my vegetable garden. "Ugh," I told her. "This looked so much better a couple of years ago."

She smiled. "You can't grow kids and a garden at the same time." Then she went back to her day.

You're right, I thought. *Never mind the garden.*

"Women who work are constantly torn between the demands of work and motherhood," CBS's *Early Show* host Hannah Storm said. "After having children, I decided to put my kids first, always. That does not mean I am any less ambitious or capable than other working moms, but I do make every decision with my kids in mind."

And here's where the trouble begins. Why can men be fathers and professionals but women can't be both mothers and professionals? It's certainly not that we're incapable.

For years, women and men have worked diligently to open up both academic and professional opportunities for women. And yet in the twenty-first century women are still locked into the status quo duties of home and child care, even if we're also working outside the home. According to the Department of Labor, the average workingwoman spends twice as much time as the average workingman on household chores, and gets an hour's less sleep a night. Even though almost as many women as men hold jobs (78 percent of women, 85 percent of men), two-thirds of all women are left preparing the meals and doing the housework on any given day compared to only one-fifth of men who help with the housework and one-third who help with meals or cleanup.

Why is that? Has nothing changed between the sexes? Why are we expected to be Wonder Woman more than men are expected to be Superman? Why shouldn't our male counterparts assume a larger role in helping with the familial obligations? Why shouldn't our society support us such that, like men, we can have careers and families and not feel guilty (or be penalized) because of it? Why should we beat ourselves up for having a career and a family?

Are women handling all the household obligations because we've never spelled out in full enough detail exactly how we need help? We have to ask for what we want. This first step in this social compact is crucial because true equality starts at home.

Yes, we have progressed from being nonpersons to being able to own property, vote, and even govern. Our lives no longer exist strictly within the four walls of our homes, but our lives and our rights there must and should be considered key to our societal respect and happiness. These are rights that should be endowed to all women, whether they seek to use them or not. If we are honored and respected inside our homes, we will be honored and respected outside of them.

We're not asking for "mommy salaries." We are asking for greater assistance in keeping our homes in working order. We need to rethink and challenge social customs and preconceived notions of a woman's role inside and outside the home. We can be and do anything that men can do. And men can be and do anything we can do (except give birth, which in itself should grant us a certain amount of respect).

So why is it still a woman's responsibility to do the wash? Look at ads for any washing machine and you will see it's about a "woman's work." And do the grocery shopping? Pack the lunches? Make the dinner? Chauffeur the kids? Mr. Clean is often the only mister that helps with the housework. Have you ever heard the saying "A man may work from sun to sun, but women's work is never done"? There's too much truth in that, isn't there?

Recently, a woman in Frankfort, Indiana, went on strike. The mother of four was encamped on a lawn chair in her front yard with a sign that said "Mom on Strike," and she was telling all who would listen that she was tired of being the sole caretaker of house and home. She demanded help from her family, and she knew that when they got dirty enough and hungry enough, they'd agree to help.

It reminded me of a woman who, with her husband, owned the dry cleaners I used when I lived in Boston. One day when I went to pick up my dry cleaning Mrs. Kim was sitting on the pavement outside the store with her arms folded, legs crossed, and lips in a pout. A sign she had created from a wire hanger's paper wrap said it all: "Me on Strike!" I suppose it came as no surprise that my laundry wasn't ready.

The following week, needing a suit for an interview, I returned to see if my cleaning was ready. Mrs. Kim happily handed over my laundry. "I guess the strike is over?" I asked as I paid.

Mrs. Kim smiled, leaned across the counter, and in a whisper proffered some wisdom I remember to this day: "He listen when he have to do all the work by himself."

Here's my idea for the home part of our social compact. If we all made a list of our daily duties—the list of to-dos that need to be accomplished on a regular basis to keep our homes running—presented them to our beloveds (husband and/or children), and said, "I need help. Which of these tasks, dear, are you able to take off my plate?" I'd bet they'd be willing to take on a little more. If not, you'll at least get a very clear picture of where you stand and just how lopsided your roles are—and that in and of itself will be nothing less than empowering.

BODY

Is it just me or are beauty magazines designed to make us feel ugly and inadequate? On a recent trip to the newsstand I took out my notebook and wrote down a few of the magazine headlines taunting me from the rack.

Glamour

- *"Always Hungry? (How to Fill Up and Not Gain Weight)"*
- *"Look and Feel Like the Sexiest Woman in the Room—The Clothes, the Hair, the Makeup, the Confidence"*

Cosmopolitan

- *"20 Sexifiers—Just for Your Eyes!"*
- *"Get Your Guy to Give You the Attention You Crave"*

Jane

- *"117 Insider Tips to Amp Your Style"*
- *"The Hottest Hair on the Planet Is Yours"*

Marie Claire

- *"Men Reveal Your Sexiest Look"*
- *"Splurge & Steal Special—224 Must-Have Beauty Buys, Secrets, Tips and Much More!"*
- *"Sexy Hair in Seconds."*

Redbook

- *"What's Your Healthy Weight? Everything You Need to Know About Your Number"*
- *"Steamy Love-Life Secrets—How Do You Compare?"*

Elle

- *"How to: Find a Man, Like Your Job, Love Yourself"*
- *"Forever Young (How to Look 21 for the Rest of Your Life)"*

Vogue

- *"Great Lengths—The New Lust for Long Hair"*
- *"Midnight Miracles—Beauty Solutions That Work While You Sleep"*

But it was *Shape* magazine that outdid them all:

- *"10 Things You Should Know About Your Breasts"*
- *"Flat Abs, Firm Butt—A Revolutionary Way to Get in Your Best Shape"*
- *"Is Your Diet Making You Sick?"*
- *"Feel Full and Lose Weight! A Diet You'll Love!"*
- *"Pant Perfection! Find the Most Flattering Pants for Your Body Shape"*

Aaaaaagh! My boobs are too small, my hair is too short, my body is misshapen, and men think I'm an old hag—is that what we're supposed to believe? Who is selling us this message? And if we're continually bombarded with such "news," are we going to buy it as the truth? It's a no-win situation for us. We're either too fat or too thin. Why is it we don't hear about men's weight? Can you imagine these headlines being directed at men rather than women?

- *"Always Hungry? (How to Eat Like a Pig and Not Get a Gut)"*
- *"Look and Feel Like the Hottest Man in the Room—The Clothes, the Back Waxing, the Confidence"*
- *"Get Your Woman to Give You the Attention You Crave"*
- *"Sexy Hair in Seconds"*
- *"How to: Find a Woman, Like Your Job, Love Yourself"*
- *"Forever Young (How to Look 21 for the Rest of Your Life)"*
- *"Midnight Miracles—Become Handsome While You Sleep"*
- *"10 Things You Should Know About Your Testicles"*

Wouldn't that be ridiculous? Would they sell a single copy? I'd bet the magazines would be laughed off the rack. So why do they continuously hawk this stuff to us? Because we're *buying it*! Not just the magazines—we're buying that we're malformed, ill-tressed, wrinkled wenches with flabby thighs who deliver lackluster bedroom performances. Perhaps these publications are beholden to the advertising dollar—all the companies on their pages hawking makeup, diet pills, and the miracle cures to what they say ails us. We are led to believe we have the malady that their product allegedly fixes, buying blindly into the promises to make ourselves "better." But wait a second—*we* are in the driver's seat both in buying the publications and in buying the products therein.

Interestingly, Dove, the maker of soaps and lotions, recently garnered much publicity for their "Tested on real curves" campaign. The campaign showed "real women" of sizes six to fourteen, rather than stick-thin models, in their undies next to the product pitch: "New Dove Firming. As tested on real curves." There was much brouhaha over the campaign, including *Chicago Sun-Times* columnist Richard Roeper's chauvinistic remark that the women were "chunky."

The marketing materials on the company's website, set up specifically for the campaign, said their philosophy is that beauty comes in different shapes and sizes. Their mission is to "make more women feel beautiful every day by broadening the definition of beauty." Though looking at "real" models is refreshing as is the message that we should feel beautiful just the way we are, the underlying message created a glaring contradiction. Dove Firming is a product to get rid of our unsightly jiggling thighs! The campaign was momentarily inspiring, but beneath its friendly, curvaceous surface, the message is once again that we are not good enough and need something to help us triumph over adversity—in this case, overcoming the lumpy flesh (aka cellulite) that comes with age and obesity to 90 percent of all women. If Dove really wanted to "help women feel that beauty is within their reach," they might just tell us that aging is natural and, according to years of medical studies, the best thing we can do for ourselves is to eat well and exercise.

All of this attention to our imperfect bodies—clothed and unclothed—only makes us feel inadequate. As Gloria, a twenty-nine-year-old mother of three, said, the one thing that could make her happier is "less media attention focused on how women look, and more focused on how women think and act." So here's my solution for the body part of our social compact: if each of us refused to buy a magazine or product that was capitalizing on our fears or what "they" allege is one of our purported weaknesses, they'd quickly catch on. When sales plummeted, they'd find things that enabled us to actually discover ourselves and celebrate our strengths, rather than fret over our supposed shortcomings. Or if you find yourself in possession of one of these insulting troublemakers, write a letter to the editor or manufacturer saying you are bothered by how shallow, how empty, how behind the times they are. If they receive enough similar remarks, they'll quickly rethink their message.

Look, if you want to buy a magazine that trumpets "How to Have Sexier Hair" and the cure for wrinkles, by all means do so. Who am I to tell you not to? It is, after all, your prerogative. But be aware of the underlying reasons *why* you're buying it, and be informed that what's in that little bottle might not be the answer to all your problems. If you really want to feel good inside and out, follow years of proven advice—eat right, exercise, and when that outfit comes along that makes you feel fabulous, buy it!

WORK

We live in a society in which economics requires that the majority of American women work, but it shouldn't be shocking that we *want* to work, and it definitely shouldn't be that we're considered abnormal for doing so. Yes, there are sexual discrimination laws, sexual harassment laws, and equal employment laws established to protect us in the workplace. As we've seen, however, no matter what our laws say, we are still viewed through a subtle yet insidious looking glass that pictures women first in our "traditional" role as wife and mother. There is a pervasive social structure that maintains both the status quo and patriarchal power. Women are entrenched in the workplace as never before, but we are regarded surreptitiously as outsiders. In short, we enter the game with the dice loaded against us, as numerous women I interviewed described.

Rikki Klieman, attorney and *Court TV* commentator: "Women continue to be held to a different standard than men. Women work harder, longer, are expected to do everything a man does in the work-place and then still may not get the credit when a man speaks up and acts as if the idea or result were his."

Sunshine, a thirty-year-old single working mother of two: "It's not harassment, but a simple 'good morning' is often accompanied by re-marks on my appearance. I would never say to a male co-worker, 'Good morning, you sure are wearing that tie really well.' Or 'Hey, nice pants. Are you losing weight?' "

Patti, a thirty-seven-year-old single engineer: "It's a power strug-gle. The condescending attitudes and comments are overwhelming. I'm stereotyped at every turn. Single—'When are you going to get married?' A female engineer—'Why'd you decide to be an engineer?' Blond—'Are you an airhead?' I'm very aware that the motives, brains, or life choices of the single blond male in the cubicle next to me are never questioned."

Several women made the point that often what's *not* said is the most threatening. One executive of a major entertainment company noted, "You definitely don't talk about the kids in the boardroom. It would be a red flag that my job wasn't my top priority." A financial analyst said that if she put a picture of her children on her desk it would "definitely make me look bad." Why is it that a man can be both family man and CEO, but if a woman has kids, she is somehow less interested in any success outside of being a mother?

What's at play here is rather insidious. Lori, a twenty-seven-year-old production assistant, added, "Look, just the fact we have to be talking about this indicates there's a problem. I'd love it if women were viewed as equally capable as men in the workplace; unfortunately that's still not the case." This is patriarchal power at play, but it's not calculated. It's just unaware. These condescending attitudes and thoughts are misguided, and it's our obligation to put up a billboard saying the status quo must change.

The women before us fought hard to enter the workplace, and now our duty—for those who came before us and to those who come after—is to redirect this underlying current. We have to communicate our concerns, taking the cue from men and being assertive and direct but not aggressive. "Girls are brought up to be listeners," explained Fifi, a seventy-six-year-old businesswoman. "Men are not required to shoulder that responsibility." It's not selfish to claim our fair share of social justice, it's healthy.

When in the summer of 1848 Elizabeth Cady Stanton and Lucretia Mott headed to Seneca Falls, New York, to consider "the social, civil and religious conditions and rights of women," Stanton boldly told a reporter to "put it down in capital letters: SELF-DEVELOPMENT IS A HIGHER DUTY THAN SELF-SACRIFICE." What does this mean for us more than 150 years later? How does that shape today's workplace? Well, for starters, it tells us that perhaps a quarrel or two might be good for us. By demanding recognition and acceptance, we're not ending the game, we're making it better. It's not about screaming and yelling, it's about speaking up. We need to untie our tongues and talk this thing through. We need social changes in order to provide women with the same career opportunities and encouragement that men are afforded, and we need to raise our voices for them, knowing it's not selfish, it's for the larger good.

First, we need to once and for all shed the view that the home is women's "place." As already discussed, men need to equally share in the work at home—or decide among a husband and wife a delineation of duties, rather than falling into them—so that when we're in the workplace it's not just the women who should expect the call from the nurse's office. This means men need to share more equally in the role as nurturer.

Second, our workplace policies and attitudes need to change so that it's no longer about "allowing" women to do what men do, but expecting it. What's good for the goose will also benefit the gander. By respecting women in the workplace, we are unshackling men from their ball-and-chain role of being the "provider."

Third, employers need to recognize and accept that it is possible to be a valuable professional and seek reasonable family time. As Geraldine Ferraro said, "The biggest roadblock for women in the workplace is that employers don't recognize the family." And it has historically been the women who are made to endure the career punishment because we're the ones looking out for others. But if we as a society have a paradigm shift such that men, as well as women, are responsible for maintaining the family, corporations would be much more willing to offer flex time, telecommuting, and at-work day care. These perks wouldn't be just for women. Quality options for caring for our children (or sick parents) would allow us (whether male or female) to be guilt-free about being good parents without fear of job repercussions.

Women should not be the only ones required to juggle home and work. Period. And until we speak up, both individually and collectively, and say that we're not going to do it by ourselves anymore, we will be faced with this conundrum at work. We must level the playing field, and we might have to squabble a bit to do it. Change with men doesn't come easy, especially when you're arguing if the ball is "in" or "out."

Fourth, when we walk in the door of our offices, we should be greeted with the same respect afforded the men we work with. If we're told, "Good morning, you look great" and that doesn't sit well with you because you knew from the eye gymnastics that what your male counterpart really meant was "Your breasts look great" or "Love the legs," you should be able to confidently say to him, "Thank you. But just the 'good morning' is fine." Or if you felt the comment was sweet, you could say, "Thanks! Love that tie, Fred."

Fifth, the glass ceiling needs to be removed from the workplace and the building reconstructed such that all employees (man or woman, white or minority) feel that there is equal opportunity to climb to the top. If you're a woman and in a workplace where you see recruitment practices that place women in limiting roles or a lack of opportunity for women in development and decision making, say something. If you're ignored, speak louder. If you're fired, the Equal Employment Opportunity Commission might like to hear from you. (See Women's Toolbox.) But if you're in a workplace that makes you unhappy or where you see that you're never going to be presented with growth opportunities, you may simply want to look elsewhere. Your talents should be recognized. Glass ceilings are nice in greenhouses and atriums, but our places of work should not impose limitations on any deserving individual.

WOMEN V. WOMEN

The last, and perhaps most important, part of our discussion should be among ourselves. Women can't "have it all" if we're pecking at each other like caged hens. With the world already against us, do we have to be against ourselves? You know what I mean.

It's not just the venomous Ann Coulter who is out for her sisters' blood. During my interviews I heard countless stories of how a female boss, colleague, or neighbor did something hurtful. From young to old, there were stories of women not helping other women or, worse, intentionally keeping them down. Jax, a thirty-two-year-old human resources specialist who is currently the stay-at-home mom of a three-month-old, said, "It amazes me that women are so competitive with each other and don't support each other more. Women do not do each other any favors and really need to start nurturing each other in the workplace and in life."

The system is against us, and yet we often help polish the glass ceiling. For example, a woman recounted this story about being interviewed by a *female* officer in a Fortune 500 company and the mother of two:

She told me all about the life/work balance (or lack thereof) she has. She said, "Take me, for example. If one of my kids is sick, the company allows me the flexibility to pencil in time to be on the phone while my nanny takes him to the doctor." Each time she finished telling me a story, she paused to see what my reaction would be. When I had none, she said, "Are you hearing what I'm saying?" in a tone that implied I should be reading between the lines. What she was saying was that she wouldn't be pleased if I came aboard and wanted to put motherhood first. Her stories were to convey that if I wanted to succeed at the company, at least in her eyes and the eyes of the other women there, then I would have to be willing to make those same sacrifices. She made no secret of her belief that women have to put their job first to be taken seriously. It's ironic that I don't even have children yet.

Linda, a twenty-nine-year-old attorney, said, "Women categorize themselves. Some of my friends, for example, think that if I were to take time off after having children I would be betraying the women who were still working by proving men's preconceived ideas about what women do when they have children. Other friends of mine think that if I don't stay home when I have children, I am a bad wife and mother."

On her TV show *The Apprentice,* Martha Stewart, the doyenne of domesticity, made this brusque point to a young female applicant who said she felt like crying: "Women in business don't cry, my dear. Cry and you're out of here." On crying, womensmedia.com advises emotional detachment: "Compartmentalizing feelings is also a good skill to learn. Practice not acting on a feeling you have."

Carrie, a forty-two-year-old FBI agent, said, "It doesn't make sense that women don't form stronger alliances to support one another. I'm always surprised that women don't more actively pursue mentoring other women within the workplace. While women often complain about gender issues in their professional lives, I also know many women who don't want to work for other women."

Elizabeth, a federal judge, put it bluntly: "Women are women's worst enemies. Every woman has a different story and different priorities. Where one woman works shorter days to be home with her kids for dinner, another woman may not be able to swing it and will resent the first woman for doing it. Or women who choose to keep their careers as top priority and maybe do not have a family resent and/or disapprove of women that try to do both."

Finger-wagging is an even worse trait than finger-pointing. Stop judging each other. Why do we need to divide ourselves into camps? The "stay-at-home moms" versus "women who work"—sounds like a reality TV show, doesn't it? Perhaps it should come as no surprise that the question in my survey that stirred the most emotion was "Do you think women are supportive of other women and the choices they make about work and/or their personal lives?"

> There is a great difference of opinion and desire in life. Today I feel women in my age group are quite confused. We appreciate the ability to work and have this independent lifestyle, but most of my girlfriends and I would like to be married with kids. *(Fiona, 31, businesswoman)*

> I think that women are very critical of each other, and I think it may be related to all the different expectations placed on women to be professionals and caregivers. There are many competing priorities. *(Liz, 29, student)*

> Some who've sacrificed having a family life may resent those who've chosen to have some balance and still succeeded. *(Eva, 43, entrepreneur)*

> I think some women view feminism as an obligation and responsibility to work, and others view it as giving women the ability to work in any field and to have the same benefits as men do. The comments I have heard seem to depend on which category the person falls into. *(Linda, 29, attorney)*

> Sometimes women are competitive or threatened by each other, which can lead to people being catty and mean—but I've also come across great female bosses who only wanted to see me succeed. *(Rachel, 33, professional)*

> Women are often expected to do everything—work plus the bulk of the child care and housework. They rarely have an ideal situation and they are often criticized whether they give up their career or pursue it wholeheartedly while their husbands are

spared the problems and criticism, so the women often end up feeling defensive. Consequently, women too, end up criticizing other women. *(Nicole, 42, former attorney, now part-time translator, mother of two)*

I think older women are unduly harsh on younger women, especially if the older woman is the supervisor. I also think that women who do not have "careers" judge those of us that do too harshly—making us feel guilty for not being home more or having kids. *(Emily, 31, lawyer)*

Most women want what someone else has. I have had to do everything—full-time mom/part-time mom; part-time employee/full-time employee. It is very difficult to find that balance between the two. So I do not judge other moms. It's hard enough keeping my own stuff straight. *(Taylor, 39, CPA and business owner, mother of two)*

We can debate ad nauseam whether or not women should stay home or work, just as we can debate how to raise our children, how short is too short for a skirt, and whether or not a man holding a door for us is courteous or boorish. But one thing is certain: we shouldn't take out our frustrations—over a society that doesn't value families and workplaces that treat women poorly—on each other. We should do something about it.

Think of Oprah Winfrey, who has built an empire on helping others. In revealing her own personal pain from weight issues and abuse, Oprah has helped countless women discover something new about themselves or find a way to overcome an obstacle. Has helping other women hurt Oprah? Quite the opposite. Barbara Corcoran, known as the queen of New York real estate, says that while building her multi-billion-dollar business from a thousand-dollar loan, she found the more she helped others out, the more it helped her out. "It's like a pyramid scheme where everyone rises to the top," she said. "I always say helping someone is a deposit in your goodwill account. People remember when you've done something to help them, especially women."

Trying to make each other fit into any sort of mold about the "ideal woman" is like sitting as a judge at the Miss America pageant. Who are we to say what the ideal is? We need to celebrate our accomplishments and get off each other's backs about any perceived shortcomings. We are all faced with the task of striking a balance between work and home. Celebrate with other women their successes, help them through their difficulties, but above all, realize that if we want social justice in this country, we must first give it to each other.

Let's make a compact between ourselves acknowledging that we all have to make our choices. Some of us marry, others don't. Some of us work outside the home, others don't. Some of us have children, others don't. But at the end of the day, we're all women who want to do the right thing for those we care about and ourselves, and we all want to be afforded equal opportunities in the eyes of society and under our laws.

STEPPING FORWARD

Recently, I participated in a panel at a conference on work and balance for women, and it did not go unnoticed by the attendees that you would never hear of a men's conference on these same issues. I attempted to put a positive spin on our conundrum by saying, "Women have to work the double shift every day. But at the end of the day when I tuck my kids in, I know the bags under my eyes are worth it."

"We're *all* in an uphill battle," another panelist commented. "As women, we're expected to be superhuman, able to multitask, work the day and night shift, and manage our time better than our male counterparts—while keeping ourselves looking good on less sleep."

Geraldine Ferraro, the first woman to run for vice president of the United States on a major party ticket, put it this way: "A man is just allowed to go out and be successful. Success for him is defined by the paycheck, but for a woman success is defined as so much more."

Remember when Miss America was our idol? The Miss America pageant was as much a part of American life as baseball and apple pie. Fifty-one of America's most talented, well-educated, and beautiful women strutted on national television in swimsuits and evening gowns in front of a panel of judges to prove that there she was—our ideal. I used to look forward to the pageant every year. On that night my two best friends and I would get to stay up late and eat bologna-and-pickle sandwiches while watching the pageant. We'd wrap towels around our short hair to make it feel longer and sing along with the contestants, using pencils as our microphones. We'd try to guess who would win. I never got it right. It seemed so arbitrary. All the women were so beautiful, poised, and talented—who could say which one was better?

Today, in our post-feminist world, Miss America is passé, and there is revived debate on what exactly "our ideal" is. Each woman's ideal is different. To some of us our ultimate goal is healthy and happy children and perhaps an adoring husband; to others our purpose is defined strictly by career success; many wouldn't have anything less than both.

"We want to be CEO and mommy," said Fox News Channel anchor and mom E. D. Hill. "It sounds really good, but it doesn't quite work out that way. If you're in a competitive business, here's the reality: on your daughter's first day of kindergarten you call in sick because you really want to be there to drop her off and pick her up. You worry that if you're honest about why you're taking the day off, your boss will think you aren't dedicated or focused enough on your job, and the greatest fear is that the guys in the office won't take the day off and they'll look like better workers."

In every interview I conducted with women while working on this book, one word came up: *balance.* Most women agreed that they were willing and happy to bring home the bacon and fry it up in the pan, but they want to feel supported and assisted in the endeavor not only by their spouses but also by our laws and society at large. At this point, frankly, we don't.

Whether married, single, widowed, or divorced, whether young or old, whether poor or rich, whether white, black, or any shade in between, we women should have a right to all the opportunities, privileges, and responsibilities granted to men. The 1977 National Women's Conference declared, "We do not seek special privileges, but we demand as a human right a full voice and role for women in determining the destiny of our world, our nation, our families and our individual lives."

As we've seen in the stories of the women chronicled here, despite the gains made since our nation's birth, equality under the law is not yet ours. Every day millions of women face discrimination, economic hardship, and limited opportunities not because they aren't capable but simply because they are women.

This isn't about being feminist. This is about finally overcoming the man-made barriers, social customs, and prejudices that have kept us down throughout time. We, and our daughters, must assume full control of our bodies, our lives, and our abilities. We've lived long enough under patriarchal orders. This is a democracy and we've got numbers too big to ignore. So let political analysts drone on about everything from NASCAR dads to undecided voters—the female voter wields a majority share of power and we're not riding in the back of the bus any longer. Remember that great Helen Reddy song "I Am Woman"? Like it says in that song, we can't be broken because we are determined to reach our goal. We will achieve equality if we, the 51 percent minority, work together to achieve it. We've come too far not to. Yes, whether mommy or president-elect, equality of rights under the law must not be denied or abridged by the United States or any state on account of sex.

WOMEN'S TOOLBOX

A guide to legal rights and remedies for the major issues facing women of the twenty-first century

Running into situations that we don't know how to handle is a fact of life. We all want to know what our rights are and where to go to seek remedies. What follows is a guide to the issues discussed in the previous chapters that will help you find solutions and set you on the path toward achieving justice. Please note that this is just to get you started; consult with an attorney before taking any drastic actions.

EQUAL PAY

If you think you are not receiving equal pay for equal work, you may file a complaint with the Equal Employment Opportunity Commission, which enforces the Equal Pay Act. If you request confidentiality, your identity will not be revealed during an investigation of an alleged equal pay violation. If a violation is found, the EEOC will negotiate with the employer for a settlement, including back pay and appropriate raises in pay scales, to correct the violation of the law. The EEOC may also initiate court action to collect back wages under the

Act. You may not sue the employer, however, if you have already been paid full back wages under EEOC supervision or if the EEOC has filed a suit in court to collect these wages. You must file suit within two years of an Equal Pay Act violation, except in the case of deliberate violations, in which case there is a three-year time limit.

Up to now, the courts have been reluctant to find that unequal pay for jobs thought to be of equal value, by itself, is proof of sex-based wage discrimination. Future court cases and interpretations by the Equal Employment Opportunity Commission, which enforces Title VII, will help to further define which practices amount to illegal sex-based wage discrimination.

Each complainant, whether through EEOC negotiations or court rulings, may recover damages for future financial losses, emotional pain, suffering, mental anguish, loss of enjoyment of life, and other non-pecuniary losses. Excluding any back pay, the amount recovered for each complainant—whether by the EEOC or in court—may not exceed:

- **$50,000 for employers with 15–100 employees**
- **$100,000 for employers with 101–200 employees**
- **$200,000 for employers with 201–500 employees**
- **$300,000 for employers with more than 500 employees**

If your suit is successful, relief can come in a number of forms:

• *Back pay.* This is the most common form of relief, which includes the wages, salary, and fringe benefits that you would have received during the period of discrimination, from the date of termination or failure to promote to the day of trial. An employee does have the duty, however, to mitigate her damages by taking reasonable efforts to find comparable employment after termination.

• *Compensatory damages.* This is an award for future loss, emotional distress, pain and suffering, inconvenience, mental anguish, and loss of enjoyment of life.

- *Attorney's fees.* The court can award attorney's fees to the winning party.
- *Punitive damages.* Punitive damages are limited to cases in which the employer's discrimination is intentional and is done with malice or reckless indifference to the individual's rights.
- *Injunctive relief.* Common examples of injunctive relief include reinstating a terminated employee or an order to the employer to prevent future discrimination.

Salary Negotiation

The National Committee on Pay Equity has a terrific website (www.pay-equity.org) that offers great tips on achieving equal pay and has detailed advice on wage and salary negotiations. Prepare your case the way a lawyer does a trial. Come armed with specific details about your skills, your responsibilities, and what you've done or will do to ensure productivity. The site advises writing a description of the job you do, detailing duties, skills, and what is necessary to perform the job well. Use this to help justify your request for an increase in salary.

The site suggests several techniques for raising awareness of your position within the organization, as well as questions you can ask and answer yourself that will empower your negotiation, such as:

- *What is your level of responsibility? Do you handle company secrets? Are you responsible for others?*
- *What skills do you have that your supervisor might not realize? Have you gotten better rates on supplies? Do you go above and beyond and help write the company newsletter?*
- *What are your working conditions like? Is there danger? Long hours? Heavy lifting?*
- *How much effort is required in your job and what are the pressures? Have you received special training?*
- *What kind of salary could you earn for the same job outside of the company?*
- *Have other women held your job?*

For More Information

www.equalrights.org

This site is sponsored by Equal Rights Advocates (ERA), a group whose mission is to protect and secure equal rights and economic opportunities for women through litigation and advocacy. If you are facing discrimination at work or at school, you can call ERA's Advice and Counseling Hotline (800-839-4372) or request information on equal pay, sex discrimination, sexual harassment, pregnancy discrimination, and problems with family/medical leave.

www.pay-equity.org

Hosted by the National Committee on Pay Equity, this site works to eliminate sex- and race-based wage discrimination and to help women achieve pay equity. Made up of a coalition of women's civil rights organizations; labor unions; religious, professional, legal, and educational associations; and commissions on women, this site announces Equal Pay Day—the day women's earnings finally catch up with men's earnings from the previous year—and reminds women to wear red that day because "we're in the red."

SEXUAL HARASSMENT

The first thing to do if you feel you are being subjected to sexual harassment is to speak up! Partly because it's the right thing to do, but also because courts have held that liability depends on the employer knowing that the situation exists and failing to take action. Make absolutely sure that the perpetrator knows how unwelcome his advances are. You're not interested, you don't think it's funny, and you have every expectation that it must stop. Document everything—create a record of the unpleasantness, noting times and dates and witnesses, being specific.

Sometimes—not always, but sometimes—sexual harassment can be nipped in the bud with the verbal equivalent of an old-fashioned slap across the face. One anonymous writer offered some creative suggestions on www.lawyer.com. For example, try the "Miss Manners" approach, which involves dramatizing your shock, thereby turning the embarrassment back on the perpetrator, where it belongs. Other suggestions for verbal judo include naming the behavior as exactly what it is; pretending not to understand the remark; noting all offenses in a notebook prominently labeled "Sexual Harassment"; and writing a letter to the perpetrator sent via certified mail, return receipt requested, describing the behavior precisely and factually and asking that it stop immediately.

Should none of these ideas work for you—or if you simply don't feel comfortable with them—the next step is to investigate what internal procedures may exist at your workplace. Go over the offender's head. With the heightened awareness that exists of sexual harassment liability today, you may find you get results. It goes without saying that being calm, cool, and collected, with paper trail in hand, is the approach here.

But be prepared for an uphill fight. The old mentality that boys will be boys and women need to be good sports about it dies hard. You may experience backlash from men and women who think this way, but rest assured that if they were on the receiving end of the kind of discomfort sexual harassment can create, they'd see it differently. In fact, they do—the EEOC reports that about 11 percent of sexual harassment complaints these days come from men, a figure that has roughly tripled in recent years.

If nothing changes, it's time to file a complaint with the EEOC within 180 days of the behavior.

According to the National Women's Law Center, sexual harassment does not have to involve sex, nor does it have to be sexual in nature. Sexual harassment also does not have to be by your supervisor, because employers now have an obligation to provide a workplace free from sexual harassment.

Sexual harassment includes:

- *Unwelcome sexual advances*
- *Request for sexual favors*
- *Verbal or physical conduct of a sexual nature*

when:

• Reaction (whether to submit to or reject) is the basis for keeping your job or getting a promotion (called quid pro quo harassment, or harassment resulting in a tangible employment action)

• Such conduct is sufficiently severe or pervasive that it creates an intimidating, hostile, or offensive work environment (called hostile environment harassment)

What to do if you believe you're being sexually harassed:

1. Tell the harasser that you want the behavior to stop, unless you fear for your safety or your job. If verbal request isn't possible or effective, write the harasser a memo telling him the behavior (be clear about what it is) must stop.

2. Use your employer's protocol to report an incident. If you're part of a union, contact the union and explain what has occurred or is occurring.

3. Document the harassment, writing down specifics, times, dates, and locations. Keep a journal, notes, and e-mail correspondence, as well as pictures and other pertinent items, and store them at home.

4. Keep a copy of your work records, performance reviews, and any correspondence regarding the quality of your work.

5. Network with others. You might find that someone else has had similar occurrences. Away from the office, rely on the support of friends and family.

6. Never give any indication that the harasser's conduct is welcome. Don't wear overly sexy clothes, speak provocatively, or give him gifts. Courts generally permit testimony regarding prior sexual history in the workplace of both parties.

7. File a formal complaint with your supervisor (or, if he is the harasser, his supervisor). Employers are legally responsible to maintain a harassment-free workplace. If there are no results (as required by law) to your complaint, file a complaint with the EEOC. The EEOC must grant a "right to sue" letter *before* you can file a lawsuit.

FOR MORE INFORMATION

www.eeoc.gov

If you are faced with what you believe is discrimination, you generally must file a short (around two-page) complaint with the Equal Employment Opportunity Commission. If an aggrieved employee tries to go directly to court without first filing with the EEOC, the judge will dismiss her suit. Congress began requiring this initial stop at the EEOC in an attempt to reduce the number of cases going to court—ideally, the EEOC helps the two parties resolve the issue while avoiding the time and expense of courtroom litigation.

In addition to sexual harassment, you can also find information about such subjects as: age, disability, equal pay, national origin, pregnancy, race, religion, retaliation, and sex. This site also gives numerous statistics and explains how to file a charge of discrimination.

EEOC's National Contact Center (NCC) customer service representatives are available to assist you in more than 100 languages between 8:00 A.M. and 8:00 P.M. Eastern Time. An automated system with answers to frequently asked questions is available on a 24-hour basis.

U.S. Equal Employment Opportunity Commission
P.O. Box 7033
Lawrence, KS 66044
800-669-4000
TTY: 800-669-6820
FAX: 703-997-4890

E-MAIL: info@ask.eeoc.gov (Include your zip code and/or city and state so that your e-mail will be sent to the appropriate office)

www.nwlc.org

The National Women's Law Center's mission is to protect and advance the progress of women and girls at work, in school, and in virtually every aspect of their lives. The site provides thorough information on the issues facing women and the laws that are both on our side and against us. The National Women's Law Center takes on only a few cases each year—those that raise new legal issues affecting large numbers of women—but the site does provide information on contacting lawyers that specialize in your type of case and a list of organizations and government agencies that may be able to help you.

www.sexualharassmentsupport.org

This site provides support and information for people who have experienced or think they may be experiencing sexual harassment. Site includes definitions, myths, actions you can take, stories from sexual harassment victims, and a chat room.

www.badbossology.com

Badbossology.com features completely free access to more than 1,200 articles and resources on solving problems with difficult managers. Besides being able to review numerous topics, you can safely e-mail material from the site anonymously—for example, to a boss who is crossing the line.

PREGNANCY

Your pregnancy rights under Title VII are:

On work duties:
• You must be treated the same as any other employee with a "disability."

• If management allows another employee to be on light duty because of an injury, they must allow you to be on light duty. However, if management forced that employee to take an unpaid leave for the duration of his injury, you can only resort to that option for protection.

On informing your employer of your pregnancy:

• It's not your employer's business to know if you're pregnant until you want to tell them.

• If you are interviewing for a job, potential employers are not allowed to ask if you are pregnant or not.

• Employers cannot refuse to hire you because you are pregnant and they cannot fire you because you are pregnant.

On your pregnancy leave:

• Title VII specifically acknowledges that women are to be entrusted with the decisions of when to work and when not to work. Your employer cannot tell you when you can or can't come back to work. That is for you to decide.

• As far as your seniority and accrual of vacation and sick days, you must be protected as much as any other temporarily disabled employee. That is to say, if your company allows for accrual of vacation and seniority during a period of temporary disability, then it must do the same for you with a pregnancy-related disability. If your employer does not allow for accrual of vacation and seniority during a period of disability, then you may not be protected.

On health care coverage:

• Your employer is also prohibited from discrimination in health care coverage. It may not charge you more for your health insurance than any other employee. It must offer the same protection to you as a female spouse of an employee as it does for a male spouse of an employee.

• Decisions whether or not to bear children are not allowed to affect health care coverage. If you feel that this has happened, you should raise the issue with your employer and health care provider and point out that you are legally protected from discrimination.

• Your pregnancy must be covered to the same extent as other medical conditions are covered. If your plan generally has very limited coverage, then you might be out of luck.

Know Your Rights

The application of these laws varies widely from state to state and company to company. One of the easiest ways to learn what your rights are as a worker and what your employer's responsibilities to you are is to contact your state's department of labor. (To find your local office, put your state's name and "department of labor" in any Internet search engine.) Some states provide extra protections for pregnant employees over and above what Title VII guarantees; you should talk to your local EEOC or county legislative office to find out about this. Go to the EEOC website (www.eeoc.gov) or visit your local EEOC office and ask lots of questions.

REVIEW YOUR COMPANY'S POLICIES

You may also need to find out from your employer:

• Whether maternity leave is paid, unpaid, or partially paid.
• Whether you're eligible for disability insurance benefits.
• Whether it has a medical disability insurance policy that pays a portion of your salary while you're on leave. Pregnancy is legally a medical disability. Find out which forms you have to complete and send them in. Follow up.
• Whether the employer's policy allows you to return to your same position.
• How much time you are allowed off. Can you use accrued benefit days to extend maternity leave?

- What about flex time or working from home?
- Does your health plan remain in effect? Will there be added costs?
- If you work for a company employing 50 people or more, then you are also protected by the federal government's Family Medical Leave Act. (You should find out how many employees your company counts—often there are many people who appear to be employees but are technically considered contract workers, consultants, or temporary workers. If you fall into one of those categories you may not be eligible for FMLA or the full benefits package.)

ASK A LOT OF QUESTIONS

Go to your employer's human resources department, or a knowledgeable colleague, and ask about company policy. Many companies have specific benefits packages for maternity leave. Ask your friends, neighbors, and co-workers how they were treated. Consider knowledge to be your armor—the more you know, the more confident you are in asking for the rights you deserve.

FILE A COMPLAINT OR HIRE A LAWYER

If you believe that your employer has behaved illegally in regard to your pregnancy rights, then go to the EEOC and charge your employer with pregnancy discrimination based on your protected rights under Title VII. Or consult with an attorney.

For More Information

www.disabilitylawyers.com

This is a comprehensive site that has a feature to help you find an appropriate attorney specializing in the issues raised by your case, as well as a helpful "regional resources" page.

smallbusiness.findlaw.com

FindLaw for Small Business provides answers to frequently asked questions regarding pregnancy discrimination, as well as other forms of employment discrimination. It also includes a handy "find a lawyer" function that locates attorneys with various specialties by zip code.

www.workplacefairness.org

Workplace Fairness is a nonprofit organization that provides information, education, and assistance to individual workers and their advocates nationwide and promotes public policies that advance employee rights. Workplace Fairness is an excellent source for pregnancy discrimination information as well as comprehensive general information about workers' rights—free of legal jargon.

AGE AND WEIGHT

Age Discrimination

The U.S. Equal Employment Opportunity Commission reports that age discrimination for women begins sooner than for men. Employers are forcing out older women and eliminating the positions they hold, typically the higher-paid positions, at faster rates than for older men. With that in mind, it is particularly important that women know their rights when it comes to age discrimination. Age discrimination in the workplace is prohibited by a federal law called the Age Discrimination in Employment Act of 1967 (ADEA). Under this law, employers who have twenty or more employees may not discriminate on the basis of age against employees and job applicants who are forty years old or more.

WHAT TO DO

You should first call the EEOC or talk to a lawyer who will help you assess whether or not you have a claim, and how you should proceed.

If you determine that your employer is guilty of age discrimination against you under the ADEA, you may file a discrimination charge with the EEOC. Note, however, that states and municipalities may enact age discrimination laws that are equivalent to the ADEA. Such laws are enforced by state and local EEOC equivalents, generally referred to as "fair employment practices agencies" or FEPAs. The decision on where to file the complaint may depend on what state you live in. Some states require that you first file with the EEOC, while others require that you first file with the state. If you are given the choice, it might be a better idea to file a charge with a FEPA instead of the EEOC, or a lawsuit in a state or municipal court instead of federal court. (Generally speaking, discrimination lawsuits in state and municipal courts are easier to win and often result in better awards.)

It may seem obvious at this point, but you will likely be forced to hire a lawyer, given how complicated the law is in this field, not to mention how adept and experienced many companies (especially large ones) are at this sort of litigation. With lawyers often charging several hundred dollars an hour, the price of trials can easily skyrocket to tens of thousands of dollars or more—a difficult price to pay, especially when you're suing precisely because you've just been denied a job or fired.

Many employment attorneys who represent plaintiffs therefore work on a contingency fee basis: rather than pay by the hour, you pay your lawyer some portion of whatever you win (that is, *if* you win). As attractive as this arrangement might initially sound, the price is steep: Contingency fees generally take a third or more of whatever the court awards. What's more, you are on the hook not only for attorney's fees but also for any other cost incurred in the course of litigation. For example, it currently costs $189 to file a lawsuit in Los Angeles Superior Court and about $1,000 to hire a stenographer to attend a deposition. Mailings, long-distance telephone costs, private investigators, and the like all quickly inflate this tab. It is, in sum, quite expensive to litigate.

That said, if you want to move forward with a complaint to a FEPA or the EEOC, you must act quickly. A 180-day statute of limitations applies for starting legal action under the ADEA, beginning on the date your alleged age discrimination occurred. If a state age discrimination law also comes into play, you'll have up to 300 days to file your charge. The problem is you may not know whether or not a state law also applies until you file your charge or see a lawyer, so it's a good idea to assume that you have only 180 days until you learn otherwise.

WHAT HAPPENS NEXT

Generally, your employer will be notified of the charge, and an investigation will begin. The EEOC or FEPA will request documents from your employer and interview witnesses, if there are any. If the EEOC or FEPA does *not* find evidence to suggest that discrimination occurred, you will be notified and given a right-to-sue letter, which allows you to pursue a private lawsuit. If the EEOC or FEPA *does* believe discrimination occurred, the agency will try to work out a settlement with the employer. The settlement could include reinstating you to your job and awarding you back pay and punitive damages. If the EEOC cannot reach a settlement, it may bring a lawsuit on your behalf or issue a right-to-sue letter, allowing you to proceed to court. About 80 percent of all employment disputes are resolved in the first year during the EEOC process. (Note that your employer cannot lawfully retaliate against you for exercising your rights under the ADEA. Your employer is also prohibited from retaliating against co-workers who testify on your behalf during related proceedings.)

IF YOU DECIDE TO PROCEED WITH A LAWSUIT

Once you've hired a lawyer and brought suit, you must prove, generally to a jury, that it was more likely than not that your employer took an adverse employment action against you on the basis of some forbidden criterion (for example, because of your age).

It is often extremely difficult to prove discriminatory practices, because sophisticated employers know not to leave smoking guns around—for example, very few employers will testify, in a candid manner, that they just don't like having women, minorities, or older people around the office. Likewise, few employers will admit that a certain employee would have received a job offer if she had been a little younger.

Recognizing this difficulty, the Supreme Court has made things somewhat easier for discrimination plaintiffs. An employee alleging that an employer refused to hire her because of her sex, for example, generally must make four initial showings:

1. That she belongs to some protected class (e.g., that she is a woman)
2. That she was qualified for a job for which the employer was seeking applicants
3. That, despite her qualifications, she was rejected
4. That, after the rejection, the position remained open and the employer continued to seek applicants from persons with the same qualifications

If you cannot make these showings, then you won't even get to go to trial; the judge will throw out the case before it ever reaches a jury. Once a plaintiff does make these showings, however, the law requires the employer to present evidence of why the employee failed to get the job. Otherwise, the employer automatically loses the case.

After the employer has presented such evidence, the court battle begins. The two sides seek to prove to the jury which explanation, the employer's or the employee's, is more plausible. In certain cases, however, the employer need not even get this far: if the employer has discriminated against an employee but it is due to the actual requirements of the job itself (for example, if a casting director is attempting to hire an actor to play a twenty-year-old college student and considers only actors who could plausibly pass for that age), then the law no longer regards the discrimination as illegal, and the judge will dismiss the suit.

Bringing an employment discrimination suit is therefore not only expensive but also a very risky proposition. This is particularly true when the employee is attempting to convince the court to break new legal ground—to protect, for example, someone who was fired not entirely on the basis of a discriminatory motive, but rather based on some combination of legitimate and illegitimate motives, or to protect someone discriminated against on the basis of a category not directly covered by the statutes, such as when an employer discriminates against an employee based on her weight.

Weight Discrimination

If you believe you have been the victim of unlawful weight discrimination, there are several legal options available to you. You may file suit under (1) Title VII (2) the Rehabilitation Act and the Americans with Disabilities Act (ADA), or (3) a state or local ordinance such as Michigan's Elliot Larsen Civil Rights Act.

TITLE VII

While the Civil Rights Act of 1964 (Title VII, 42 U.S.C. §2000 et seq.) establishes basic federal law on employment discrimination, it does not identify weight as a protected characteristic. However, the differential application of weight standards to members of protected classes (such as classes defined by age or gender) *may* constitute unlawful discrimination under Title VII. For example, in *Gerdom v. Continental Airlines Inc.*, the court determined that the airline's weight restriction program treated employees differently based on sex because it was designed to apply only to females, and "it was not merely slenderness, but slenderness of female employees which the employer considered critical." The airline argued it had a marketing strategy that required flight attendants to be attractive and that a slender female was a bona fide occupational qualification. The court rejected this argument holding that customer preference unrelated to the ability to do the job cannot justify discriminatory policies.

If you believe that you have been discriminated against because of your weight and you believe that discrimination was directly linked to your age or gender (or other protected-class characteristic), you should consider filing a Title VII claim with the EEOC and/or contacting a lawyer.

REHABILITATION ACT AND THE AMERICANS WITH DISABILITIES ACT (ADA)

The Rehabilitation Act and the ADA provide protection against employment discrimination if a person can establish that he or she is an individual with a disability within the meaning of the acts. This includes anyone who has a physical disability that substantially limits one or more "major life activities" of the individual. The EEOC defines "major life activities" as "functions such as caring for oneself, performing manual tasks, walking, seeing, hearing, speaking, breathing, learning and working." According to this regulation, obesity will not be considered as a disability except in "rare circumstances" (29 C.F.R. §1630.2).

It is important to note that simply being overweight is not considered a disability. While the line of demarcation between being considered overweight and obese must be considered on a case-by-case basis, it is generally accepted that when one's body weight is 100 percent or more over normal weight, one has a disability as defined by the EEOC. Note also that an obese individual is not protected by the ADA when that person is discriminated against on some other basis, such as her appearance. On the other hand, if an obese person is discriminated against by an employer because that employer regards her as substantially limited in one or more major life activities, that individual may be protected by the ADA even though he or she does not have a substantial limitation. In addition, if an obese person has a physiological disorder, such as hypertension or a thyroid disorder, that either causes or is caused by obesity, those physiological disorders are, by definition, disabilities.

If you believe that you have been discriminated against because of your obesity and/or your employer perceives you as being disabled as a result of your obesity, you should consider filing a claim with the EEOC under the Rehabilitation Act and the ADA and/or contacting a lawyer.

STATE OR LOCAL ORDINANCE

The state of Michigan, the District of Columbia, and the California cities of Santa Cruz and San Francisco explicitly prohibit discrimination on the basis of weight (regardless of whether one might be considered obese). If you live or work in one of these jurisdictions and believe that you have been discriminated against because of your weight, you should consider filing a complaint with either the EEOC or its local equivalent (FEPA) and/or consulting a lawyer.

For More Information

www.eeoc.gov

Provides everything you need to know about filing a complaint with the EEOC, as well as a great summation of the Age Discrimination in Employment Act of 1967 (ADEA) and concise explanations of when it might apply.

www.obesity.org

The American Obesity Association website focuses on changing public policy and perceptions about obesity. The site includes a wealth of information about obesity research, prevention, and treatment, as well as obesity discrimination and stigma.

www.employeeissues.com/age_discrimination.htm

A free resource for general information about employee rights in the United States. According to the site, "EmployeeIssues.com helps employees and employers to help themselves, to better understand U.S. employee rights."

MARRIAGE AND DIVORCE

Before getting married, lay the groundwork for having a successful marriage by discussing how the partnership will be and asking (and answering) each other's important questions. Include such financial questions as:

1. How will the income that both parties receive be handled every year?
2. Will you file separate or joint tax returns?
3. How will the monthly expenses be paid? Equally or on some percentage basis?
4. How will credit cards be handled? Will they be in a single spouse's name or joint?
5. Is there a personal business involved? What will happen to it should there be a divorce?
6. If one spouse helps another through school, how will that spouse be compensated if a divorce occurs?
7. Whose house will you live in? How will the other spouse be compensated for using his or her home? Will you share the proceeds if the other property is sold?
8. If either spouse inherits anything during the marriage, how will it be treated?
9. If you decide to purchase any new property while married, how will it be titled and how will it be paid for?
10. How will each spouse's funds be distributed in case either party dies during the marriage?
11. Will the house be sold if either party dies, or will the surviving spouse be able to live there until he or she dies or remarries?

12. Will either party pay alimony or support in case of a divorce or separation?
13. Will any children be living with you at any time? If so, who pays their expenses and handles their care?
14. How will family holidays be spent?

Other great questions and ideas can be found in books like these:

- *101 Things I Wish I Knew When I Got Married: Simple Lessons to Make Love Last,* by Linda Bloom and Charlie Bloom
- *1001 Questions to Ask Before You Get Married,* by Monica Mendez Leahy
- *Don't You Dare Get Married Until You Read This! The Book of Questions for Couples,* by Corey Donaldson
- *The Hard Questions: 100 Essential Questions to Ask Before You Say "I Do,"* by Susan Piver
- *The Marital Compatibility Test: Hundreds of Questions for Couples to Answer Together,* by Susan Adams
- *Getting Ready for Marriage Workbook: How to Really Get to Know the Person You're Going to Marry,* by Jerry D. Hardin and Dianne C. Sloan

Prenuptial Agreements

To provide a framework for complete and enforceable premarital agreements the following states have adopted the Uniform Pre-Marital Agreement Act: Arizona, Arkansas, California, Connecticut, Delaware, the District of Columbia, Hawaii, Idaho, Illinois, Indiana, Iowa, Kansas, Maine, Mississippi, Montana, Nebraska, Nevada, New Mexico, North Carolina, North Dakota, Oregon, Rhode Island, South Dakota, Texas, Utah, Virginia, West Virginia, Wisconsin.

Financial planner David Latko, author of *Financial Strategies for Today's Widow: Coping with the Economic Challenges of Losing a Spouse,* offers this advice on prenups:

1. Both parties should have their own lawyer to advise them on the merits of the legal agreement.

2. Both parties must give complete disclosure about what assets they have before the marriage. If either party tries to withhold assets, a judge could later void the whole contract or claim fraud.

3. Nothing can be oral. Everything must be in writing, with the final agreement signed by both parties. Some states will require your signatures to be notarized.

4. If you decide to go ahead with a prenuptial agreement, have the lawyers videotape the signing. This way, no one can later claim they were coerced.

5. Don't make the agreement too lopsided for one side or the other. A judge may look very unfavorably on this at a later date.

6. Have the document signed well before the wedding date. Courts hate to see a prenuptial signed on the Friday before the Saturday wedding. It makes it look like a last-minute decision that neither party had time to fully contemplate.

Wills

MAKING A WILL

One of the most important and powerful privileges we possess is the ability to specify the new owners of our property when we die. Even so, surveys reveal that between 60 and 75 percent of Americans die without having written a will. Numerous explanations have been offered for this, such as a reluctance to contemplate one's own mortality, a general lack of time, and just plain indifference. The fact is, though, if you fail to make a will before your death, the state (in its "infinite" wisdom) will determine who gets your property—and a judge may decide who will raise your children. Writing a will empowers you to make these decisions yourself.

IS A BASIC WILL ENOUGH?

For the most part, if you are under age fifty and don't expect to leave property valuable enough to be subject to estate taxes, you can probably get away with making just a basic will. As you get older and acquire more assets, you may want to refine your plan.

Here are a few examples of real-life situations where a basic will is probably sufficient.

- Jane, a widow with three grown children, owns property with a net worth of $275,000. She creates a will leaving all her property equally to the children. She indicates that if any child dies before her, that child's share is to be divided equally between the surviving children.
- Elizabeth is a single mother with two young children. Though she's not on great terms with her ex-husband, he's a decent father and pays child support more or less on time. Elizabeth's will leaves all her property equally to her children. Because she does not want her ex-husband managing money left to her children if she dies, she uses her will to appoint her sister Rhonda to manage each child's property until that child turns eighteen.
- Bob and Susan, in their late twenties, own property with a net worth of $110,000. They have one small child. Each prepares a will leaving all his or her property to the other. If they die at the same time, the couple's child is to receive all their property. Bob and Susan agree that Bob's brother will care for the couple's child and manage the property until the child turns eighteen.

WILL I AVOID PROBATE WITH A BASIC WILL?

Probably not. If you leave anything greater than a small amount of property through a will, a proceeding in probate court will likely be necessary after your death. (Probate involves inventorying and appraising the property, paying debts and taxes, and distributing the remainder of the property according to the will.) Although the process varies from state to state, probate can take six months or a year and consume 3 to 5 percent of your estate in lawyers' and court fees. Moreover, your beneficiaries will probably get little or nothing until probate is complete.

Even so, if you need only a basic will, you have little reason to concern yourself now with probate. If you are relatively young and healthy and you don't have a mountain of money, your real concern should be to make legal arrangements for the unlikely event that you will die suddenly and unexpectedly. You almost certainly have time to come up with a plan for avoiding probate later.

DO I NEED MORE THAN A BASIC WILL?

If one of the following applies to your situation, then you probably need something more than a basic will:

- You have children from a previous marriage and you fear there could be a dispute between them and your current spouse.
- You have a child with a special need that you wish to attend to in your estate plan.
- You anticipate owing estate tax when you or your spouse dies.
- You suspect someone might challenge your will, claiming that you were not of sound mind when making it, or that the will was born of fraud or duress.
- You want to have control over what happens to your assets after death—for example, you want to leave some property in trust for your child, and have it go to your grandchildren when your child passes.

Steps to get started on your will

1. Make a list of what property you want included in your will. Your significant assets should be listed. Also list other items

you want to leave that you are not going to include in your will and which will be left by other methods.

2. If you are married, each spouse must make his or her own will. If you and your spouse both have your names on the title to something you own, you each own half an interest. If an item you own doesn't have a title document, in general you own it if you paid for it or if you received it as a gift. Property inherited by one spouse alone is separate property, and if the property is owned by one spouse before the marriage, that too is his/her separate property. It is virtually impossible to cut your spouse out of your will. In most states, there are laws that allow a surviving spouse to take a certain portion or percentage of the deceased spouse's estate if he or she was not taken care of in the will.

3. In most states, getting divorced automatically revokes a will, which means you need to make a new will, and especially if you get remarried. Your new will should explicitly revoke your old one, to be safe.

4. Choose whom you want to leave your assets to. You should also choose contingent beneficiaries (alternatives), in case your first-choice beneficiaries do not survive you. Only very close relatives, such as surviving spouses, children, or grandchildren, can ever claim a right to an inheritance.

5. Choose an executor. An executor is the person whom you want to carry out the terms of your will. Make sure that you choose someone who is willing to serve as an executor and notify that person that you want to choose him or her. It is common to name your spouse or child as executor, but you can name someone else besides family. An executor can accept or decline the responsibility. An executor can also resign at any time. You can name an alternative in the will in case these scenarios arise. If an alternative is not named, the court will appoint an executor. An executor gets paid for this duty.

6. Choose a guardian for your children if they are under

eighteen years of age. A guardian will help raise them if the other parent is unable to do so.

7. Arrange for someone to manage your children's property. If you don't do it, the court will do it for you if the children are under eighteen.

8. You can leave a trust for your children. Your will names a trustee who handles the money and property for the child until the child reaches the age of inheritance that you specify in the document. If you leave a trust and the beneficiary of the trust is already at the age of inheritance you named in the document, the trust never comes into being and the child can inherit. A trustee must act in the best interest of the child and according to your written instruction.

9. You must have at least two witnesses watch you sign your will. They must also sign the will, and the will needs to be notarized.

10. Finally, make sure you store your will safely but accessibly; your executor should be able to easily find the will when that time arrives.

Things you can't leave in your will

• Property you hold in joint tenancy, tenancy by the entirety, or community property with right of survivorship. This is because this type of property is jointly owned with your spouse or another, and at your death your share automatically passes to the surviving co-owner. The only time a provision in your will leaving this property to someone else would be valid is if all co-owners died simultaneously.

• Property you've transferred to a living trust (see page 219).

• Life insurance proceeds for which you've already named a beneficiary.

• Pension plans, IRAs, 401(k)s, or other types of retirement plans. In those situations, the beneficiary is named on the forms provided by the account administrator.

• Stocks or bonds called TOD—transfer on death—for which

there is a beneficiary. To change the beneficiary you must contact the brokerage firm directly.

• If you want the money in a POD—payable on death—account to go to a different beneficiary than was already named, go to the bank to fill out the form.

When you need to or will want to change your will

• You get married.
• You get divorced.
• You are unmarried but have a partner—your partner will not get anything if you do not include him or her in the will.
• You have a new baby.
• You get remarried and have stepchildren. Stepchildren have a legal right to inherit from you only if you legally adopt them. If you don't adopt them and want to leave them property in your will, you need to write them into your will.
• You acquire new or substantial assets.
• You move from a community property state to a common-law property state.

> • *Community property state:* Money earned by either spouse during marriage and all property bought with those earnings are considered community property, equally owned by both spouses. This includes debts incurred during marriage. The surviving spouse receives the deceased spouse's property at death unless a will says otherwise. You can still own separate property if you are married in these states. Spouses don't have to follow these rules; it is a more flexible system. If they choose, they can sign a written agreement that makes some or all community property the separate property of one spouse, or vice versa.
> • *Common-law property state:* If only your name is on the deed, registration document or other title paper, it's yours. You are free to leave your property to whomever

you choose, subject to your spouse's right to claim a certain share of your estate after your death. If you and your spouse both have your names on the title, you each own a half interest. Your freedom to give away or leave that half interest depends on how you and your spouse share ownership.

- You decide that you want to remove from your will a person you named as a beneficiary.

AVOIDING PROBATE WITH A LIVING TRUST

People often work hard and save money not only because they want to raise their own standard of living but also because they want to leave something behind for their children. Understandably, they don't want a substantial portion of their money to be eaten up by probate lawyers' fees.

That is where living trusts can be useful. A living trust is a device in which you hold property as a "trustee," and your surviving family members can transfer your property quickly and easily, without probate (and without probate fees). The bottom line is that more of the property you leave goes to the people you want to inherit it.

IS A BASIC LIVING TRUST SUFFICIENT IN MOST CASES?

Unless you expect to owe federal estate tax at your death or your spouse's, a basic living trust to avoid probate is probably all the trust you need. (Fewer than 2 percent of estates—those worth more than $2 million—owe estate tax.)

Note: A married couple can use one basic living trust to handle both co-owned property and the separate property of either spouse.

HOW TO CREATE A BASIC LIVING TRUST

To create a basic living trust, you create a document called a declaration of trust. You name yourself as trustee (the person in charge of the trust property). If you create a trust jointly with your spouse, you will be co-trustees.

Then you transfer ownership of some portion or the entirety of your property to yourself as trustee. For example, you might sign a deed transferring your home from yourself to yourself "as trustee of the Mary Johnson Revocable Living Trust dated June 18, 2006." Because you're the trustee, you don't give up any control over the property you put in trust.

In the declaration of trust document, you name the parties you want to inherit trust property after your death. You can change those choices if you want; you can also revoke the trust altogether if you wish.

WHEN YOU DIE

When you die, the person you named in the trust document to take over—the successor trustee—transfers ownership of trust property to the parties you want to receive it. Most of the time, the successor trustee can handle the whole thing in a few weeks with some simple paperwork. No probate court proceedings are required.

FOR MORE INFORMATION

www.abanet.org/rppt/public

On this site, the American Bar Association provides answers to the most common questions about the estate planning process, probate and administration of estates, transfer taxes and tax planning for your assets, and disability planning.

www.aarp.org/money/financial_planning

This estate planning guide on the AARP's site provides a wealth of information about wills, trusts, and related issues such as "power of attorney" and probate. It also provides helpful links to further information.

www.nolo.com

Nolo is a site aimed at providing do-it-yourself legal solutions for consumers and small businesses. Since 1971, Nolo has offered affordable, plain-English books, forms and software on a wide range of legal issues, including wills, estate planning, retirement, elder care, personal finance, taxes, housing, real estate, divorce, and child custody. Nolo also offers materials on human resources, employment, intellectual property, and starting and running a small business.

www.lawyers.com

This site provides state-specific estate planning information as well as contact information for estate planning attorneys near you.

Divorce

Since divorce laws are different in every state, what follows are the most common errors women make in divorce. For more specific information discuss your case with your lawyer.

WHAT TO DO

When faced with the difficult situation of divorce, it is important to be overprepared.

1. Do your homework. Know the laws, know your assets, know what to expect. There is an abundance of websites and legal resources out there for divorcing couples.
2. Consider mediation. The less you fight your battles in court, the better for both you and your wallet.
3. Do your best to stay calm and act logically. Understand that divorce is a long and frustrating process. Most of the biggest mistakes in divorces happen as a result of frustration and emotion. Meditate, vent to your family and friends, or go for a run to blow off steam . . . but do *not* allow your frustration to get the better of you.

4. Know what you have. Go through your household records, find anything with your name on it or anything that was acquired jointly, and make a list of all these items, with financial institution name, address, account number, balance, interest rate, etc. Knowing exactly what is at stake financially will help preclude surprises later.

5. Know what you need and want. Do a realistic analysis of what you need to live on, then do a realistic analysis of what you want out of the divorce. If you don't know what you want, how can you ask for it?

6. Know what is going to be asked of you by lawyers and courts, mostly about your financial history and roles in your marriage. To this end, get your finances together, pay down your debts, and know your credit history and income. You should also figure out how much time and money you lost in caring for children (i.e., time taken off and salary lost for part-time work).

WHAT NOT TO DO

In divorce, knowledge trumps emotion, an important lesson that should not be learned the hard way. Here are some emotion-based moves you should avoid.

1. Do not transfer, assign, borrow against, conceal, or in any way dissipate or dispose of any marital property without the consent of your spouse.

2. Do not cancel any insurance policy that covers either your spouse or your children or that names your spouse or the children as beneficiaries.

3. Do not harass, threaten, or abuse your spouse and do not make disparaging remarks about your spouse to or in the presence of the children or to your spouse's employer.

4. Do not relocate children outside the state, or more than 100 miles from the home you've shared with your spouse, except

if you fear physical abuse against either yourself or the children. Most courts see behavior like this as irrational and uncooperative and will tend to favor the other side if you engage in it. There are even states where this behavior is illegal; it remains to be seen whether legislation will effectively limit such irrational behavior.

FIRST SIX THINGS TO DO IF YOU'RE FILING FOR DIVORCE

Make careful, logical steps toward a divorce settlement.

1. Get all financial records, including receipts, check registers, canceled checks, and tax returns (personal and business), and either copy them or get them out of the house to a location under your control. Don't incur any more liabilities with your spouse except to pay taxes. Put away your pen and shut your mouth (loose lips sink ships).
2. Since this is going to be about money, plan in advance and, if you can, start socking it away from any source possible. Get as many accounts as possible in your name alone, or withdraw at least half of the funds. Put it in a shoebox if necessary. Avoid issues that require his signature. Get valuables and separate property out of the house if possible—replace real jewelry with copies if necessary.
3. Get what you can copied off the computer, including e-mails, financial statements, Excel documents, etc. You never know where this could lead. If you can't get the necessary password(s), then you need to hire a professional firm to get data off the computer. This is especially true if a girlfriend (or boyfriend) is in the picture. Go through his car and office if possible.
4. Organize a support group.
5. If parenting is an issue, become a supermom and don't let him do the caregiving, transportation, etc.
6. Try to sweet-talk him into signing property over to you.

FOUR THINGS YOU MUST ASK YOUR ATTORNEY

This assumes your attorney has been thoroughly checked out. Don't find an attorney in the phone book. Ask someone who did well in their divorce.

1. What do you want me to do that I haven't done?
2. What will you do to protect me and to get him out of the house?
3. Who pays for what and who selects experts? Send me to your financial person.
4. What is the worst I can expect?

MISTAKES WOMEN MAKE WHEN FILING FOR DIVORCE

There are a few mistakes that you *must* avoid.

1. Sleeping with your divorce attorney.
2. Telling your spouse about your extramarital love life or boyfriends or girlfriends. There are some counselors out there who want you to have a cathartic experience. Don't. Deny, deny, deny unless under oath. Don't even tell your best friend. No sex when the children are in the home, no overnight visitors.
3. Believing that your soon-to-be ex will keep your best interests in mind. He won't. Neither will his friends or family.
4. Not planning for the worst. For example, don't break up with a new boyfriend until you get the case resolved. The boyfriend could become your soon-to-be ex's best friend and witness.
5. Leaving a paper trail. Pay cash and lose the receipts unless your attorney tells you to do otherwise in order to establish your need for maintenance.

6. Computers, e-mail, and phones are not your friends—
   remember, anything electronic can be discovered.

CAVEATS

1. Anybody can get your cell phone records if they try hard
   enough: they are not private.
2. Find out if your spouse is using two cell phones. It may be a
   way to prove he has a girlfriend.
3. All new phones have GPS on them so they can be tracked.
   You can even tell which cell tower a caller used. Authorities
   use this GPS feature to track lost hikers, kidnappers, etc. You
   can no longer activate a non-GPS phone.
4. Don't get involved in an actual or faux Internet romance.
   Your spouse may be reading and copying your e-mails
   without your knowledge. Courts are skeptical of defining this
   kind of e-mail as merely innocent fantasizing, or day-
   dreaming or whatever you want to call it.
5. Change your e-mail password immediately and keep
   changing it on a regular basis. Avoid using wireless devices
   for confidential transmissions unless you have a really good
   firewall. Avoid using a laptop; it is too easy for it to be stolen.
   Copy your data to a secure backup device or securely stored
   removable media regularly, and then erase what's on your
   computer (but remember that simply deleting data does not
   mean that they cannot be recovered; there are programs
   available to make files truly unrecoverable).

FOR MORE INFORMATION

www.divorcenet.com

DivorceNet is an excellent resource, offering state-specific articles, an
online community, and a nationwide directory of divorce lawyers, me-
diators, and financial professionals.

www.womansdivorce.com

This site is dedicated to helping women take control of their divorce by providing comprehensive information on the legal, financial, and emotional aspects of divorce, as well as articles about starting over.

www.ivillage.com

A great resource for women covering all aspects of divorce—e.g., advice on how to cope emotionally, financially, and legally. Just go to the home page and type "divorce" into the search bar.

www.child-support-collections.com

This free site is designed to help you understand your state's child support collection laws and assist you in learning how to go about collecting past due or back child support payments (possibly with interest). Use the online arrearage calculator to figure out the approximate amount of back support you can collect.

DOMESTIC VIOLENCE

First and foremost, if you have been abused, you are not to blame. You are not the cause of another person's violent behavior. Sometimes a woman is not sure if she is the victim of abuse. Maybe you haven't been seriously injured. Maybe you haven't been hit at all. But if your partner does things that make you afraid or keeps you from friends or family, you may be a victim of abuse.

Warning Signs of Domestic Violence

You may be in an abusive relationship if your partner:

- *Keeps you from seeing friends and relatives*
- *Calls you names and humiliates you in front of others*
- *Grabs, pulls, or pushes you or hits you in places where the bruises won't show*

- *Threatens to harm or kill you, your children, your family, or your pets*
- *Forces you to have sex or do sexual things that make you uncomfortable*
- *Accuses you of flirting or cheating*
- *Shows you weapons or destroys things to scare you*
- *Threatens to have you deported*
- *Takes away your house or car keys*
- *Prevents you from working*

Offering Help

If you know or suspect that someone is in a violent relationship, don't be afraid to offer help—it just might save someone's life. Peace at Home, Inc., recommends some basic steps you can take to help someone who may be in an abusive relationship:

- *Approach them in a non-blaming way.*
- *Acknowledge that it is difficult and scary to talk about domestic violence.*
- *Discuss how abuse is based on power and control.*
- *Support by being a good listener.*
- *Ask if she's reported the assault to the police or gone to the hospital.*
- *Provide information and numbers of emergency services and legal advice.*
- *Inform her about legal protection that is available.*
- *Plan how to get out safely from the relationship.*

Victim's Rights

In order to inform abuse victims of their rights and to answer many questions they may not have thought to ask, many states provide a "Notice of Victim's Rights." Here is an example of one, issued in Johnson County, Indiana:

- A victim has the right to be treated with fairness, dignity, and respect throughout the criminal justice process.
- A victim has the right to be informed, upon request, when a person who is accused of committing or convicted of committing a crime perpetrated directly against the victim, is released from custody, or has escaped. This includes release or escape from mental health facilities.
- A victim has the right to have the victim's safety considered in determining release from custody of a person accused of committing a crime against the person.
- A victim has the right to information, upon request, about the disposition of the criminal case involving the victim or conviction, sentence, and release of a person accused of committing a crime against the victim.
- A victim has the right to be heard at any proceeding involving sentence or post-conviction release decision. A victim's right to be heard may be exercised at the victim's discretion, through an oral or written statement, or submission of a statement through audio- or videotape.
- A victim has the right to make a written or oral statement for use in preparation of the pre-sentence report. The victim also has the right to read pre-sentence reports relating to the crime committed against the victim in order that the victim can respond to the pre-sentence report.
- A victim has the right to confer with a representative of the prosecuting attorney's office after a crime allegedly committed against the victim has been charged; before the trial of a crime allegedly committed against a victim, and before any disposition of a criminal case involving the victim.

This right applies in any of the following situations:

- The alleged felony was directly committed against the victim.
- The alleged felony or misdemeanor was an offense against the

person, which includes the crimes of Battery, Domestic Battery, Aggravated Battery, Battery by body waste, Criminal recklessness, Intimidation, Harassment, Invasion of privacy, or Pointing a firearm, and the alleged felony or misdemeanor was committed against the victim by a person who is or was a spouse of the victim, is or was living as if a spouse of the victim, or has a child in common with the victim. (For other misdemeanors, a victim must file a request for notice, which includes a current telephone number and address.)

- A victim has the right to pursue an order of restitution and other civil remedies against the person convicted of a crime against the victim. A victim has the right to be informed of the victim's constitutional and statutory rights.
- A victim does not have the right to direct a prosecution.

Rape

Rape is any kind of compelled sexual activity that occurs without your consent. It can range from touching to penetration. Rape is a crime—even if you already know the person who attacked you, including a spouse, a co-worker, a friend, or a family member. It's a crime even if you didn't resist. It's a crime even if you were drinking, taking drugs, given drugs, or unconscious. Anyone—men, women, children, and the elderly—can be raped. Rape is never the fault of the victim.

Tips to avoid rape
- Secure your home with good lighting, effective door locks (deadbolts are best), and locks on windows and sliding glass doors.
- Have a good lock on your bedroom door and a phone in the room.
- Plug a lamp into an automatic timing device so that a light will be on when you get home, or leave a light or a radio on before you leave in the morning.

- If you rent, remember that the landlord is required by law to provide adequate lighting in hallways and locks on doors and windows.
- Be aware of places where someone could hide: laundry rooms, alcoves, dark hallways, stairwells, bushes, alleys, garages.
- Use only your first initial and last name on your mailbox and in phone book listings, or add "dummy names" to create an illusion. Keep up this illusion; never reveal to a phone caller or someone at the door that you are alone.
- Avoid giving out information about who is home and how long anyone is expected to be gone.
- Require proper identification of all repairmen, utility workers, and deliverymen. If you have any doubts, verify identification before allowing anyone inside: call the phone number of the company the telephone operator gives you, *not* the one he gives you.
- Stay at the front of the elevator, near the side control panel that has the alarm button. (Note: on some elevators, pushing the alarm button stops the elevator.)
- If someone gets on an elevator with you who seems suspicious, push other buttons so that the elevator will stop at all floors, and get off.
- If someone suspicious is already on the elevator, stay out of it. Wait for the next one.
- Lock all doors when entering and exiting your car. Have your keys handy as you approach, and check to see whether anyone seems to be underneath or crouched beside it.
- Be wary of someone hanging around a car next to yours. Wait until he enters a car or leaves.
- Before entering your car, check the front and back seats. Make sure your car's dome light is working.
- Open windows just enough for ventilation or to ask directions, but not enough so that someone could reach inside.
- If you suspect your car is being followed, honk your horn pe-

riodically, put on your hazard lights, and drive to the nearest police or fire station, open gas station, or all-night restaurant.

• If someone taps the rear end of your car while you're stopped or if someone flags you down, be cautious; it could be a setup.

• Avoid talking to strangers. If you feel you have to answer, do so simply but firmly. No one needs to be closer than three feet to be heard.

• If a stranger insists on speaking to you, keep moving toward your destination, and stay aware of what he's doing.

• Avoid being maneuvered into alleyways, doorways, or cars.

• If someone harasses you or tries to prevent you from leaving, make eye contact and tell him "Leave me alone" or "Go away" in a loud, controlled voice. Be resolute about what you want, and be as public as you can. Attract attention: if necessary, move into the street, shatter windows, knock things over, damage property. Yell "Fire!"

• Never wait to be grabbed; start yelling. A rapist often follows the same pattern, and disrupting that pattern might give you time to get away. Throw your books or packages into his face to distract him, and run.

• If you are physically accosted, your main objective must be to get away safely. The choice of whether or not to physically resist can be made only by you. Studies have shown that women who act quickly and confidently and use multiple strategies are much more likely to avoid being raped than women who only plead with an attacker or try to talk him out of it. Women who give in are often injured in addition to being raped.

• Target the attackers' vulnerable areas. Kick his kneecaps, elbow him in the face, strike with stiffened fingers into the hollow of the throat, knee him in the groin, or smash the heel of your hand hard up under his nose. Keep it up until he lets go of you. Keep yelling and run away toward a place of greater safety as soon as you are able.

DATE RAPE

Date rape is the most common form of rape—78 percent of rapes are committed by someone the victim is acquainted with. One in four women is expected to fall victim to rape or attempted rape before she reaches twenty-five, and three out of five rapes occur before a woman reaches age eighteen.

Date rape is forced sex between partners, dates, friends, or general acquaintances. Date rape can be forced both physically and emotionally—some emotional tactics include threats to reputation and threats to break up if the victim fails to comply. If a woman is intoxicated, she cannot consent to sex, and sex with her is legally rape.

There are certain "date rape" drugs that render the victim unconscious and limit memory—using these drugs is a federal crime with a possible twenty-year sentence. They go by many names, including Rohypnol, GHB, ActiveSeX, roofies, ruffies, Roche, R-2, rib, and rope. These drugs are odorless and tasteless and difficult to detect when in drinks or mixed with other drugs. While date rape drugs may be difficult to trace, evidence of intercourse is not, and in cases where use of these drugs is suspected, standards for evidence of rape are lower.

Signs that a sexual assault has taken place can include soreness or bruising in the anal or genital area, bruising, used condoms nearby, and traces of semen or vaginal fluids on clothes, the victim's body, or nearby furniture.

Tips to avoid date rape
• Trust your instincts. Take note of people who don't listen, don't respect your limits, display volatile anger, or do things that make you feel uncomfortable.
• Limit your use of intoxicants so you can be clear about what is happening.
• Know your sexual desires and determine the extent of sexual contact you want prior to going out. You have a right to set limits. Communicate them clearly; say "no" or "stop" loudly and clearly.

Protecting yourself from date rape drugs

• Don't accept open beverages from others who you do not know or do not trust.

• When in bars or clubs, always get your drink directly from the bartender and do not take your eyes off the bartender or your order.

• At parties, only accept drinks in closed containers.

• Never leave your drink unattended.

• Do not drink from open beverage sources such as punch bowls, pitchers, or tubs.

• Stay alert; if there is talk of date rape drugs or if others seem unusually intoxicated given what they have taken, leave the party or club immediately.

• Consider using Drink Safe, drink testing strips or coasters that change color when they come in contact with a date rape drug. The strips fit in your purse or pocket and can be used quickly and discreetly. To find out more about Drink Safe, visit www.drinksafetech.com.

WHAT TO DO IF YOU'VE BEEN RAPED

If you've been raped, the first thing you should do is get to a safe place, away from your attacker. Then you should go straight to a hospital emergency room. Do not change clothes or bathe before you go. Just get there as quickly as possible. You can call the police from the hospital.

WHAT HAPPENS AT THE HOSPITAL

The doctor in the emergency room will examine you for injuries and evidence. The attacker may have left behind clothing fibers, saliva, hairs, or semen that could lead to his identification. In most hospitals, a rape kit is used to help collect this evidence. A rape kit generally contains microscope slides and plastic bags for collecting and storing evidence. Samples of any evidence obtained may be used in court.

The doctor will then need to do a blood test. Female rape victims will be checked for pregnancy, and all rape victims are tested for sexually transmitted diseases. Cultures of the cervix may be sent to a lab to check for disease as well. The results of these tests will come back in several days or a few weeks. It's important for you to see your own doctor to review the results of these tests. If any of your results are positive, you'll need to talk with your doctor regarding treatment.

WHAT KIND OF TREATMENT YOU MIGHT NEED

If you take birth control pills or have an intrauterine device (IUD), the chances of your becoming pregnant are slim. If you don't take the pill, you may consider pregnancy prevention treatment. Pregnancy prevention consists of taking two pills when you first get to the hospital and two more pills twelve hours later. This treatment reduces the risk of pregnancy by 60 to 90 percent. This treatment may also lead to some nausea.

The chances of getting a sexually transmitted disease during a rape are about 5 to 10 percent. Your doctor can prescribe medicine for gonorrhea, syphilis, and chlamydia when you first get to the hospital. If you haven't already been vaccinated for hepatitis B, you should get that vaccination while you are at the emergency room. Then you'll get another vaccination in one month and a third in six months. The doctor will also talk to you about human immunodeficiency virus (HIV) infection. The risk of getting HIV from a rape is less than 1 percent, but if you want preventive treatment, you can take two medicines—zidovudine (brand name Retrovir) and lamivudine (brand name Epivir)—for four weeks.

WHAT ELSE YOU SHOULD KNOW ABOUT RAPE

The emotional impact of rape can be profound. You may experience any number of emotions, such as fear, rage, disbelief, anxiety, and guilt. About half of all people who are raped experience depression in the first year after the attack. You may have an upset stomach or feel nervous. Be sure to tell your doctor about any emotional, physical, or sexual problems you may be having, even if you don't think they're related to the rape.

For More Information

NATIONAL DOMESTIC VIOLENCE HOTLINE
800-799-SAFE
TTY: 800-787-3224

www.bwjp.org

Battered Women's Justice Project is a collaborative effort on civil and criminal justice responses to domestic violence. See the website, or call 800-903-0111.

www.endabuse.org

The Family Violence Prevention Fund is an organization dedicated to stopping domestic violence through education and political action. An active player in the national public policy arena, this organization helped develop the first comprehensive national legislation to address issues of violence against women—the Violence Against Women Act of 1994—and continues to serve as a reliable and respected resource to Congress and the executive branch.

www.ncadv.org

The National Coalition Against Domestic Violence serves as a national information and referral center for the general public, media, battered women and their children, and allied and member agencies and organizations. It has a strong track record of providing programs with information and technical assistance, and has promoted the development of innovative programs that address the special needs of all battered women.

www.rainn.org

The Rape, Abuse, and Incest National Network is a national hotline that connects callers with their closest rape crisis center. You can call them at 800-656-HOPE.

www.loveisnotabuse.com

Information and tools sponsored by Liz Claiborne, Inc., that men, women, children, teens, and corporate executives can use to learn more about the issue of domestic abuse and find out how they can help or get help.

www.pandys.org

Pandora's Aquarium, a free message board and chat room for rape and sexual abuse survivors, has been an online community since 1999. The first survivor message board of its kind, it remains one of the largest and most active, with more than 2,500 members, 200,000 archived posts, and 300 new posts each day. Its community includes a message board, chat room, and blogging feature.

BODY

If You're Pregnant

While there are many organizations and websites that offer advice and counseling to help pregnant women and girls make decisions about their pregnancies, nearly all are affiliated with religious or political groups that also work to make abortion illegal. Their counseling starts from the premise that abortion is an immoral act, against God, self, and child, that requires repentance and forgiveness for healing.

The last thing we need when we're making such a difficult choice is politics. So here are two sites that approach the decision with an understanding that each woman's situation is different, and offer help before, during, and after.

www.pregnancyoptions.info

This site provides unbiased information on pregnancy options, including pregnancy decision making, medical abortion with RU-486, surgical abortion, adoption, childbirth, parenting, and more. Put together by a group of people who deal with different aspects of pregnancy choices and believe that each woman must decide what is right for her situation, the site offers things to think about and ways to make important decisions, including a Pregnancy Options Workbook.

www.4exhale.org

Exhale is based not on shoulds but on what is and offers a free After-Abortion Talkline that provides emotional support, resources, and information. The talkline, at 866-4EXHALE (866-439-4253), is available to women and girls who have had abortions and to their partners, friends, allies, and family members. All calls are completely confidential, and counselors are nonjudgmental.

Common Questions About Contraception:

Can a pharmacist refuse to fill my birth control prescription?

In some cases, yes. In some states, officials have introduced "conscience clause" legislation that explicitly grants pharmacists the right to refuse to dispense even contraceptive drugs on moral grounds. For an updated accounting of "conscience clause" legislation in your state, go to www.ncsl.org/programs/health/ConscienceClauses.htm. To contact elected representatives and let them know what you think of "conscience clause" legislation, go to www.congress.org.

Should my prescription contraception be free if I have insurance coverage?

As with most prescriptions, there will likely be a co-pay requirement for your contraception. However, anti-discrimination law requires that contraception be covered in the same way as other comparable prescriptions.

What if my prescription is covered by my insurance but the co-pay seems excessive?

This may not be fair. According to a 2000 EEOC decision on this question, "Respondents [employers] must cover the expenses of prescription contraceptives to the same extent, and on the same terms, that they cover the expenses of the types of drugs, devices, and preventive care." This wording does not explicitly mention co-pays, but if there is a discrepancy in payment for birth control and other prescriptions, you should talk to your employer about this.

What are the differences between federal, state, and private insurance requirements for contraception?

Twenty-five states have contraceptive equity laws, which regulate insurance company plans to include prescription contraception. However, many of these states have "conscience clauses," which permit certain companies to deny coverage on moral grounds.

The federal laws apply to self-insured or state-insured employers.

How can I find out if my employer is self-insured?

You can ask your human resources director, benefits administrator, or supervisor. Self-insured companies are required to have fifteen or more employees and are subject to Title VII discrimination laws, just like companies that are not self-insured.

Does my state have a contraceptive equity law in place?

Your state law may or may not ensure that you get your contraception covered. If you need help finding out about whether your state law applies to you, contact your local Planned Parenthood affiliate.

For More Information

www.plannedparenthood.org

Each year, Planned Parenthood–affiliated health centers nationwide provide high-quality, affordable reproductive health care and sexual health information to nearly five million women, men, and teens. This site is a great source for reproductive health information, as well as information about where to find a clinic near you, links to accessing low-cost and emergency contraception, and up-to-date information regarding reproductive health and the law.

www.reproductiverights.org

The Center for Reproductive Rights examines legal issues surrounding contraceptive care in the United States, including discrimination against women by insurance companies that refuse to cover contraception. It also provides state-specific information regarding contraception equity laws and pending legislation affecting reproductive health.

www.now.org

The National Organization for Women site is an excellent source of information regarding women's rights in general, and women's reproductive health rights in particular.

ACKNOWLEDGMENTS

I can think of no one I'd rather work with on a project like this than Bruce Littlefield. He's the friend and compatriot that every woman (and every man) needs, and I am grateful for his kindness, his ideas, and his true friendship.

Putting together a book is a team effort, and I had an ace team of legal interns: Sari Goldmeer, Maura Kugelman, Karina Shpits, Michelle Witten, Andy Hoffman, Marina Bejarano, and Stephanie Petrak. We all had our eyes opened at the legal and social inequities women are dealt in this country.

Special thanks to all the women who filled out my survey with honesty and candor; and to the many others who told and trusted me with their stories.

My agent Todd Shuster at Zachary Shuster Harmsworth has been a great adviser and friend, as has the incredible team at Ballantine: Gina Centrello, Kim Hovey, Brian McLendon, Sarina Evan, Gene Mydlowski, Barbara Bachman, Penelope Haynes, Elana Bensoul, and especially Jane von Mehren, whose vision is as sharp as her pencil. She is the editor every writer should be so lucky to have.

At Fox: Iren Halperin, Gwen Marder, and Karen Corvelli, for making me look presentable; Roger Ailes, for giving me the chance; and Bill O'Reilly for providing the opportunity to present my point of view, even if it's not his.

To my children Jacob and Dani, I adore you; I'm honored to be your mom; and thank you for forgiving me for forgetting to turn in the baseball uniform and Brownie cookie money.

And to Mickey, thanks for your love and for making me laugh.

BIBLIOGRAPHY

More than three hundred women gave me their thoughts and opinions for this book. In addition, I consulted the following sources.

Chapter 1: EQUAL = EQUAL

Cox, Ana Marie. "Women Who Make the World Worse." *New York Times Book Review,* 15 January 2006.

Crawford, Darlisa. "Election Focus 2004: Women Voters in the 2004 Election." U.S. Department of State, 14 April 2004.

Davey, Monica. "Global Leaders, Women Still Fight Old Views." *New York Times,* 4 February 2006.

Dewar, Helen. "President, Senate Reach Pact on Judicial Nominations." *Washington Post,* 19 May 2004.

Dowd, Maureen. "Who's Hormonal? Hillary or Dick?" *New York Times,* 8 February 2006.

"Equality Now: Agents of Change." www.equalitynow.org Annual Report 2004.

Estrich, Susan. "Pregnancy." Creators Syndicate, 6 July 2006.

Fackler, Martin. "Japanese Princess Expects, and Many Hope (for a Boy)." *New York Times,* 8 February 2006.

Fox, Margalit. "Betty Friedan, Who Ignited Cause in 'Feminine Mystique,' Dies at 85." *New York Times,* 5 February 2006.

Gallagher, Maggie. "The World Friedan Made." *New York Post,* 10 February 2006.

Howe, Julia Ward. "Mother's Day Proclamation." 1870.

In Touch. "Oprah Nominated for President!" 20 February 2006.

Kagan, Elena. "Remarks on the Status of Women in the Legal Profession." Harvard Law School. 7 November 2005.

Newsweek. "How Women Lead." 24 October 2005.

Orin, Deborah. "Laura's Court Appeal: Surprises W. with Call for Woman." *New York Post*, 13 July 2005.

Polgreen, Lydia. "Liberia's Harvard-Trained 'Queen' Is Sworn In as Leader." *New York Times*, 17 January 2006.

Quindlen, Anna. "The Value of the Outsider." *Newsweek*, 24 October 2005.

Richards, Camden, and Lela Shephard. "Bush Administration Rolling Back Progress for Women and Girls." National Women's Law Center, 8 April 2004.

Rohter, Larry. "A Leader Making Peace with Chile's Past." *New York Times*, 15 January 2006.

Rohter, Larry. "What Is Missing in This Woman's Victory? Coattails." *New York Times*, 15 January 2006.

Rossi, Alice S. *The Feminist Papers: From Adams to de Beauvoir.* Columbia University Press, 1973.

Sciolino, Elaine. "Blow to French Patriarchs: Babies May Get Her Name." *New York Times*, 20 January 2005.

Smith, Kati Cornell. "Lil' Jail Time: Gets Off Easy as Judge Cites Martha." *New York Post*, 7 July 2005.

Warner, Judith. "The Parent Trap." *New York Times*, 8 February 2006.

Winik, Lyric Wallwork. "A Woman for President?" *Parade*, 19 February 2006.

Women's Campaign Fund. "Parties of Your Choice." Annual New York dinner, 7 March 2005.

Yafie, Roberta C. "Woman's Touch." *New York Post*, 18 January 2006.

Yafie, Roberta C. "One 'How-To' of Start Up: Female Intuition." *New York Post*, 18 January 2006.

Chapter 2: EQUAL PAY

Ash, Arlene, and Phyllis Carr. "Compensation and Advancement of Women in Academic Medicine: Is There Equity?" American College of Physicians, 2004.

Bosman, Julie. "Stuck at the Edges of the Ad Game." *New York Times*, 22 November 2005.

Campaign for America's Future. "Economic Security for Women and Children: What Will It Take?" 28 February 2001.

Friedan, Betty. "Judge Carswell and the 'Sex Plus' Doctrine." Testimony before the Senate Judiciary Committee, 1970.

Jacobs, Mindelle. "We've Come a Long Way, Baby; Feminists Have Made

Great Strides, but Mindelle Jacobs Says There's Still a Long Way to Go." *Toronto Sun,* 6 March 2005.

Myers, Betsy. "A Shortsighted President Shortchanges Women." *Boston Globe,* 10 April 2001.

Morris, Betsy. "How Corporate America Is Betraying Women." *Fortune,* 10 January 2005.

Quirk, Barbara. "We Can't Afford Apathy on Women's Issues." *Capital Times,* 20 July 2004.

The Economist. "Helping Women Get to the Top." 23 July 2005.

The Economist. "The Conundrum of the Glass Ceiling." 23 July 2005.

The Work and Family Legal Center. "A Better Balance." Fall 2005.

Tucker, Judith Stadtman. "Doing the Math on Earnings Inequality." U.S. Census Bureau Special Report.

Equal Pay Cases

Borne v. Haverhill Golf & Country Club (Massachusetts, 2003)

Corning Glass Works v. Brennan (Supreme Court, 1974)

Ortiz-Del Valle v. NBA (New York, 1999)

Schultz v. Wheaton Glass Co. (3rd Circuit Court of Appeals, 1970)

Wheatley and Grogan v. Wicomico County, Maryland (Supreme Court, 2006)

Chapter 3: SEXUAL HARASSMENT

Associated Press. "No Nudes Is Good Nudes." *Tulsa World,* 1 July 1998.

Associated Press. "Tanning Salon Ordered to Pay in Peeping Case." 16 September 2003.

Associated Press. "Adrian Tanning Salon Owner Ordered to Pay $50,000 to Woman He Videotaped." 11 August 2004.

Associated Press. "Ex–New York Rangers Cheerleader Accuses Management of Sexual Harassment." 18 October 2004.

Associated Press. "Using Peepholes Has Loopholes." 8 February 2005.

Associated Press. "Delegate to Seek Law Against Upskirt/Downblouse." 10 November 2005.

Bode, Nicole, et al. "Goin' Toe-to-Toe in Sex Suit Flap: Fired Execs and Isaiah Dueling in the Press." *Daily News,* 26 January 2006.

Campanile, Carl, and Dareh Gregorian. "Ranger Gal Ices Garden with Sex Suit." *New York Post,* 19 October 2005.

Crowley, Kieran, and Bill Hoffmann. "Sex Pol Wins." *New York Post,* 11 November 2005.

DCBA.org. "Facts About Women and the Law." October 1999.

DeMare, Carol. "Secretary Asks $9M in Harassment Case." Albany *Times Union,* 5 August 2005.

Federal Communications Commission. "Understanding Workplace Harassment." 21 April 2004.

Findlaw.com. "One in Five Americans Has Experienced Employment Discrimination, Says New Findlaw Survey." 20 July 2004.

Georgiades, William. "The Real Dirt." *New York Post,* 13 March 2005.

Ginsberg, Alex. "Hospital Sicko." *New York Post,* 20 June 2005.

Green, Leonard. " 'Source' of Sex Harass." *New York Post,* 12 April 2005.

Hayek, Eve. "Report Shatters Myths About U.S. Women's Equality." 1 October 2005. National Organization for Women.

Knight, Dana. "Sexual Harassment and Bias Complaints Surging Among the Young." *Indianapolis Star,* 14 August 2005.

Lewis, Diane. "Working It Out." *Boston Globe,* 16 January 2000.

Londono, Ernesto. "Mooning Deemed 'Disgusting' but No Crime in Md." *Washington Post,* 4 January 2006.

Meyer, Dick. "Whistleblowing in the Wind." CBSNews.com, 1 June 2006.

National Center for Victims of Crime. "Video Voyeurism Laws." 26 February 2006.

National Conference of State Legislatures. "50 State Summary of Breastfeeding Laws." 25 October 2005.

New York State, Office of the Governor. "Governor Signs Video Voyeurism Legislation into Law." Press release, 23 June 2003.

Newsweek. "Policing Video Voyeurs: The Feds join the battle against perverts with cameras." 14 February 2005.

O'Keeffe, Michael. "Trading Shot." New York *Daily News,* 26 January 2006.

Playboy, interview of then-governor Jimmy Carter. November 1976.

Sandomir, Richard. "Hockey Cheerleader Is Suing the Garden." *New York Times,* 19 October 2004.

Selvin, Molly. "Law Spurs a Boom in Harassment Training: Consultants Can Charge $1,500 to $3,000 a Day to Help Companies Comply with New State Rules." *Los Angeles Times,* 6 August 2005.

Sexual Harassment Litigation Reporter. "Court Allows Privacy Claims Based on Rest Room Camera." 5 April 2005.

Smith, Kati Cornell. "$10 Mil Sex Suit vs. Top Dog." *New York Post,* 12 December 2005.

Sramcik, Tim. "Heading Off Harassment: Prevention Is the Best Medicine to Stop Workplace Harassment; Employee Relations." *Motor Age*, June 2005.

Stratton, Jim. "Ex-Deputy Files Sexual-Harassment Suit." *Orlando Sentinel*, 5 August 2005.

The Smoking Gun. "Pump Judge Gets Popped: Charge Former Oklahoma Jurist with Exposing Himself on Bench." 26 February 2006.

University of Oregon Counseling and Testing Center. "Sexual Harassment Myths and Realities." 2004.

Weiss, Gail Garfinkel. "A Physician's Guide to Antidiscrimination Law: Federal EEOC Requirements—and Their Local Equivalents—Govern Hiring, Firing, and Everything in Between; Equal Employment Opportunity Commission." *Medical Economics*, 22 July 2005.

Whistleblower.org. "National Whistleblower Center Proposes Legislation to Restore Whistleblower Rights." 4 July 2006.

Sexual Harassment Cases

Cleveland Board of Education v. Lafleur (Supreme Court, 1974)
Green v. Waterford Board of Education (Supreme Court, 1974)
Jenson v. Eveleth Taconite Co. (8th Cir. Minn. 1997)

Chapter 4: PREGNANCY

American Psychological Association. "New Longitudinal Study Finds That Having a Working Mother Does No Significant Harm to Children." News release, 18 February 1999.

Associated Press. "Former National Employees Win $1.9 Million." 16 July 1987.

Armour, Stephanie. "Pregnant Workers Report Growing Discrimination." *USA Today*, 17 February 2005.

Campanile, Carl. "$100M Bias Suit—Gal Slaps Drug Giant." *New York Times*, 18 February 2005.

Catholic World News. "Actress Wins Pregnancy Discrimination Lawsuit." 23 December 1997.

CBS News.com. "More Pregnancy Bias Complaints." 7 October 2003.

Childbirth Solutions. "'Don't Work in the Dark': Know Your Rights." www.childbirthsolutions.com, 26 February 2006.

Cooper, Cynthia L. "Pregnant and Punished." Ford Foundation, 2003.

Crittenden, A. *The Price of Motherhood: Why the Most Important Job in the World Is Still the Least Valued.* Metropolitan Books, 2001.

Doyle, John, et al. "My Little Angel: 'DWI' Dad Wails over Girl He Fatally Ran Down: Kin." *New York Post*, 20 September 2005.

Equal Employment Opportunity Commission. "Celebrating the 40th Anniversary of Title VII." 23 June 2004.

Friedman, Dana E. "Workplace Flexibility: A Guide for Companies." Familiesandwork.org, 26 February 2006.

Fursman, Lindy. "Ideologies of Motherhood and Experiences of Work: Pregnant Women in Management and Professional Careers." Center for Working Families, University of California, Berkeley, 2002.

Harvard Women's Law Journal. "Beyond the Maternal Wall: Relief for Family Caregivers Who Are Discriminated Against on the Job." 2003.

Human Rights Watch. "Mexico's Maquiladoras: Abuses Against Women Workers." 17 August 1996.

Kamen, Al. "Court Upholds Pregnancy Leave Laws; Special Benefits for Women Rule No Violation of Rights Statutes." *Washington Post*, 14 January 1987.

Oakland Tribune. "Bias Suit Captivates Capitol." 1 March 2003.

Paltrow, Lynn M. "Do Pregnant Women Have Rights?" www.alternet.org, 22 April 2004.

Pechman, Louis. "Appearance Based Discrimination." Berke-Weiss & Pechman, LLP, New York City, 26 February 2006.

Quirk, Barbara. "We Can't Afford Apathy on Women's Issues." *Capital Times*, 20 July 2004.

Ramirez Jr., Domingo. "Single Mom Files Pregnancy Discrimination Case." Fort Worth *Star-Telegram*, 23 April 2005.

Roberts, Penny Brown. "Jury Deliberating in Family-Leave Lawsuit." *The Advocate*, 29 October 2004.

Saul, Stephanie. "12 Women File Bias Suit Against Large Drug Maker." *New York Times*, 18 February 2005.

Schneider & Wallace, Attorneys at Law. "California Regents Approve $10.6 Million Class Action Settlement in Gender Discrimination Class Action Against Lawrence Livermore National Laboratory." San Francisco, California, 26 February 2006.

Shellenbarger, Sue. "Baby Blues: The Dangers of the Trend Towards Shorter Maternity Leaves." *Wall Street Journal*, 20 May 2004.

Stewart, Sean. "PDA, FMLA, and Beyond: A Brief Look at Past, Present and Future Sex Discrimination Laws and Their Effects on the Teaching Profession." Brigham Young University, 2003.

The Lawyer. "Retaining Employment Rights While on Maternity Leave." www.thelawyer.com, 26 February 2006.

Wiseman, Lesley J. "A Place for 'Maternity' in the Global Workplace: International Case Studies and Recommendations for International Labor Policy." *Ohio Northern University Law Review,* 2001.

Women's Law Journal. "Supreme Court Narratives on Equality and Gender Discrimination in Employment: 1971–2002," 10 April 2004.

Zack, Margaret. "Illegally Fired Receptionist Awarded $19,000 in Damages." Minnesota *Star-Tribune,* 1 September 1987.

Pregnancy Cases

Bainlardi v. SBC Warburg, Inc. (Southern District New York, 1998)

Board of Education v. LaFleur (Supreme Court, 1974)

Carr v. Barnaby's Hotel (App. Div. Five, 1994)

Carrington v. Frank (D. Nebraska, 1989)

Cerra v. East Stroudsburg Area School Dist. (Pennsylvania, 1971)

Communications Works of Am. v. Illinois Bell Telephone Co. (N.D. Ill., 1980)

Dukes v. Wal-Mart Stores (N.D. California, 2004)

EEOC v. Continuity Programs, Inc. (E.D. Michigan, 1993)

EEOC v. Hacienda Hotel (9th Circuit, 1989)

Jennifer Erickson v. Bartell Drug Co. (Washington, 2001)

Polly A. Gammon v. Precision Engineering Co. (Minnesota, 1987)

Green v. Waterford Bd. of Education (2nd Circuit, 1973)

Freda Leichter v. St. Vincent's Hospital, et al. (Southern District New York, 2001).

Maddox v. Grandview Care Center, Inc. (11th Circuit 1986)

In re Pan Am, World Ways (11th Circuit 1990)

Peralta v. Chromium Plating & Polishing Corp. (Eastern District New York, 2000)

Cynthia Quaranta v. Management Support (Arizona, 2003)

Jennie Sbrogna v. ChipCom Corp. (Massachusetts, 1997)

Schiffman v. Cimarron Aircraft Corp. (W.D. Oklahoma, 1985)

Shafrir v. Assoc. of Reform Zionists of Am. (Southern District New York, 1998)

Debbie Sherman v. AI/FOCS, Inc., (Massachusetts, 2000)

Tamimi v. Howard Johnson Co. (11th Circuit, 1987)

Kimberly Wilson v. Training Plus, Inc. (Kansas, 2003)

Rochelle Woodworth v. Concord Management (Ohio, 2000)

Chapter 5: AGE AND WEIGHT

Associated Press. "Obese Woman Angry That Doctor Advised Weight Loss." 24 August 2005.

Boston College Law Review. "Weighing In Against Obesity Discrimination." 1994.

Buffa, Denise. "Woman: I Was Sacked for Being 75." *New York Post,* 27 March 2006.

California Law Review. "Addressing the Problem of Weight Discrimination in Employment." January 2002.

Catholic University Law Review. "A Growing Problem: Why the Federal Government Needs to Shoulder the Weight." Winter 2005.

Fernandez, Elizabeth. "Exercising Her Right to Work." *San Francisco Chronicle,* 7 May 2002.

Goldberg, Carey. "Weight-Based Bias More Extensive Than Ever Before." *San Francisco Examiner,* 5 November 2000.

Gortmaker, Steven. "Social and Economic Consequences of Overweight in Adolescence and Young Adulthood." *New England Journal of Medicine,* October 1993.

Kolata, Gina. "Women Pay Price for Being Obese." *New York Times,* 30 September 1993.

Kuntzman, Gersh. "Casino Gals' Fat Chance." *New York Post,* 18 February 2005.

Lo, Danica. "How Not to Look Fat." *New York Post,* 28 November 2004.

Meece, Mickey. "Mind-Set: Only the Svelte Need Apply." *New York Times,* 22 March 2000.

Roe, Daphne A., and Kathleen R. Eickwort. "Relationships Between Obesity and Associated Health Factors with Unemployment Among Low Income Women." *Journal of the American Medical Women's Association,* 1976.

Saul, Stephanie. "Selling Dreams and Drugs." *New York Times,* 22 September 2005.

Sobel, Beth. "The New F-word." *New York Post,* 29 March 2005.

Zakrzewski, Karen. "The Prevalence of 'Look'ism in Hiring Decisions." *University of Pennsylvania Journal of Labor and Employment Law,* winter 2005.

Representative Age/Weight/Appearance Cases

Banks v. The Travelers Company (2nd Circuit, 1998)

Cassita v. Community Foods, Inc. (California, 1993)

Cook v. Rhode Island Department of Mental Health, Retardation and Hospitals (Rhode Island, 1994)
Craft v. Metromedia (8th Circuit, 1985)
Engstrand v. Pioneer Hi-Bred International, Inc. (Iowa, 1996)
Frank v. United Airlines (9th Circuit, 2000)
Gallo v. John Powell Chevrolet, Inc. (Pennsylvania, 1991)
Hazeldine v. Beverage Media, Inc. (New York, 1997)
Lamoria v. Sun Valley Manor, Inc. (Michigan, 1999)
Malarkey v. Texaco, Inc. (New York, 1992)
Yanowitz v. L'Oréal USA, Inc. (California, 2003)

Chapter 6: MARRIAGE

Associated Press. "Roe v. Wade for Men Suit Filed." 9 March 2006.
Adams, Susan. *The Marital Compatibility Test: Hundreds of Questions for Couples to Answer Together.* Addicus Books, 2002.
Eaton, Leslie. "A New Push to Loosen New York's Divorce Law." *New York Times,* 30 November 2004.
Haltzman, Scott. *The Secrets of Happily Married Men.* Jossey-Bass, 2005.
Kiplinger's. "Prenups for the Not So Rich and Famous." 10 April 2002.
Hardin, Jerry D., and Dianne C. Sloan. *Getting Ready for Marriage Workbook: How to Really Get to Know the Person You're Going to Marry.* Nelson Impact, 1992.
Latko, David. *Everybody Wants Your Money.* Collins, 2006.
Maldonado, Solangel. *U.C. Davis Law Review.* "Deadbeat or Deadbroke: Redefining Child Support for Poor Fathers." March 2006.
McAree, Dee. "Deadbeat Dads Face Ban on Procreation." *National Law Journal,* 10 June 2004.
Mendez, Monica. *1001 Questions to Ask Before You Get Married.* McGraw-Hill, 2004.

Marriage and Divorce Cases
Sherrer v. Sherrer (Supreme Court, 1948)
United States of America v. Sage (2nd Circuit, 1996)
Wendt v. Wendt (Connecticut, 1997)

Chapter 7: VIOLENCE AGAINST WOMEN

ABC News Law & Justice Unit. "Tears as Alleged Duke Rape Victim ID'd Suspects." 11 May 2006.

Anderson, Michelle J. "Understanding Rape Shield Laws." National Center for Victims of Crime, September 2004.

Becker Liu, Lara. "Fallen Angel: The Short, Tragic Life of Charkendra Baker, Part 2." *Rochester Democrat and Chronicle,* 15 August 2005.

Bolton, Michael. Speech on domestic violence. Michael Bolton Charities, Inc. April 2005.

Buel, Sarah M. "Access to Meaningful Remedy: Overcoming Doctrinal Obstacles in Tort Litigation Against Domestic Violence Offenders. *Oregon Law Review,* 2004.

Carter, Darla. "Preventing Sexual Assault: Students Can Protect Against Attacks." Louisville *Courier-Journal,* 11 April 2005.

Damon, Anjeanette. "Marshal Tracks Domestic Abuse Offenders." *Reno Gazette-Journal,* 14 February 2000.

de Kretser, Leela. "Victim Now a Victor: Abused Gal's Fight Title." *New York Post,* 23 August 2005.

Domestic Violence Services of Greater New Haven. "A Brief History of Domestic Violence Services." 2006.

Edelman, Susan. "Murder-by-Beau: 'Intimate' Slayings a Citywide Epidemic." *New York Post,* 26 September 2004.

Graham, Ginnie. "Doing Something About Crime: Stopping the Cycle of Domestic Violence." *Tulsa World,* 11 July 2004.

Greenhouse, Linda. "Women Lose Right to Sue Attackers in Federal Court." *New York Times,* 16 May 2000.

Henneberger, Melinda. "Calls to Spouse-Abuse Hotlines on the Rise." *New York Times,* 26 June 1994.

Kiewra, Karin. "Miscarriage of Justice: By Awarding Custody and Visitation Rights to Abusive Men, Family Courts Transgress the Rights of Women and Children." *Harvard Public Health Review,* winter 2005.

Letter from the president. Michael Bolton Charities, Inc. May 2005.

Lewin, Tamar. "The Simpson Case: The Syndrome; Case Might Fit Pattern of Abuse, Experts Say." *New York Times,* 19 June 2004.

Lithwick, Dahlia. "The Shield That Failed." *New York Times,* 8 August 2004.

Liz Claiborne, Inc. Policy on Domestic Violence. 5 March 2006. Available on www.loveisnotabuse.com.

Mongelli, Lorna, et al. "Cops Seek Beau of Slain Bx. Gal: Threatened to Kill Her if She Left Him." *New York Post,* 21 March 2005.

Namako, Tom, et al. "Mom's Protector: Gutsy 4-yr.-Old Girl Uses Broomstick to Fight off Crazed Dad." *New York Post,* 20 June 2005.

National Legal Research Group, Inc. "The Impact of Domestic Violence on Property Division in Divorce," Charlottesville, Virginia, 2004.

National Organization for Women. "VAWA Passes in Congress, Ready for President's Signature." www.now.org, 20 December 2005.

Neil, Martha. "Bryant Case Leads to Calls for Change in Rape-Shield Laws." *ABA Journal,* 6 August 2004.

Parks, Ann. "Top Court: Spouses Can Sue Each Other." Baltimore *Daily Record,* 13 August 2003.

"The Police Called It a Family Matter." Letter to the editor, *New York Times,* 30 June 1994.

Public Agenda (Ghana) *All African Global Media.* 15 August 2005.

Quindlen, Anna. "Public & Private: Remember Nicole Simpson." *New York Times,* 22 June 1994.

Resnik, Judith. "Asking About Gender in Courts." Binghamton University, summer 1996.

Smith, Devin. "Beastly Hubby Gets Cage: 4 Years for Torturing Wife Near Live Leopards." *New York Post,* 31 January 2006.

State Bar of California, Domestic Violence Committee of the Family Law Section. Pamphlet on Domestic Violence. 2006.

Stevenson, John. "First DNA Link Possible in Lacrosse Case." *Durham Herald Sun,* 11 May 2006.

Sujo, Aly, and Hasani Gittens. "Violence Surging at Home: Hotline Calls Up 70 Percent." *New York Post,* 29 September 2004.

U.S. Newswire. "In Light of Advancements, Domestic Violence Advocates Urge Congress to Strengthen and Reauthorize Violence Against Women Act." 19 July 2005.

Venezia, Todd, and Barry Bortnick. "Kobe Settles Sex Suit: $$ Deal Due by Weekend." *New York Post,* 2 March 2005.

Domestic Violence Cases

Hakkila v. Hakkila (New Mexico Court of Appeals, 1991)

Henriksen v. Canmeron (Maine, 1993)

Town of Castle Rock v. Jessica Gonzales (Supreme Court, 2005)

Twyman v. Twyman (Texas, 1993)

U.S. v. Morrison (Supreme Court, 2000)

Stalking Cases

People v. Krawzec (2nd District, 1994)

U.S. v. Jordan (Wisconsin, 2006)

Colorado v. Sullivan (Colorado, 2002)

H.E.S. v. J.C.S. (New Jersey, 2003)

Estate of Amy Boyer v. Docusearch, Inc. (New Hampshire, 2003)

Chapter 8: MY BODY

Advocates for Youth. "Current Research." March 2001.

Alford, Sue. "What's Wrong with Federal Abstinence-Only-Until-Marriage Requirements?" Advocates for Youth, March 2001.

Associated Press. "South Dakota to Vote on Abortion Law." 19 June 2006.

BBC Monitoring International Reports. 24 August 2005. Xinhua News Agency.

Bollinger, Caroline. "Find Out Why Growing Numbers of Doctors and Pharmacists Across the US Are Refusing to Prescribe or Dispense Birth Control Pills." *Prevention,* 2 July 2004.

Business Day. "Human Rights: Folly to Ban Virginity in the Name of Human Rights." 12 August 2005.

Clinton, Hillary Rodham. "Remarks by Senator Hillary Rodham Clinton to the NYS Family Planning Providers." 24 January 2005.

Connolly, Ceci. "Some Abstinence Programs Mislead Teens, Reports Say." *Washington Post,* 2 December 2004.

Contreras, Joseph, et al. "Latina Liftoff." *Newsweek,* Latin America Edition, 22 August 2005.

Davidoff, Judith. "Now It's the Pill They're After; Right-to-Life Movement Calls It Chemical Abortion." *Capital Times,* 1 August 2005.

Denogean, Anne T. "Court OKs Albertson's Birth-Control Benefits." *Tucson Citizen,* 13 February 2004.

Edelman, Susan. "Hidden Clause in Gals' Lives." *New York Post,* 5 March 2006.

Evans, Patrick, and Sikander Hashmi. "Activists Speak Out Against Sharia." *Toronto Star,* 13 August 2005.

Fattah, Hassan M. "Kuwait Grants Political Rights to Its Women." *New York Times,* 17 May 2005.

Feldt, Gloria. "Awakening: The Courage to Act." Planned Parenthood Federation of America, Inc., 22 March 2002.

Feldt, Gloria. "Hypocrisy, Theocracy, and Reclaiming Our Birthright of Freedom." Speech, Planned Parenthood Federation of America, Inc., 16 May 2003.

Gannon, James P. "A Religious Test? Let's Not." *USA Today,* 3 August 2005.

Gallup/CNN/USA Today Poll. Public Opinion Online, Question Number 284, July 7–10, 2004.

Goldstein, Amy, and Jo Becker. "Memo Cited 'Abortion Tragedy': Roberts Backed Service for Fetuses." *Washington Post*, 16 August 2005.

"Health Plan Coverage." *Seattle Post-Intelligencer*, 11 September 2001.

Hesse, Katherine A., and Doris R. MacKenzie. "Prescription Benefit Plans—Excluding Prescription Contraceptives as Sex Discrimination." *Benefits Quarterly*, 1 April 2002.

Hinsliff, Gaby. "Aids Fear as Bush Blocks Sex Lessons: US Undermines Global Declaration." London *Observer*, 5 May 2002.

Howard, Simon. "Jobfile: City Maternity Ploy That We All Have to Pay For." Timesonline.co.uk., 30 January 2005.

Kershaw, Sarah. "A 1909 Washington State Law Shielding a Woman's Virtue is Being Challenged." *New York Times*, 26 January 2005.

Kirkpatrick, David D. "Alito Hearings Unsettle Some Prevailing Wisdom About the Politics of Abortion." *New York Times*, 16 January 2006.

Kristof, Nicholas D. "Bush's Sex Scandal." *New York Times*, 16 February 2005.

Liptak, Adam. "In Abortion Rulings, Idea of Marriage Is Pivotal." *New York Times*, 2 November 2005.

MacArthur, John. "Ugliness of Illegal Abortion—What's at Stake in the Roberts Appointment." Editorial, *The Providence Journal*, 2 August 2005.

McGough, Michael. "Analysis: Alito's Abortion Views May Not Be Far from O'Connor's." Post-Gazette.com, 3 November 2005.

Meek Gordon, James. "Abort Showdown: Court to Hear 'Partial-Birth.' " New York *Daily News*, 22 February 2006.

Monday Business Briefing. "Exclusion of Prescription Contraception Is Sex Discrimination." 18 December 2001.

Munro, Neil. "Slamming the Court." *National Journal*, 30 July 2005.

National Organization for Women. "Conservatives Oppose New Cervical Cancer Vaccine." 22 December 2005.

National Organization for Women. "NOW Condemns Utah Murder Prosecution for Delayed Cesarean Delivery." 12 March 2004.

Neal, Terry. M. "The Fight Behind the Fight." *Washington Post*, 1 August 2005.

Norris, Michele, and Jerome Socolovsky. "Swedes Back Away from Feminism." National Public Radio, 12 August 2005.

Page, Susan. "Roe v. Wade: The Divided States of America." *USA Today*, 17 April 2006.

Painter, Steve. "Kansas Attorney General Sues to Stop State-Funded Abortions." *Wichita Eagle*, 19 August 2005.

Peters, Keith. "Unborn Victims Act Faces Challenge." *Family News in Focus*, 16 March 2004.

Pew Research Center for the People and the Press. "Abortion and the Rights of Terror Suspects Top Court Issues: Strong Support for Stem Cell Research." Pewforum.org, 3 August 2005.

Planned Parenthood Federation of America, Inc. "Abstinence-Only Education Is Irresponsible (and Dangerous)." 8 April 2002.

Planned Parenthood Federation of America, Inc. "Planned Parenthood Federation of America Mission and Policy Statements." 5 March 2006.

Planned Parenthood Federation of America, Inc. "The Fate of Reproductive Rights Rests with Your Generation." 23 January 2002.

Reuters. "Blanco Signs Law That Would Ban Abortions." 17 June 2006.

Roberts, Sally. "Plan Agrees to Cover Contraceptive Drugs: Bartell Case Was Closely Watched." *Business Insurance*, 17 March 2003.

Roth, Rachel. "Policing Pregnancy." *The Nation*, 16 October 2000.

Sage, Alexandria. "Drug Allegations a Factor in Murder Case Against Utah Mother." Associated Press, 17 March 2004.

Shanahan, Jessica. "It's Time for High Court to Overturn Roe v. Wade." *Buffalo News*, 15 August 2005.

Smeath, Doug. "Rowland Says State Is Making Example of Her." *Deseret Morning News*, 16 March 2004.

Stacy, Mitch. "Judge Dooms Terri: Pulls Feed Tube as Congress Bids to Step In." *New York Post*, 19 March 2005.

Steinem, Gloria. "The Time 100: Most Important People of the Century, Margaret Sanger." *Time*, 13 April 1998.

Sullivan, Andrew. "Hillary's Pro-Life Message." *New York Post*, 29 January 2005.

Sullivan, Andrew. "The Case for Compromise on Abortion." *Time*, 7 March 2005.

Szalai, Michelle. "Erickson v. Bartell Drug Company: Requiring Coverage of Prescription Contraceptives." *St. John's Law Review*, 1 April 2002.

Teenpregnancy.org. "State Abstinence-Only Programs." 5 March 2006.

Toledo Blade.com. "The Abortion Strategy." 22 June 2006.

Toner, Robin, and Adam Liptak. "In New Court, Roe May Stand, So Foes Look to Limit Its Scope." *New York Times*, 10 July 2005.

U.S. Newswire. "Planned Parenthood Negotiates Victory for Fairness for Women in Landmark Erickson v. Bartell Drug Contraceptive Coverage Case." 4 March 2003.

Vanderkam, Laura. "If 'Roe' Were Overturned." *USA Today,* 26 July 2005.

"The War Against Women." Editorial, *New York Times,* 12 January 2003.

Weiss, Deborah. "Reducing Teenage Pregnancy." Planned Parenthood, 2001.

Yoder, Steve. "Distortion 101: In Spite of the Facts, Bush's Department of Health and Human Services Keeps Pushing Abstinence." InTheseTimes .com, 14 April 2006.

Body Cases

Jennifer Bach v. United Parcel Service, Inc. (Florida, 2002)

Cooley, Jackson, Love and Branham v. Daimler-Chrysler Corp. (7th Circuit, 2004)

Eisenstadt v. Baird (Supreme Court, 1972)

Erickson v. Bartell Appellate Summary, Court of Appeals (9th Circuit, 2002)

Griswold v. Connecticut (Supreme Court, 1965)

Hodgson v. Minnesota (Supreme Court, 1990)

Planned Parenthood v. Casey (Supreme Court, 1992)

Planned Parenthood of Central Missouri v. Danforth (Supreme Court, 1976)

Roe v. Wade (Supreme Court, 1973)

Lisa Smith Maudlin v. Wal-Mart (Georgia, 2002)

Thornburg v. American College of Obstetricians and Gynecologists (Supreme Court, 1986)

Webster v. Reproductive Health Services (Supreme Court, 1989)

Chapter 9: THE SOCIAL COMPACT

Angier, Natalie, and Kenneth Chang. "Gray Matter and the Sexes." *New York Times,* 24 January 2005.

"Declaration of Sentiments." Seneca Falls, New York, 1848.

Healy, Orla. "Unleash Your Inner Jolie." *New York Post,* 17 January 2005.

Podhoretz, John. "Parenthood 101." *New York Post,* 18 February 2005.

Potts, Malcolm. "Why Can't a Man Be More Like a Woman?" *Obstetrics and Gynecology,* November 2005.

"Revived Debate: Babies, Careers and Having It All." Letters to the editor, *New York Times,* 22 September 2005.

Ripley, Amanda. "Who Says a Woman Can't Be Einstein." *Time*, 7 March 2005.

Rosenbloom, Stephanie. "Big Girls Don't Cry." *New York Times*, 13 October 2005.

Sanders, Holly M. "New Dove Ads Stir a Huge Soap Opera." *New York Post*, 28 July 2005.

"Special Report: Leading Women." *Newsweek*, 24 October 2005.

Steinberg, Jacques. "It's Not Atlantic City, but Miss America Pageant Adjusts Easily." *New York Times*, 21 January 2006.

Tierney, John. "The Happiest Wives." *New York Times*, 28 February 2006.

Tierney, John. "What Women Want." *New York Times*, 24 May 2005.

INDEX

ABOUT THE AUTHOR

LIS WIEHL is one of the nation's most prominent trial lawyers and a highly regarded legal commentator. She is Fox News's full-time legal analyst, and goes head-to-head with Bill O'Reilly as his co-host on the nationally syndicated daily radio show *Radio Factor*. A graduate of Harvard, she's never lost a case. She lives with her two children and husband in Westchester County, New York, and is the author of *Winning Every Time*.

ABOUT THE TYPE

This book was set in Caslon, a typeface first designed in 1722 by William Caslon. Its widespread use by most English printers in the early eighteenth century soon supplanted the Dutch typefaces that had formerly prevailed. The roman is considered a "workhorse" typeface due to its pleasant, open appearance, while the italic is exceedingly decorative.